FOR ORGANS, PIANOS & ELECTRONIC KEYBOARDS

E-Z PLAY® TODAY

392

2nd Edition

P9-AFS-514

Disney FAVORITES

ISBN 0-634-01577-X

Wonderland Music Company, Inc.

Walt Disney Music Company

DISTRIBUTED BY

HAL•LEONARD®
CORPORATION

7777 W. BLUEMOUND RD. P.O. BOX 13819 MILWAUKEE, WI 53213

In Australia contact:
Hal Leonard Australia Pty. Ltd.
4 Lentara Court
Cheltenham, Victoria, 3192 Australia
Email: ausadmin@halleonard.com

Visit Hal Leonard Online at
www.halleonard.com

Disney FAVORITES

The Age of Not Believing
from Walt Disney's BEDKNOBS AND BROOMSTICKS

Registration 2
Rhythm: Fox Trot

Words and Music by Richard M. Sherman
and Robert B. Sherman

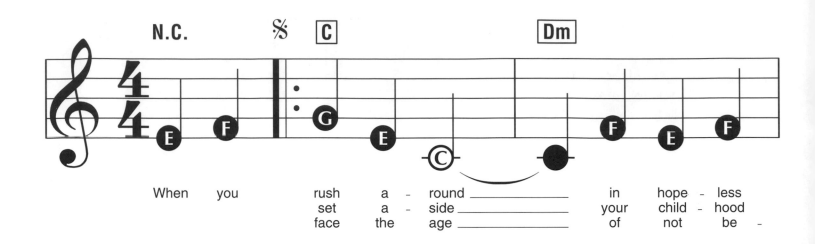

When you rush a - round _____ in hope - less
set a - side _____ your child - hood
face the age _____ of not be -

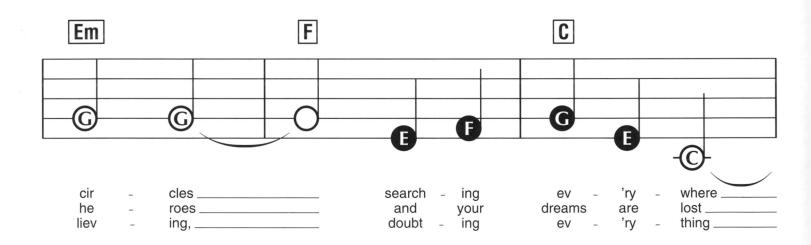

cir - cles _____ search - ing ev - 'ry - where _____
he - roes _____ and your dreams are lost _____
liev - ing, _____ doubt - ing ev - 'ry - thing _____

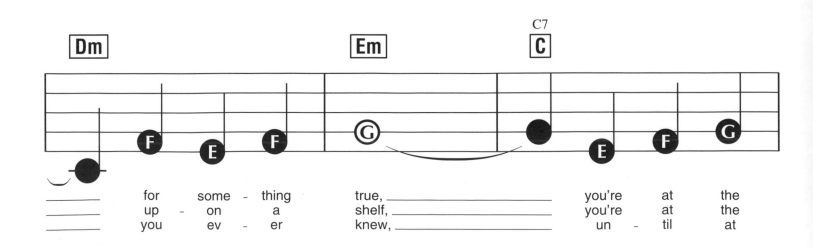

_____ for some - thing true, _____ you're at the
_____ up - on a shelf, _____ you're at the
_____ you ev - er knew, _____ un - til at

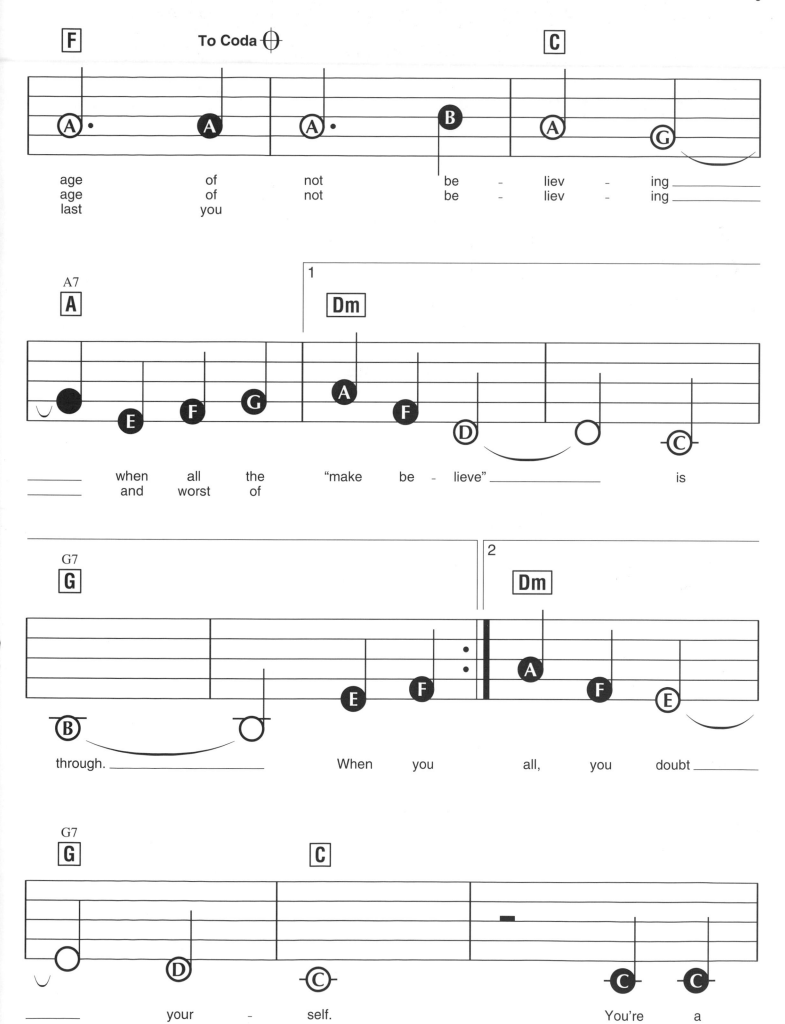

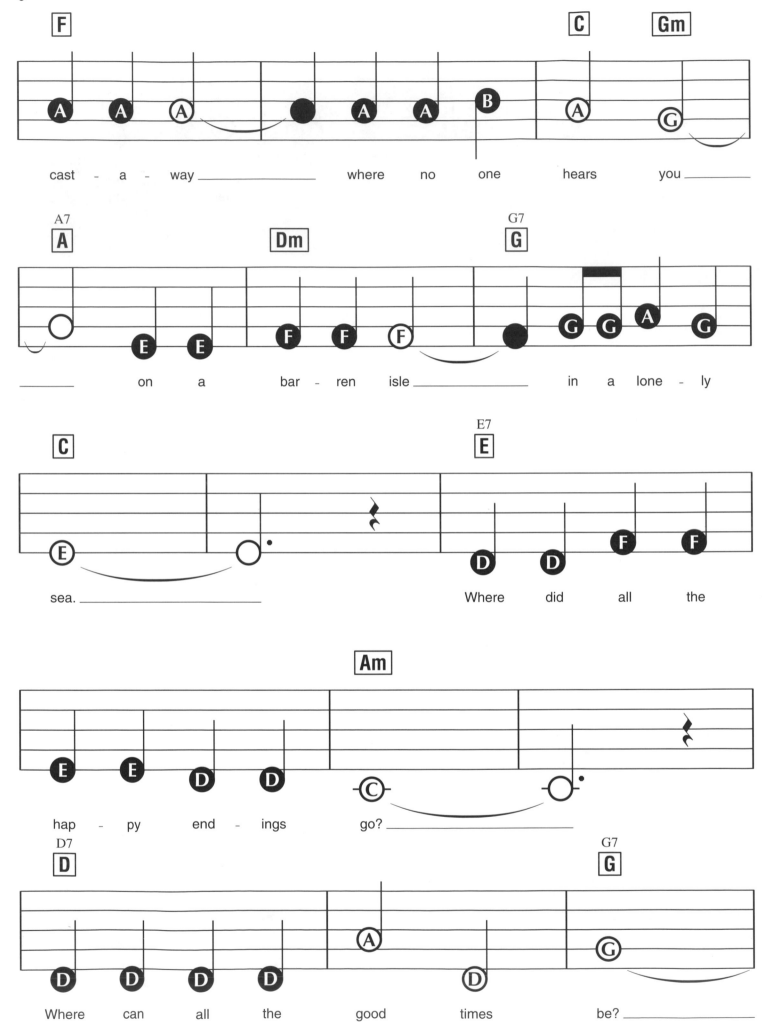

D.S. al Coda
(Return to %
Play to ⊕ and
Skip to Coda)

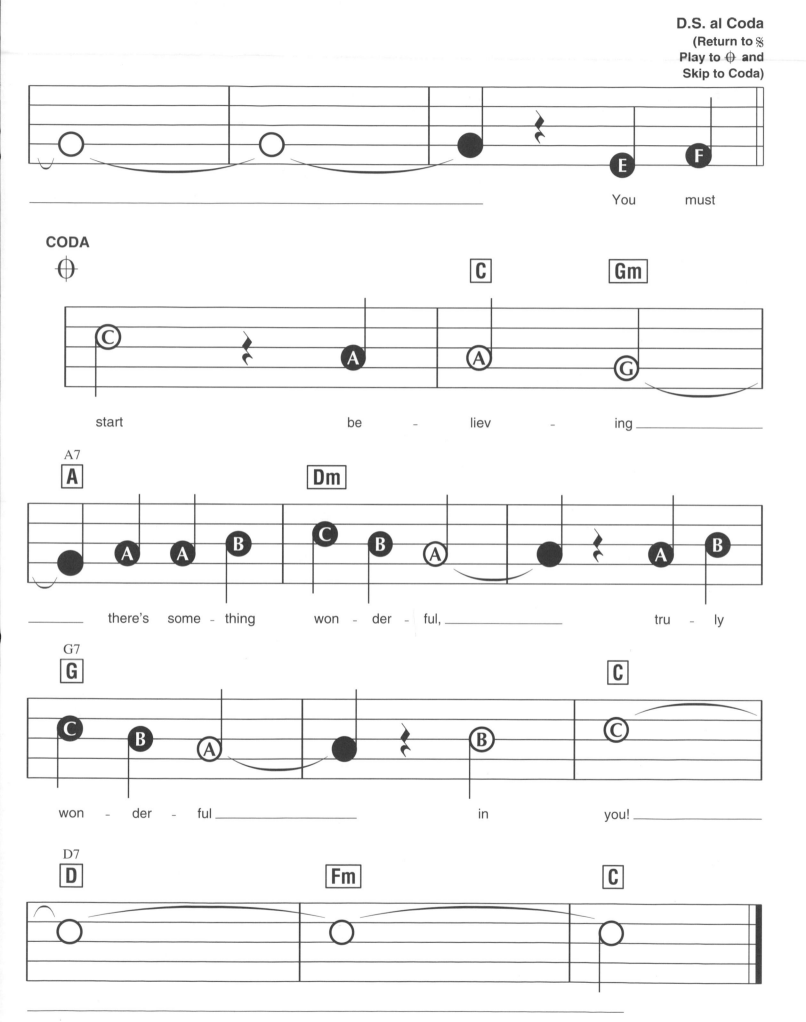

Alice in Wonderland
from Walt Disney's ALICE IN WONDERLAND

Registration 8
Rhythm: Fox Trot

Words by Bob Hilliard
Music by Sammy Fain

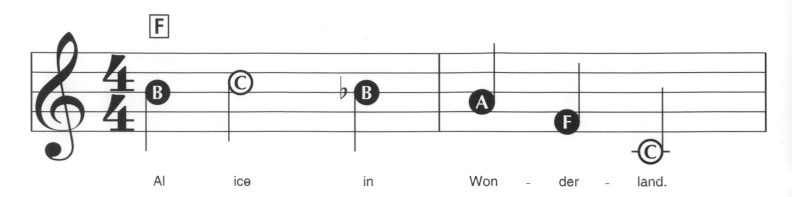

Al - ice   in   Won - der - land.

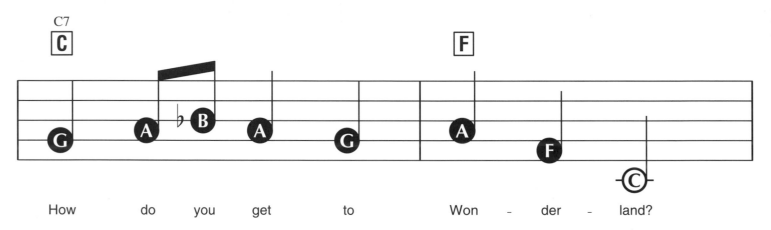

How   do   you   get   to   Won - der - land?

O - ver the hill   or   un - der - land   or

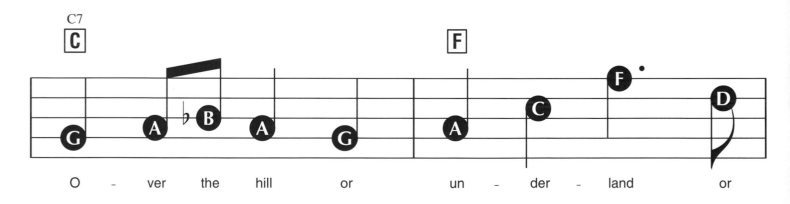

just   be - hind   the   tree.   When   clouds   go

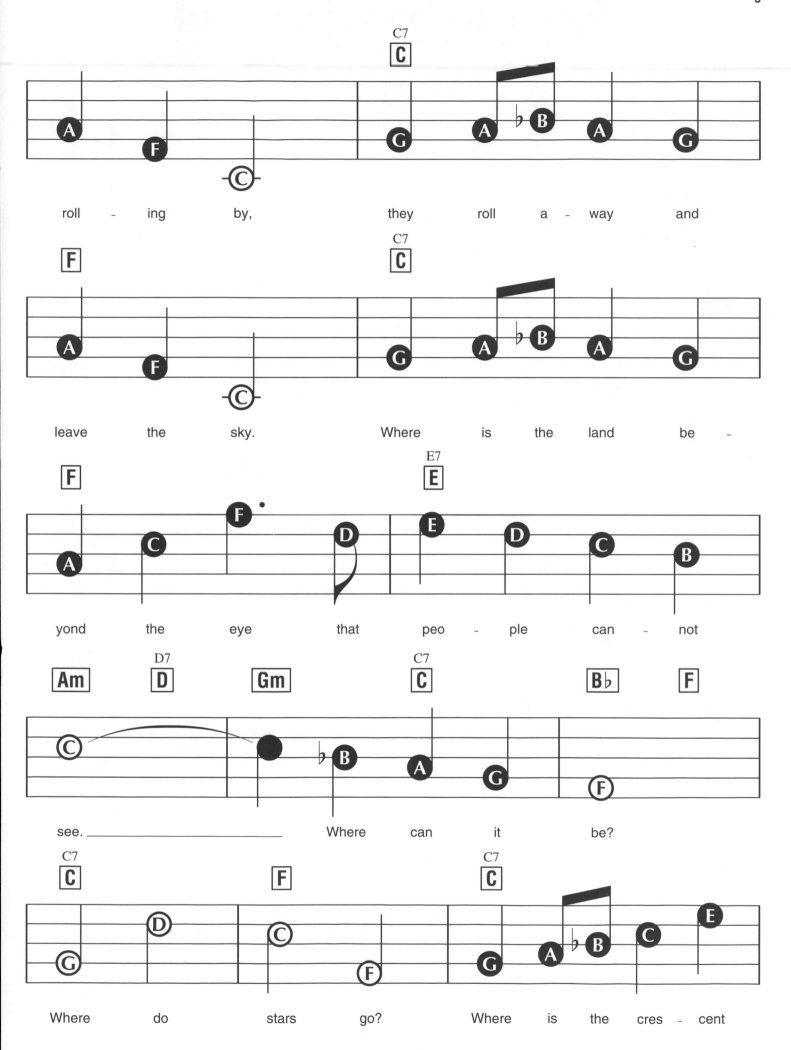

10

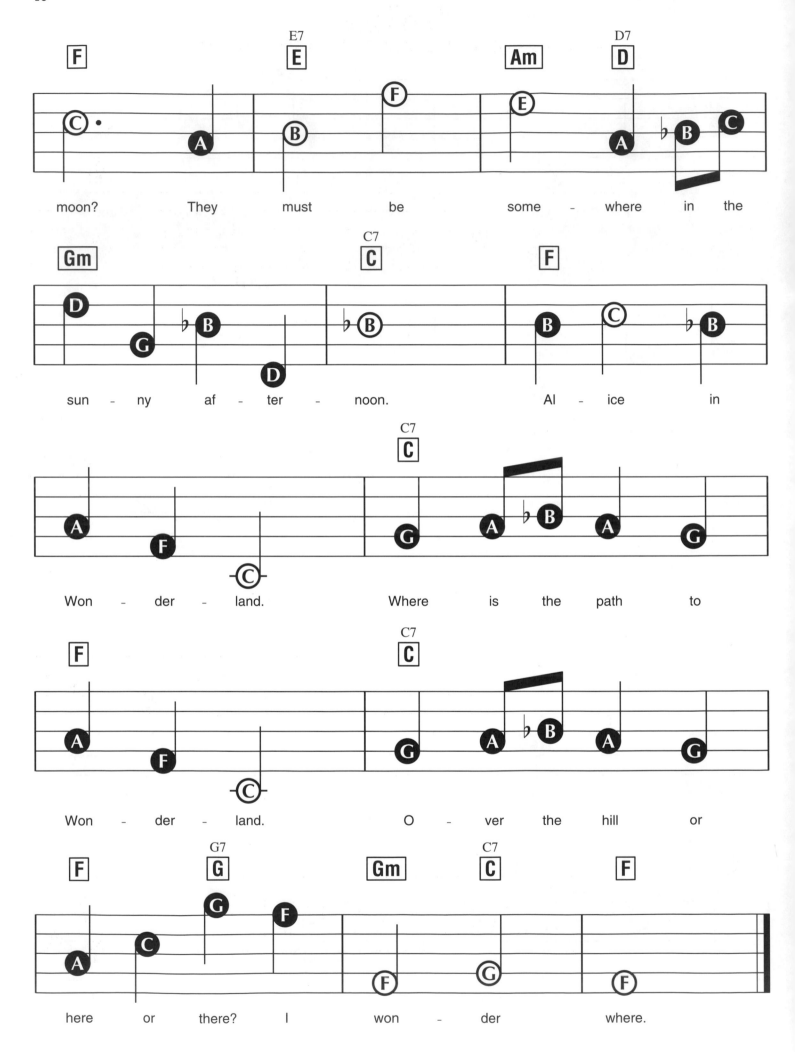

Belle
from Walt Disney's BEAUTY AND THE BEAST

Registration 9
Rhythm: March or Polka

Lyrics by Howard Ashman
Music by Alan Menken

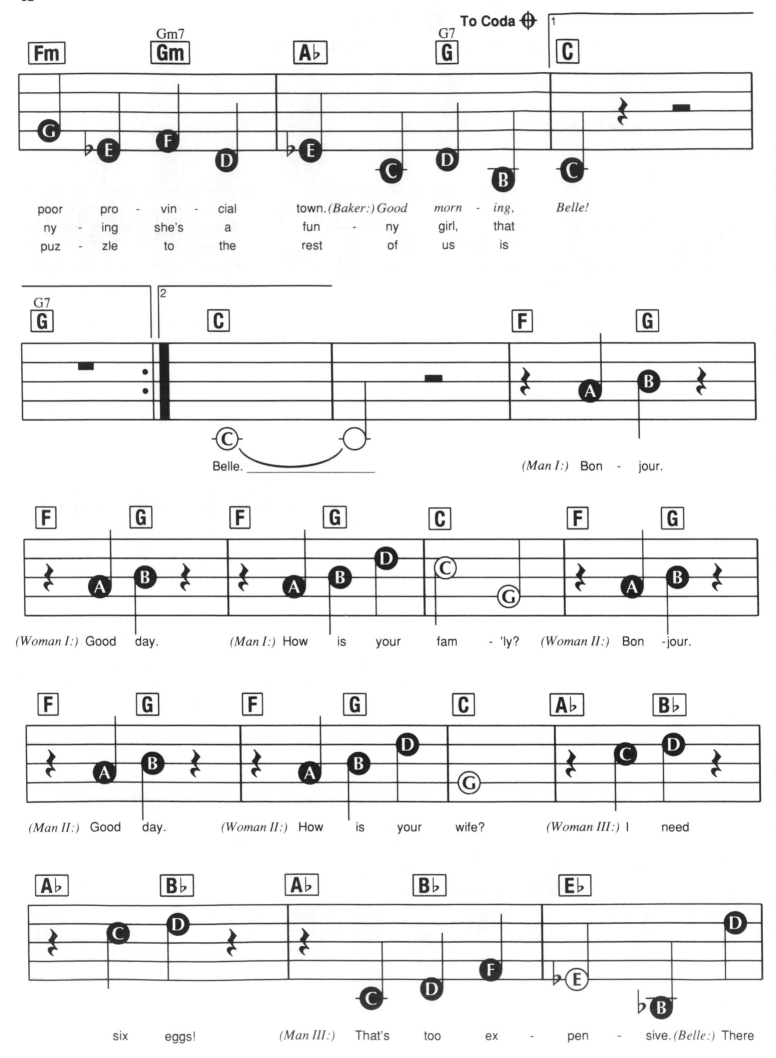

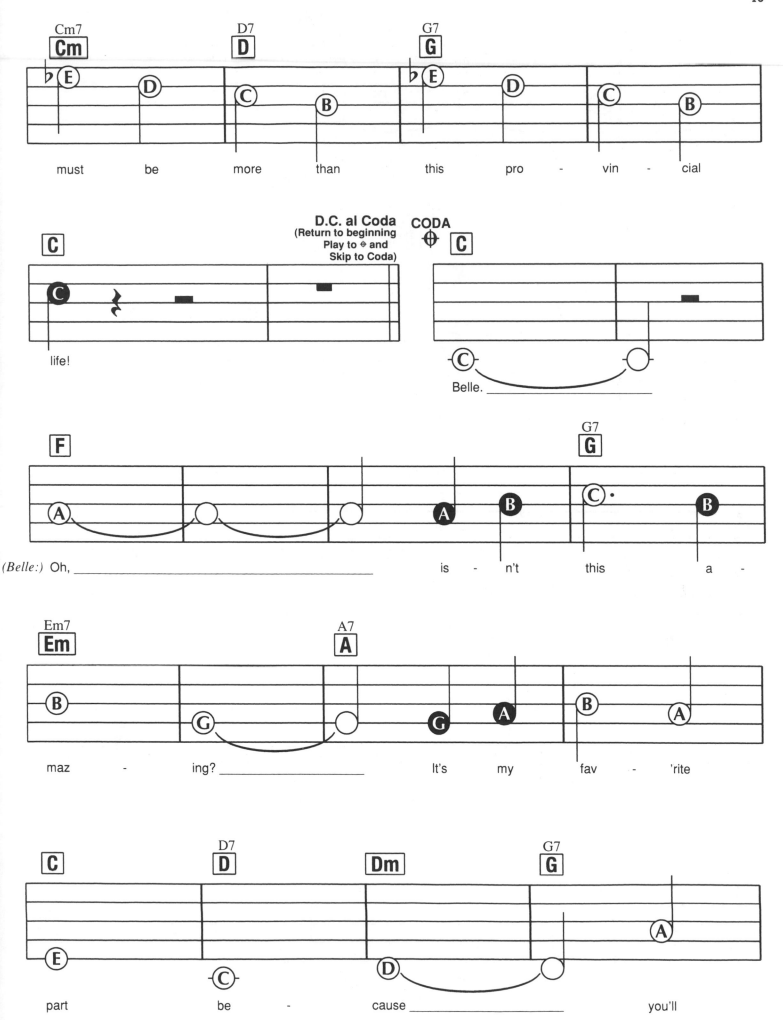

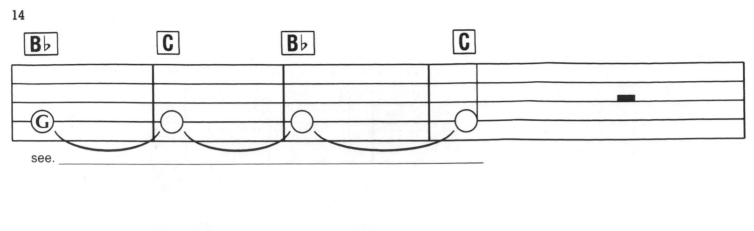

see.

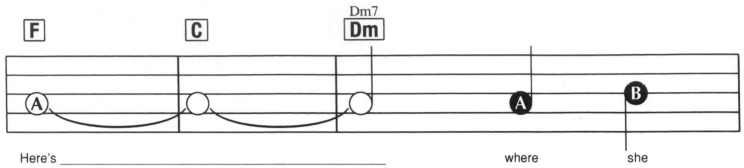

Here's _____ where she

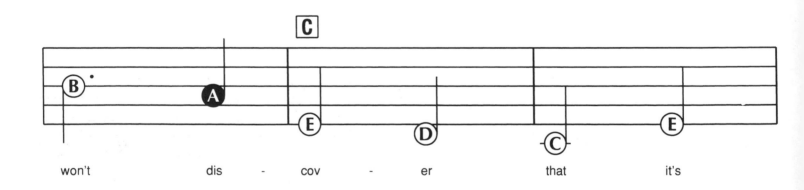

meets Prince Charm - ing, _____ but she

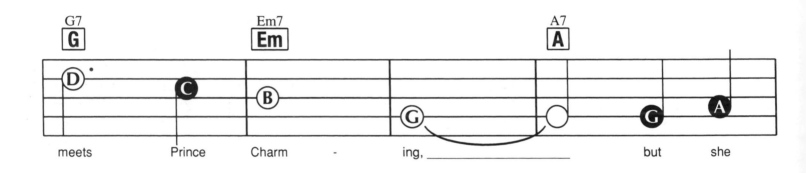

won't dis - cov - er that it's

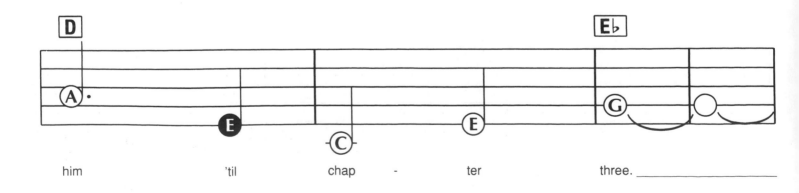

him 'til chap - ter three. _____

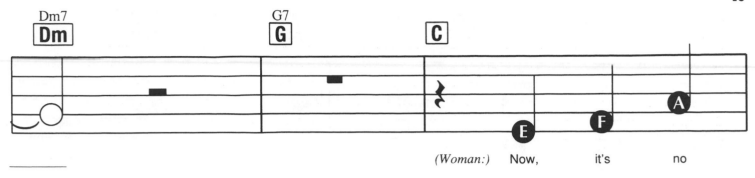

(Woman:) Now, it's no

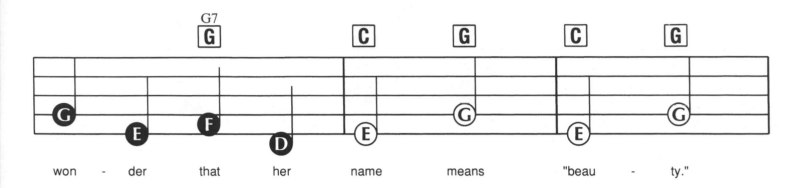

won - der that her name means "beau - ty."

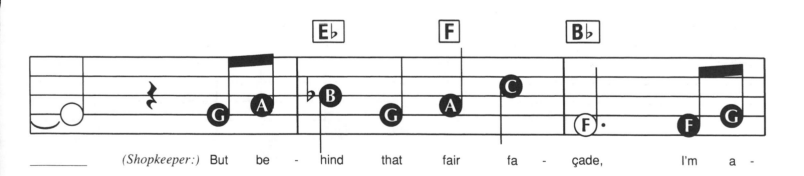

Her looks have got no par - al - lel. _____

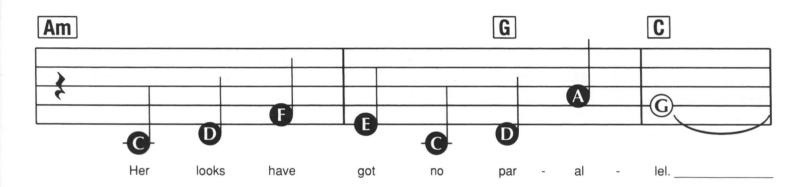

(Shopkeeper:) But be - hind that fair fa - çade, I'm a -

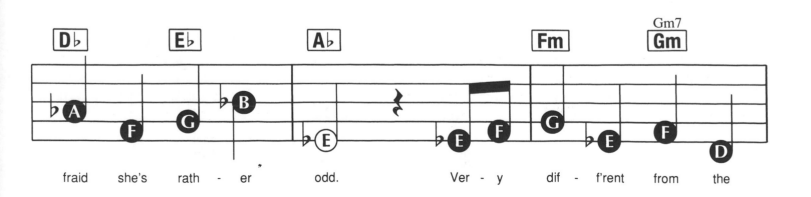

fraid she's rath - er odd. Ver - y dif - f'rent from the

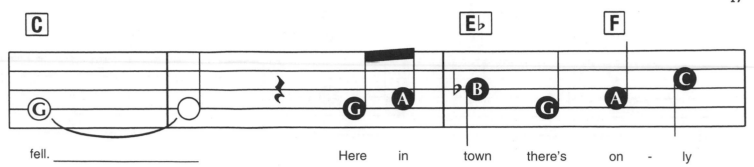

fell. _____ Here in town there's on - ly

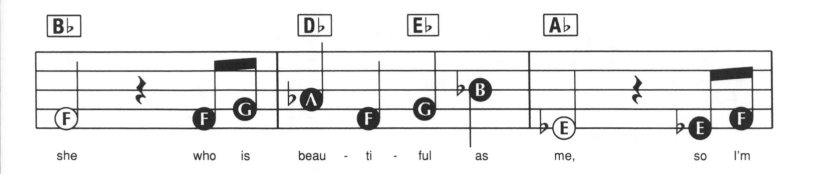

she who is beau - ti - ful as me, so I'm

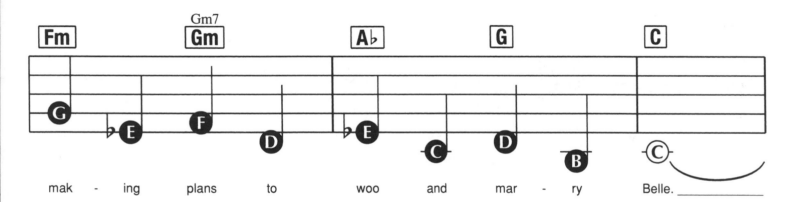

mak - ing plans to woo and mar - ry Belle. _____

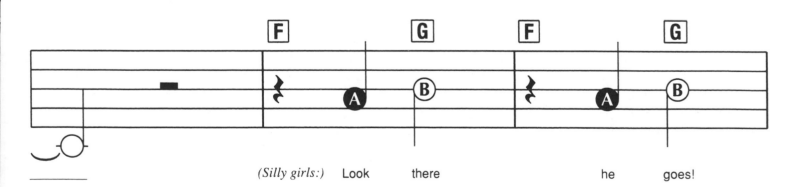

_____ *(Silly girls:)* Look there he goes!

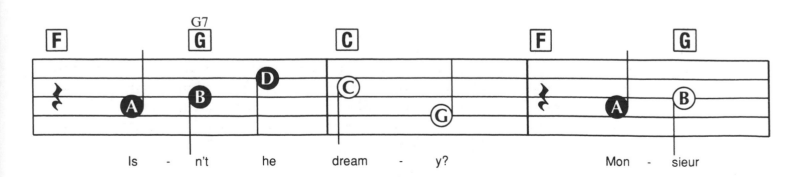

Is - n't he dream - y? Mon - sieur

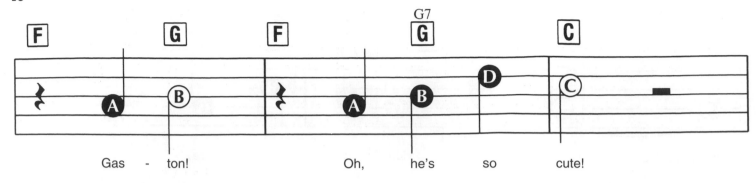

Gas - ton! Oh, he's so cute!

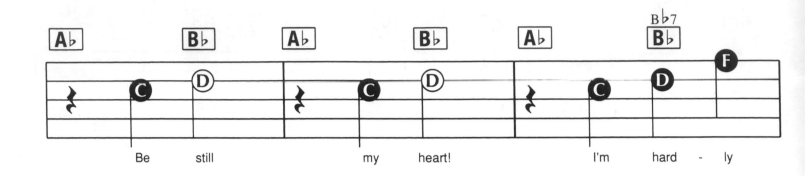

Be still my heart! I'm hard - ly

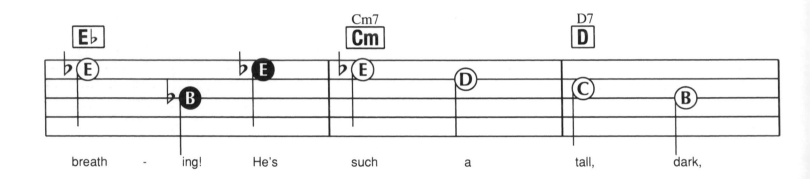

breath - ing! He's such a tall, dark,

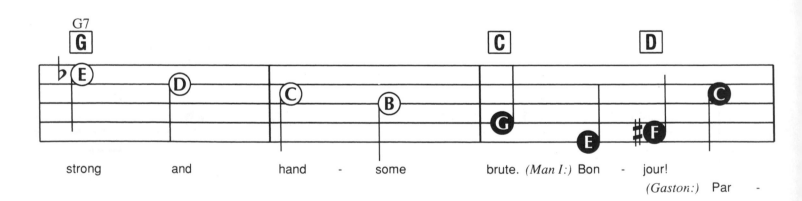

strong and hand - some brute. *(Man I:)* Bon - jour!

(Gaston:) Par -

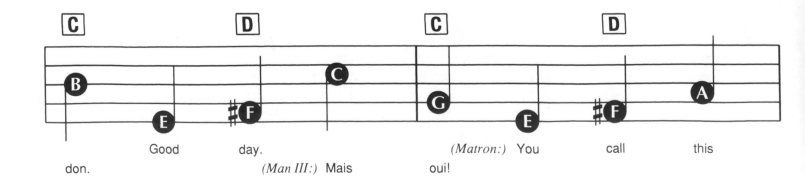

don. Good day.

(Man III:) Mais oui! *(Matron:)* You call this

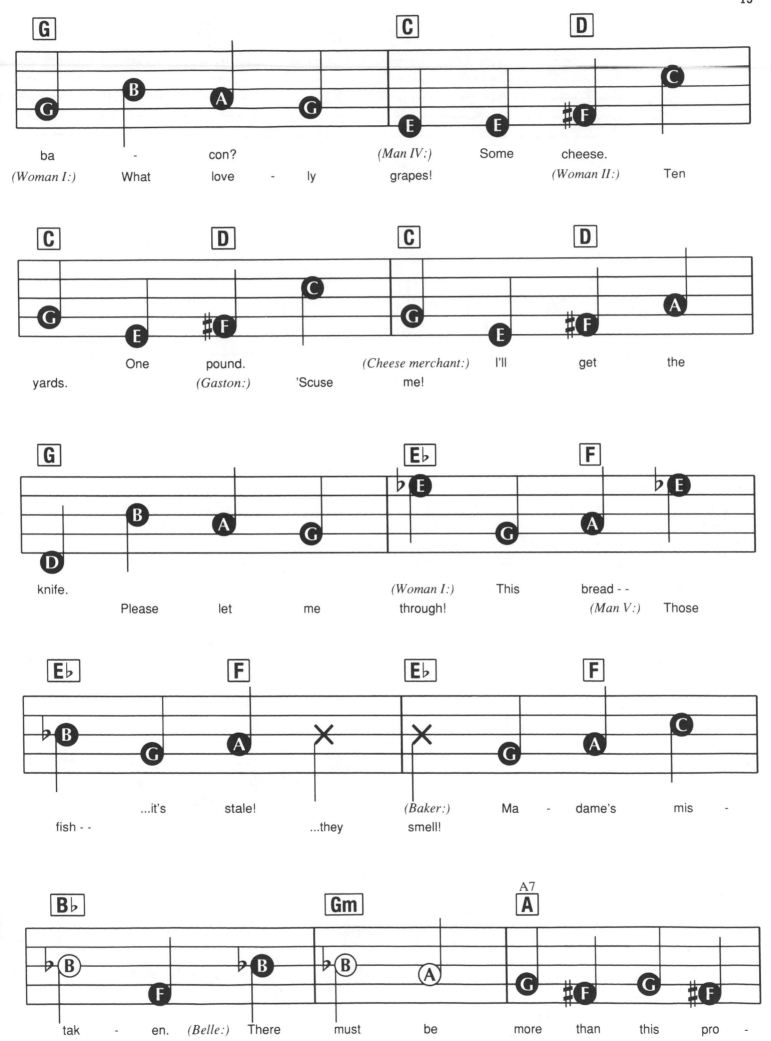

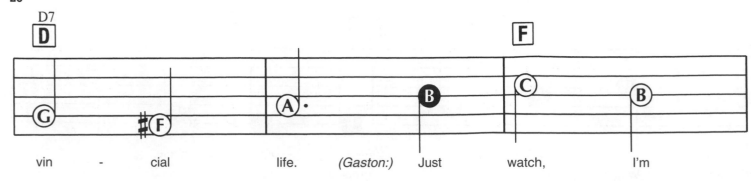

vin - cial life. *(Gaston:)* Just watch, I'm

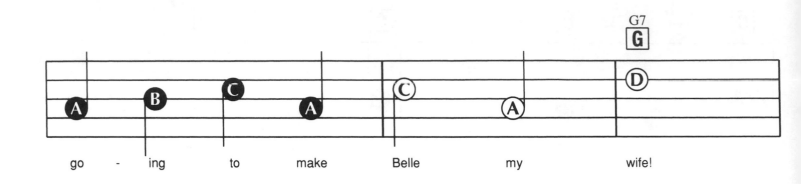

go - ing to make Belle my wife!

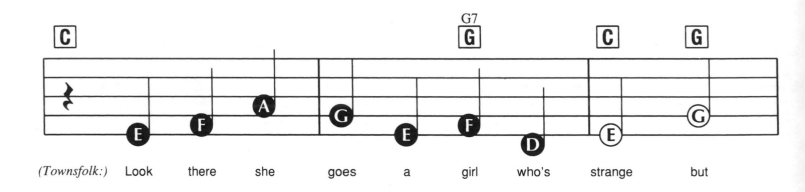

(Townsfolk:) Look there she goes a girl who's strange but

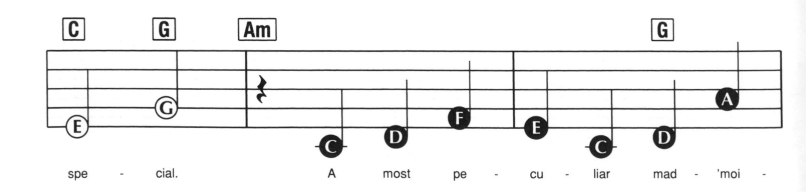

spe - cial. A most pe - cu - liar mad - 'moi -

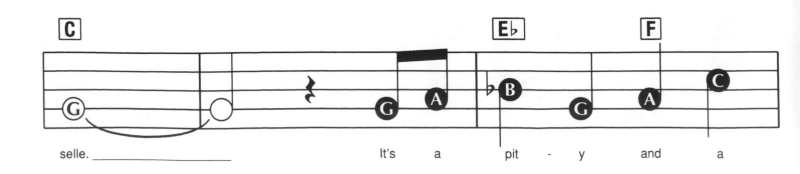

selle. _____ It's a pit - y and a

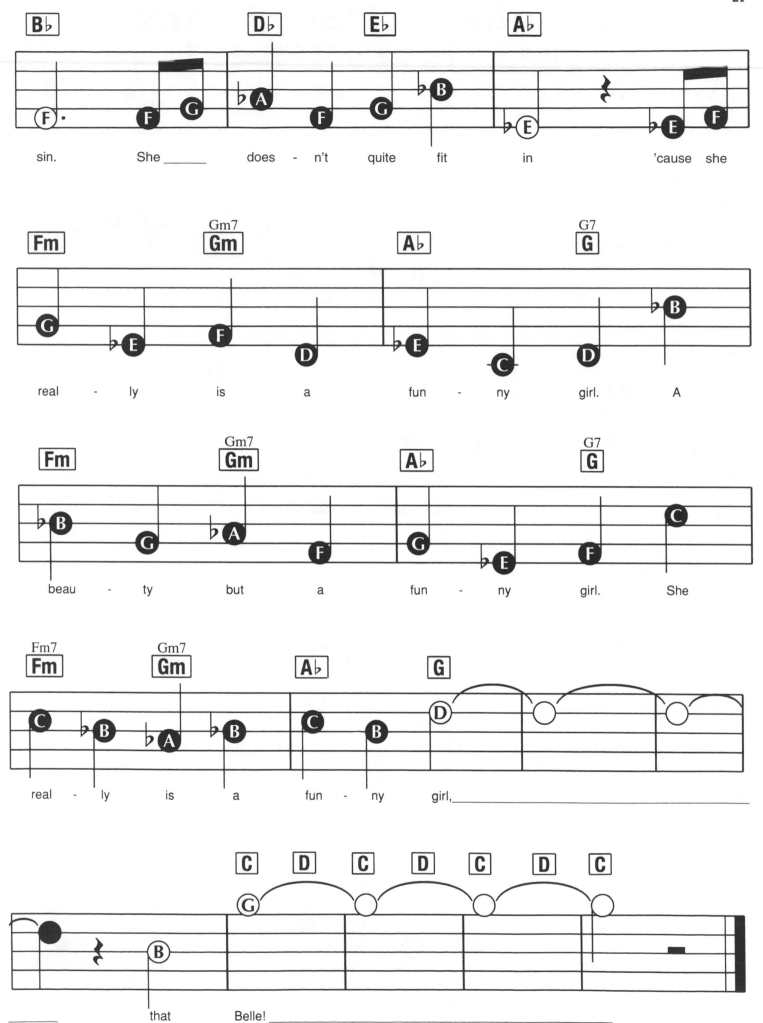

The Ballad of Davy Crockett
from Walt Disney's DAVY CROCKETT

Registration 2
Rhythm: Fox Trot or Swing

Words by Tom Blackburn
Music by George Bruns

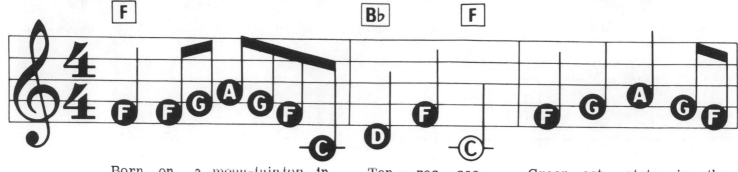

Born on a moun-tain top in Ten - nes - see, Green - est state in the

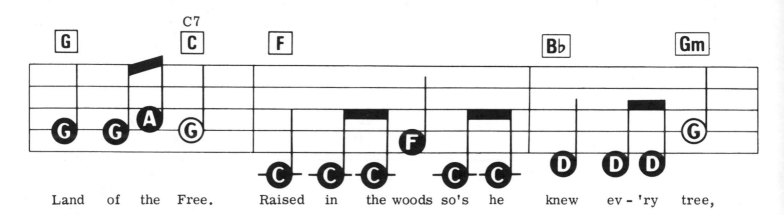

Land of the Free. Raised in the woods so's he knew ev - 'ry tree,

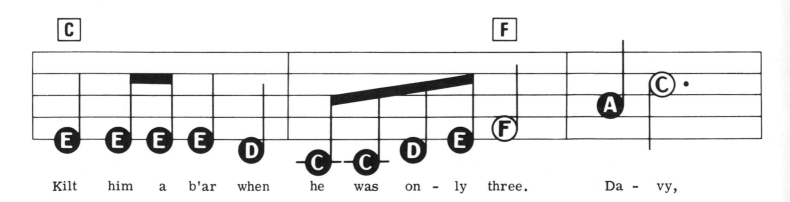

Kilt him a b'ar when he was on - ly three. Da - vy,

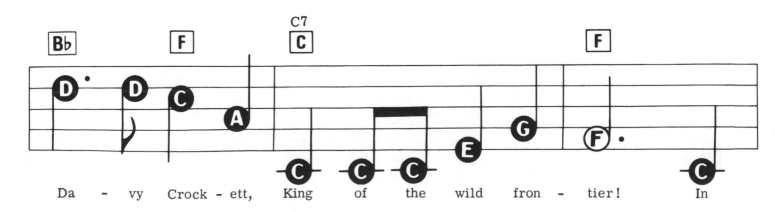

Da - vy Crock - ett, King of the wild fron - tier! In

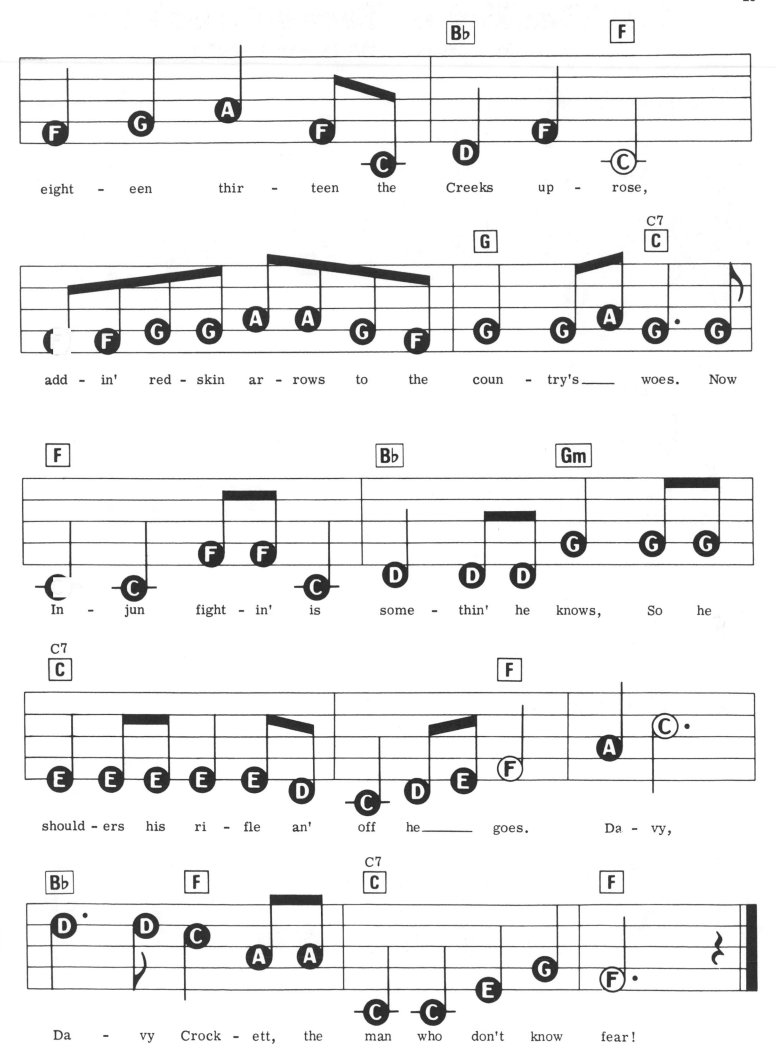

The Bare Necessities
from Walt Disney's THE JUNGLE BOOK

Registration 4
Rhythm: Fox Trot or Swing

Words and Music by
Terry Gilkyson

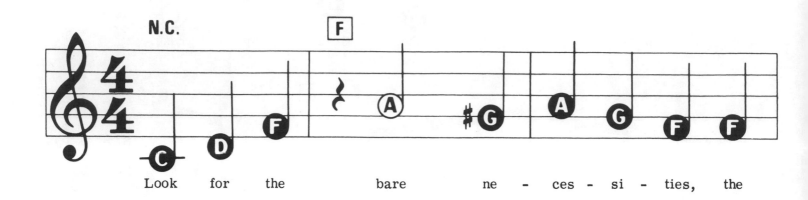

Look for the bare ne - ces - si - ties, the

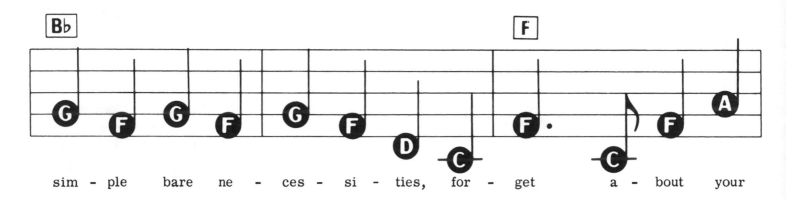

sim - ple bare ne - ces - si - ties, for - get a - bout your

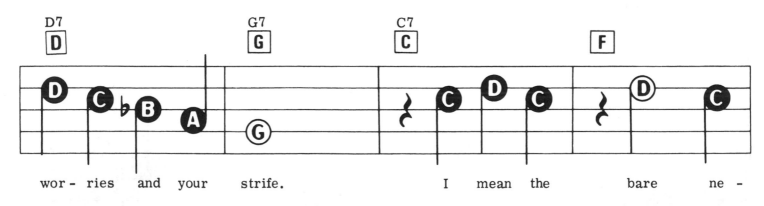

wor - ries and your strife. I mean the bare ne -

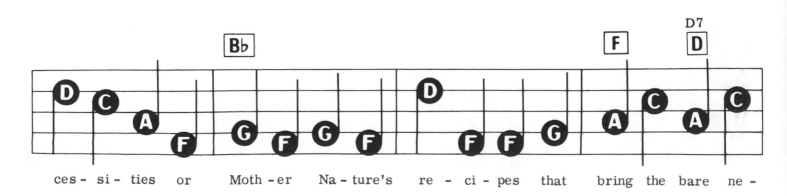

ces - si - ties or Moth - er Na - ture's re - ci - pes that bring the bare ne -

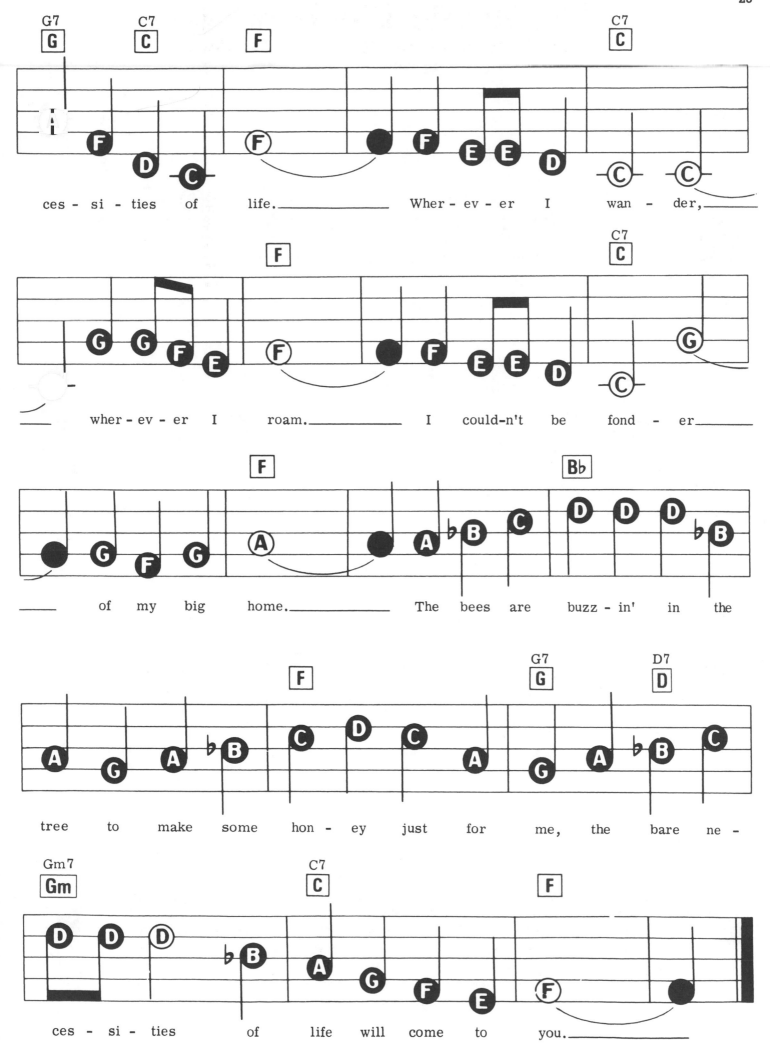

Be Our Guest
from Walt Disney's BEAUTY AND THE BEAST

Registration 5
Rhythm: March or Polka

Lyrics by Howard Ashman
Music by Alan Menken

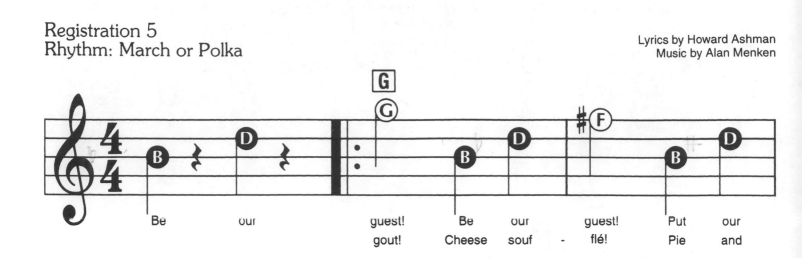

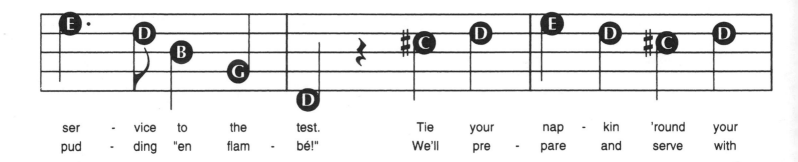

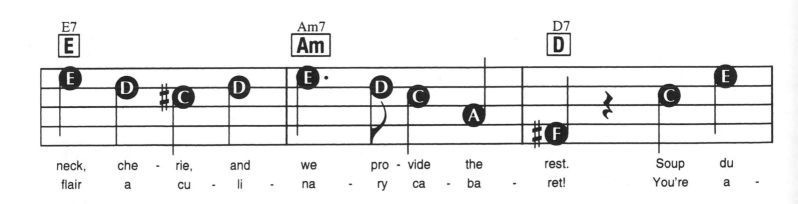

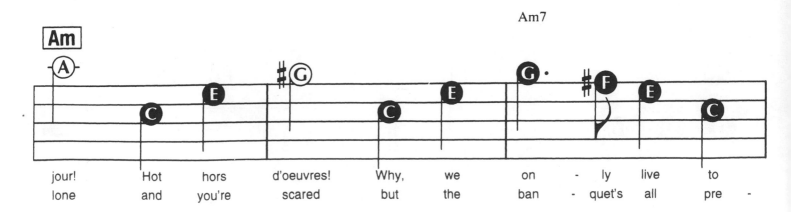

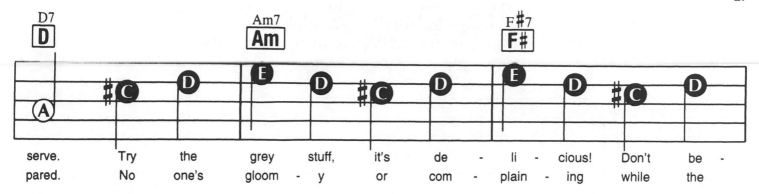

serve. Try the grey stuff, it's de - li - cious! Don't be -
pared. No one's gloom - y or com - plain - ing while the

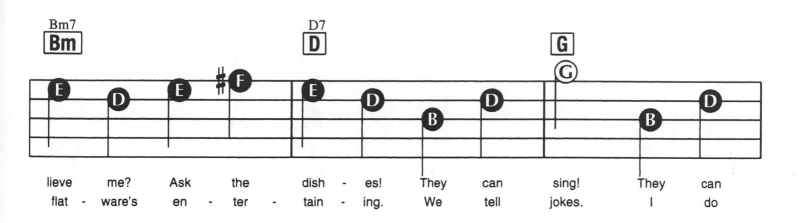

lieve me? Ask the dish - es! They can sing! They can
flat - ware's en - ter - tain - ing. We tell jokes. I do

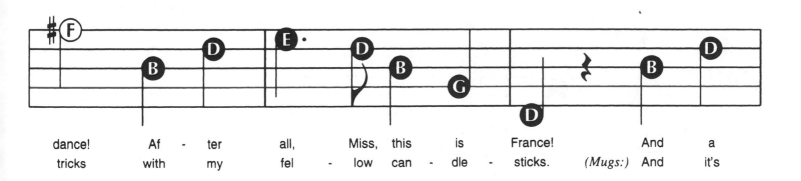

dance! Af - ter all, Miss, this is France! And a
tricks with my fel - low can - dle - sticks. *(Mugs:)* And it's

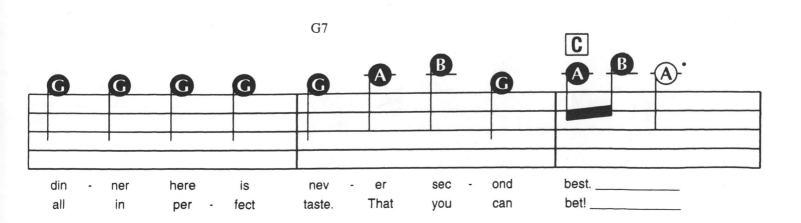

din - ner here is nev - er sec - ond best. _____
all in per - fect taste. That you can bet! _____

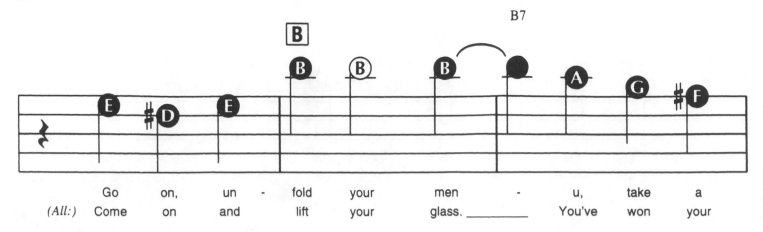

Go on, un - fold your men - u, take a
(All:) Come on and lift your glass. _____ You've won your

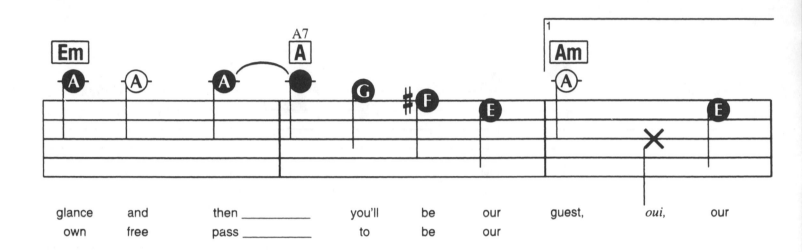

glance and then _____ you'll be our guest, *oui,* our
own free pass _____ to be our

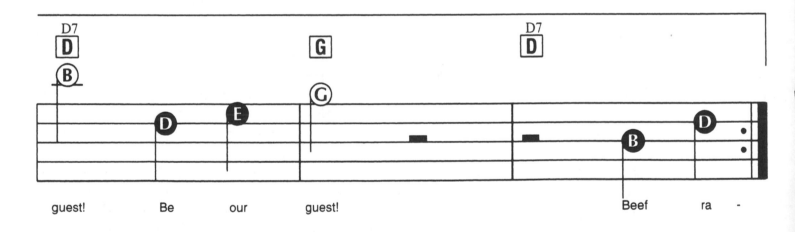

guest! Be our guest!   Beef ra -

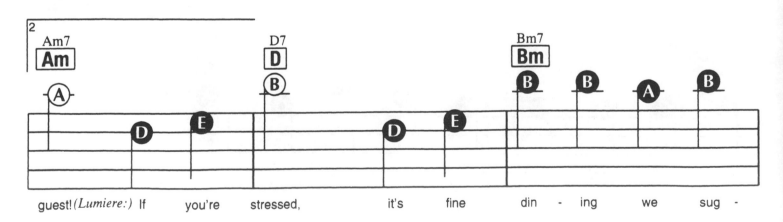

guest! *(Lumiere:)* If you're stressed, it's fine din - ing we sug -

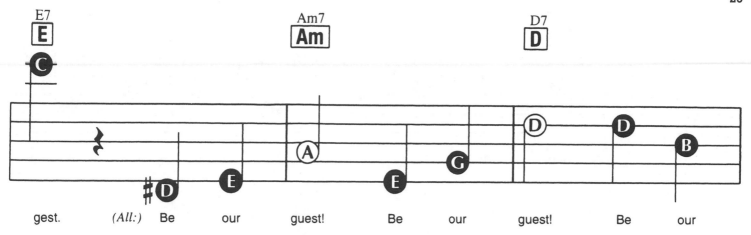

gest. *(All:)* Be our guest! Be our guest! Be our

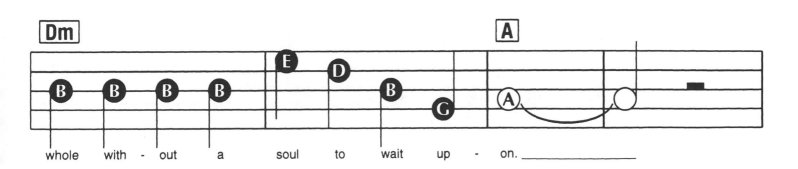

guest! *(Lumiere:)* Life is so un -

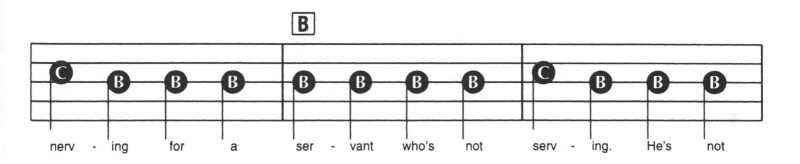

nerv - ing for a ser - vant who's not serv - ing. He's not

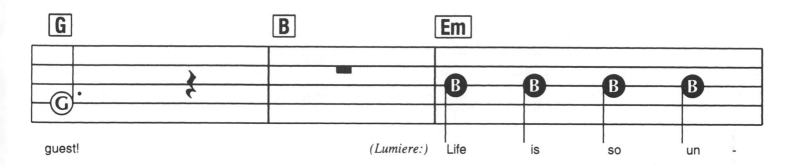

whole with - out a soul to wait up - on. _____

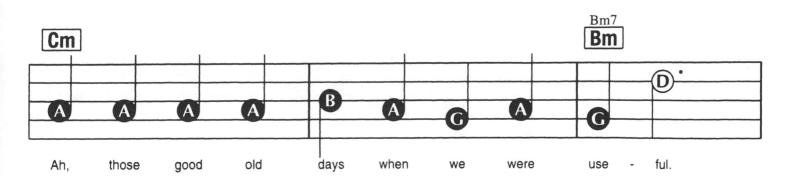

Ah, those good old days when we were use - ful.

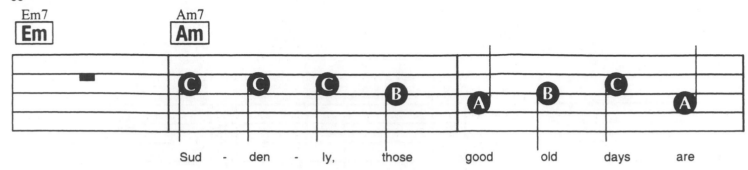

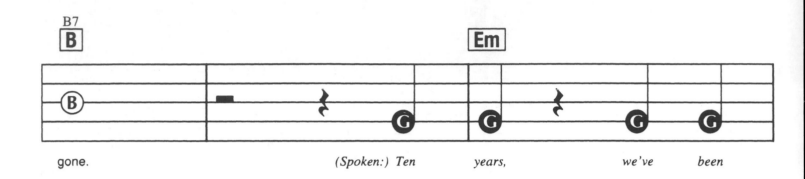

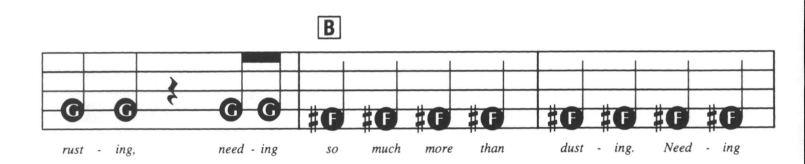

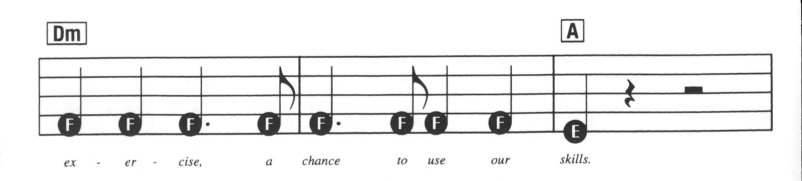

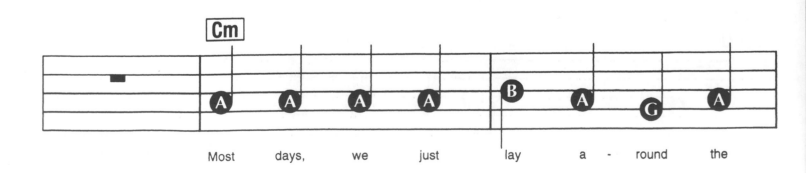

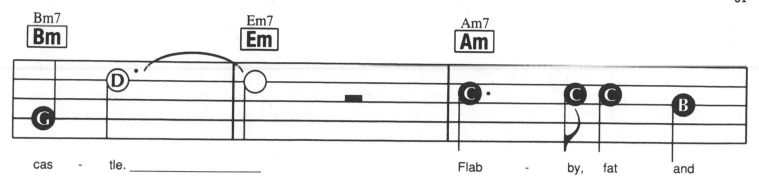

cas - tle. _____ Flab - by, fat and

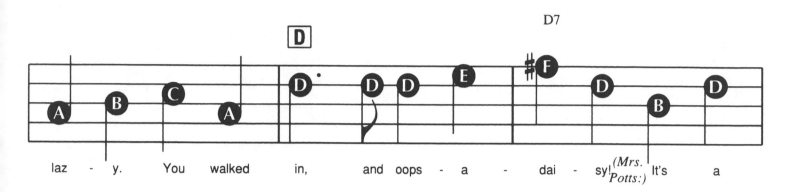

laz - y. You walked in, and oops - a - dai - sy! *(Mrs. Potts:)* It's a

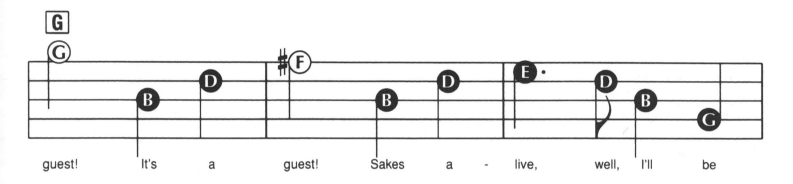

guest! It's a guest! Sakes a - live, well, I'll be

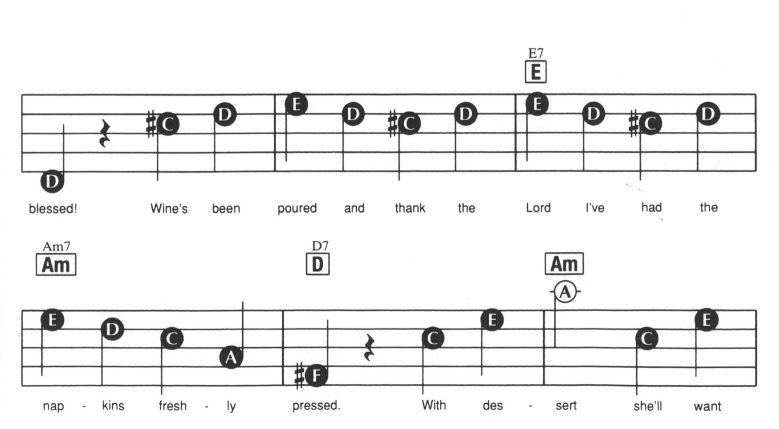

blessed! Wine's been poured and thank the Lord I've had the

nap - kins fresh - ly pressed. With des - sert she'll want

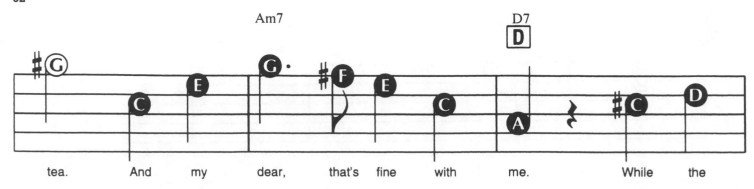

tea. And my dear, that's fine with me. While the

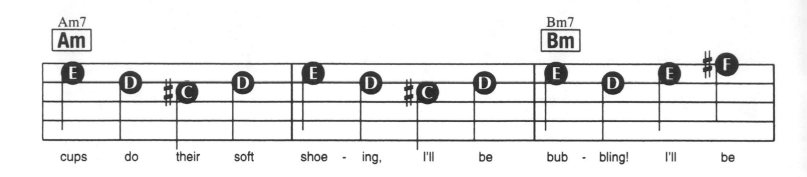

cups do their soft shoe - ing, I'll be bub - bling! I'll be

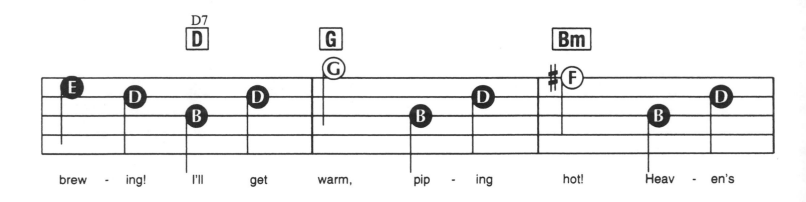

brew - ing! I'll get warm, pip - ing hot! Heav - en's

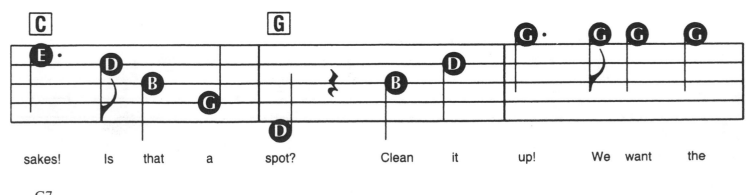

sakes! Is that a spot? Clean it up! We want the

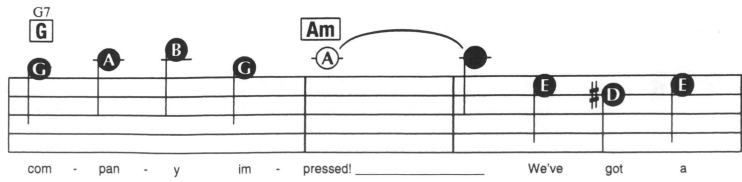

com - pan - y im - pressed! _____ We've got a

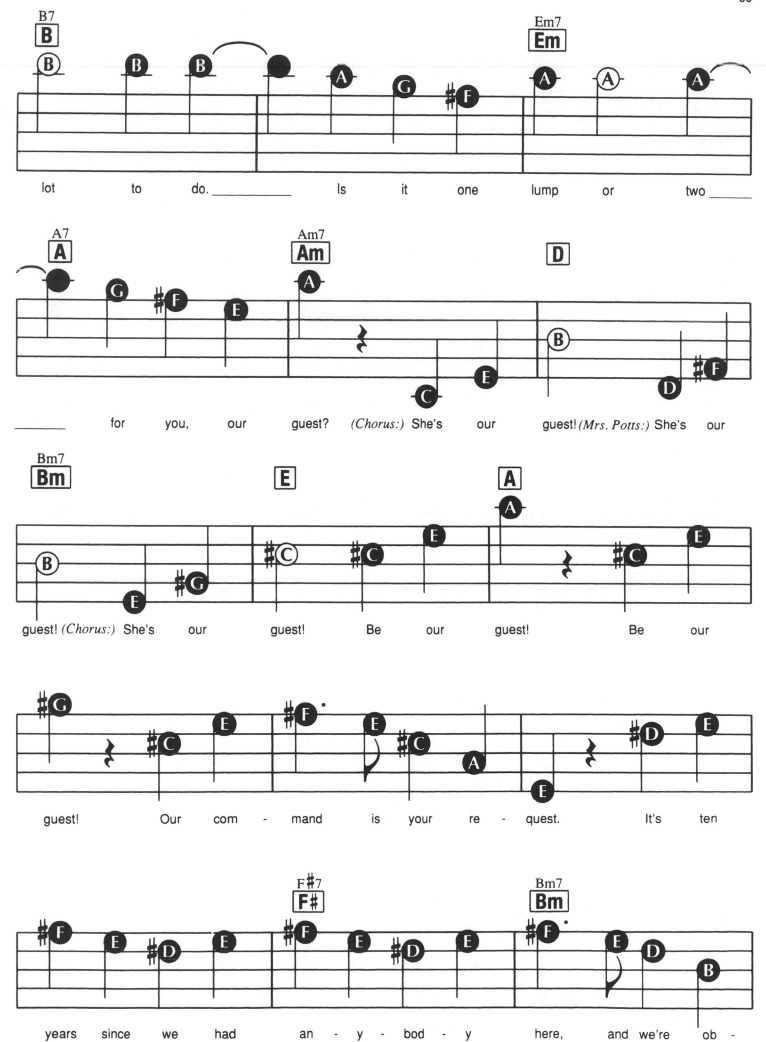

34

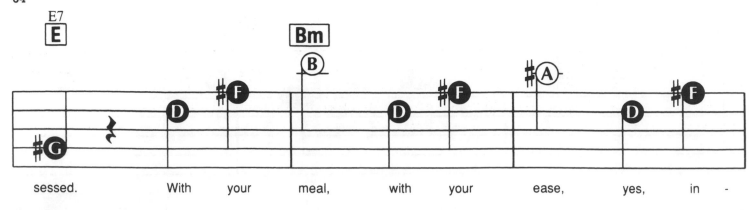

sessed. With your meal, with your ease, yes, in -

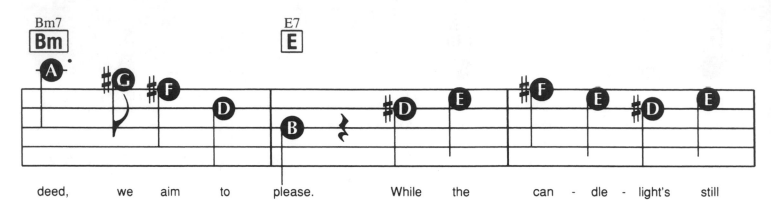

deed, we aim to please. While the can - dle - light's still

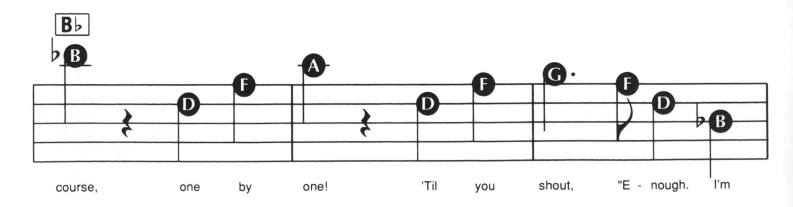

glow - ing let us help you, we'll keep go - ing course by

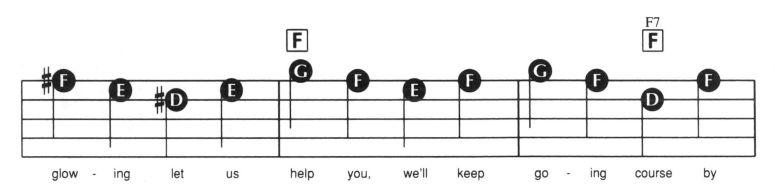

course, one by one! 'Til you shout, "E - nough. I'm

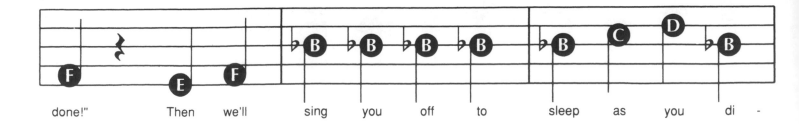

done!" Then we'll sing you off to sleep as you di -

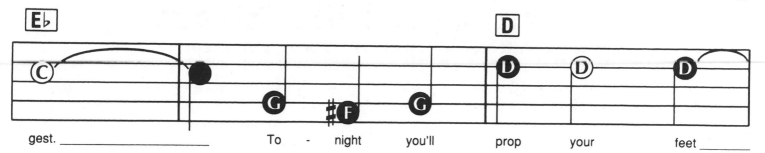

gest. _____ To - night you'll prop your feet _____

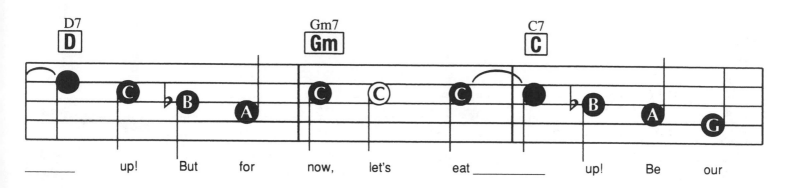

_____ up! But for now, let's eat _____ up! Be our

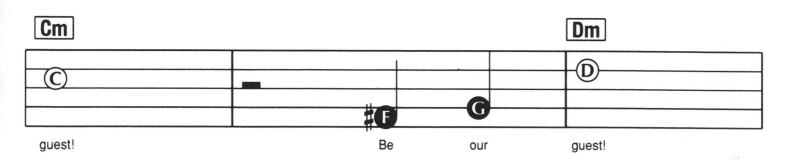

guest! Be our guest!

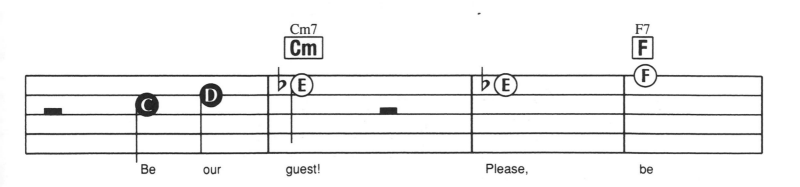

Be our guest! Please, be

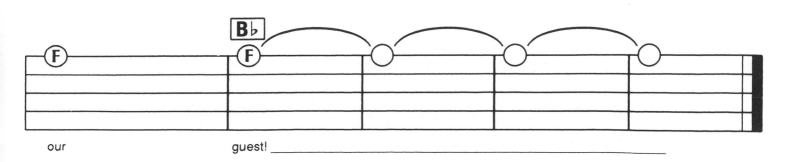

our guest! _____

Beauty and the Beast
from Walt Disney's BEAUTY AND THE BEAST

Registration 1
Rhythm: Pops or 8 Beat

Lyrics by Howard Ashman
Music by Alan Menken

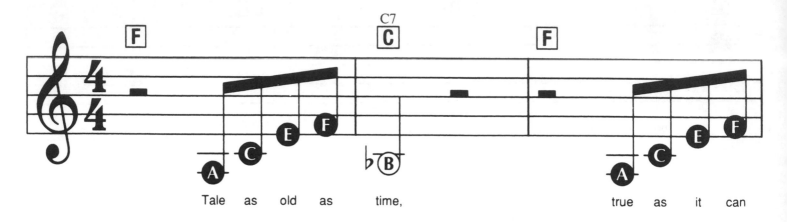

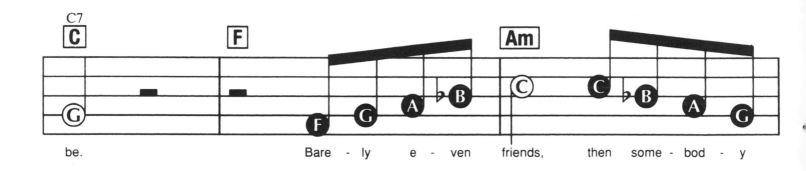

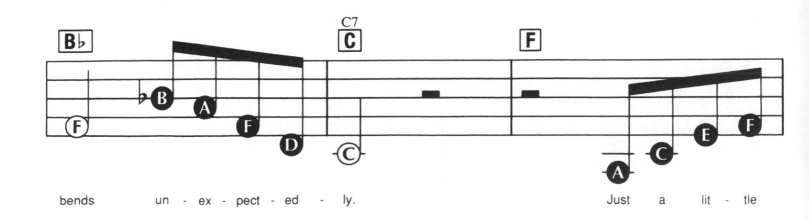

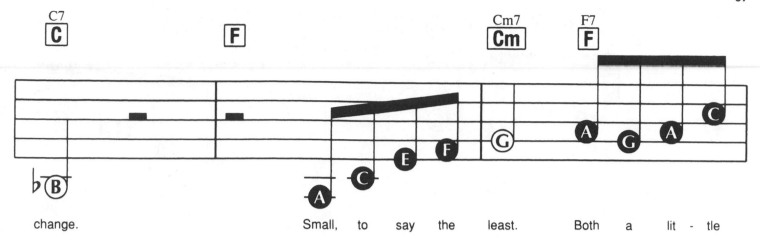

change.   Small, to say the least.   Both a lit - tle

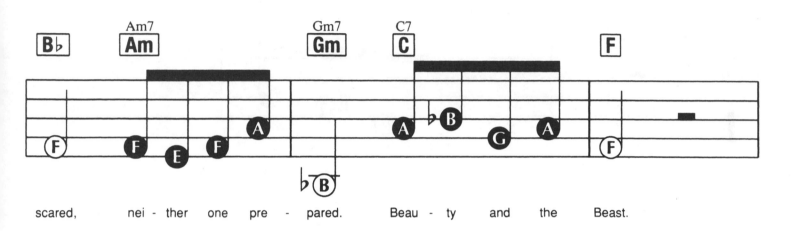

scared,   nei - ther one pre - pared.   Beau - ty and the Beast.

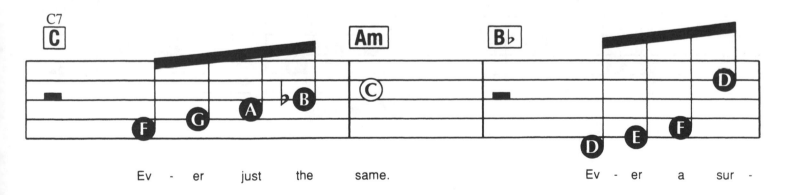

Ev - er just the same.   Ev - er a sur -

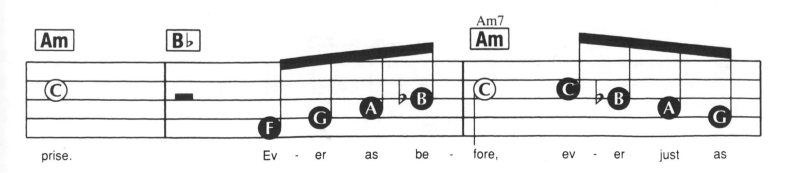

prise.   Ev - er as be - fore,   ev - er just as

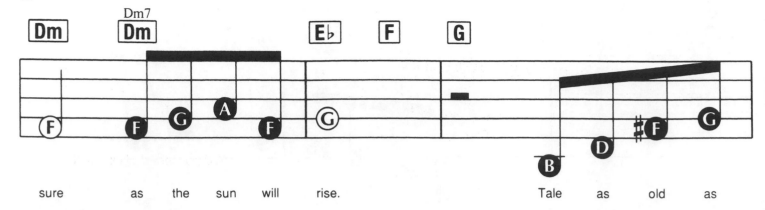

sure   as   the   sun   will   rise.   Tale   as   old   as

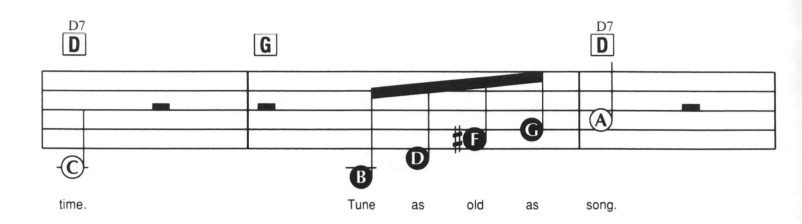

time.   Tune   as   old   as   song.

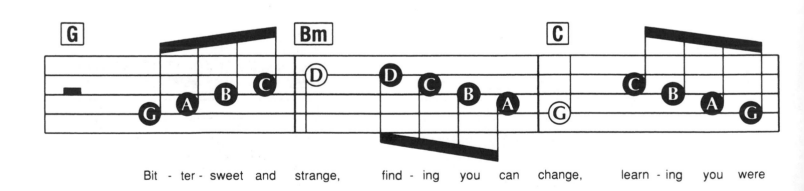

Bit - ter - sweet and strange,   find - ing you can change,   learn - ing you were

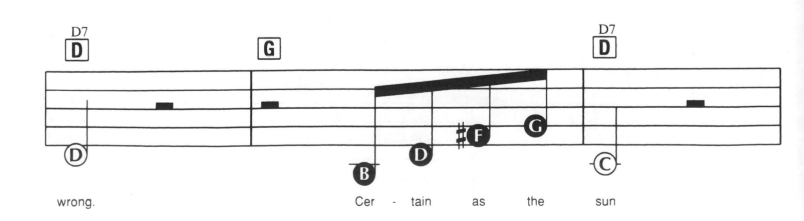

wrong.   Cer - tain   as   the   sun

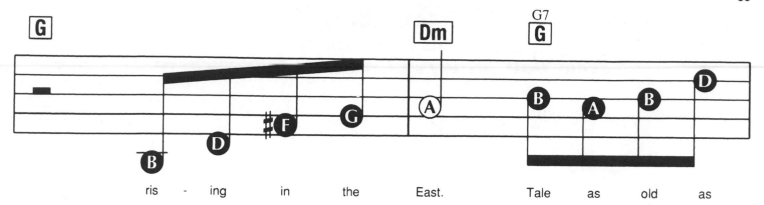

ris - ing in the East. Tale as old as

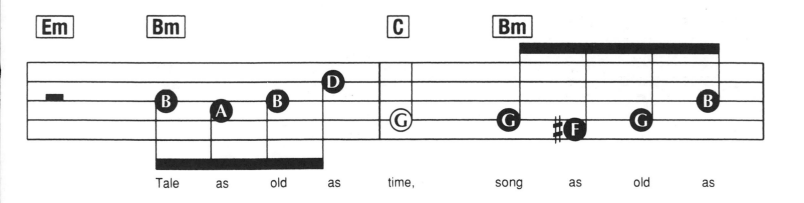

time, song as old as rhyme. Beau - ty and the Beast.

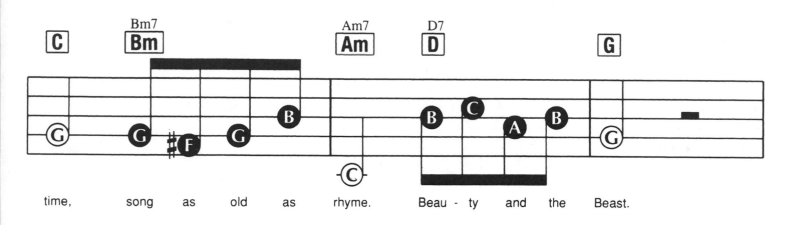

Tale as old as time, song as old as

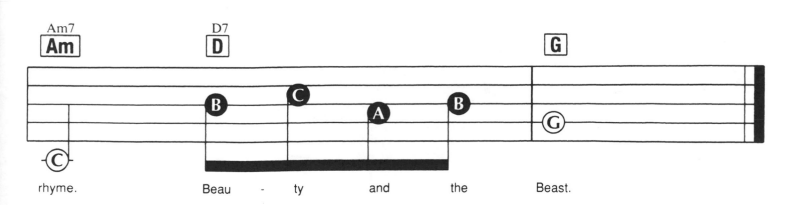

rhyme. Beau - ty and the Beast.

Bella Notte
(This Is the Night)
from Walt Disney's LADY AND THE TRAMP

Registration 7
Rhythm: Fox Trot or Swing

Words and Music by Peggy Lee
and Sonny Burke

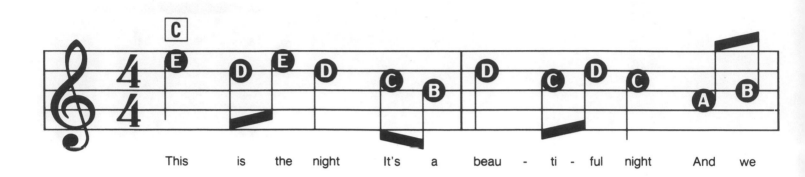

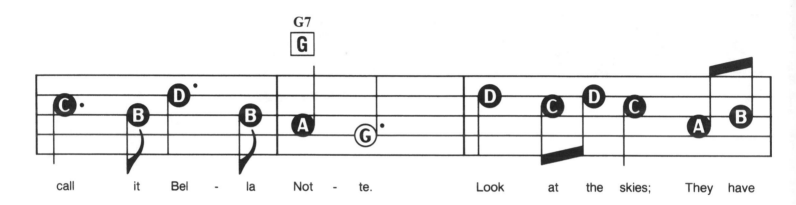

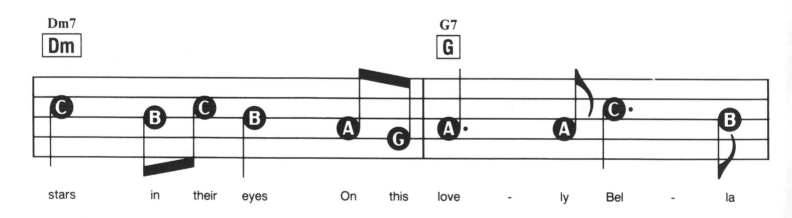

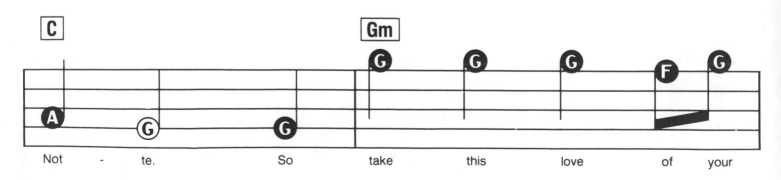

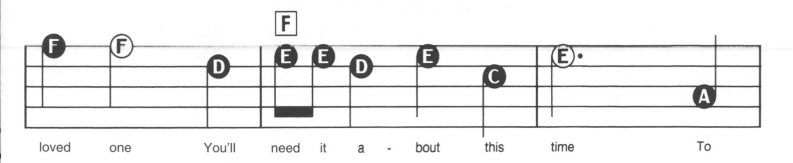

loved one   You'll   need   it   a - bout   this   time   To

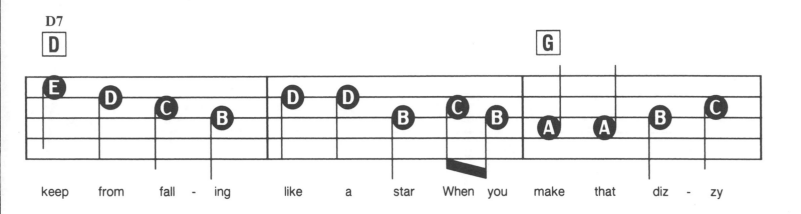

keep   from   fall - ing   like   a   star   When   you   make   that   diz - zy

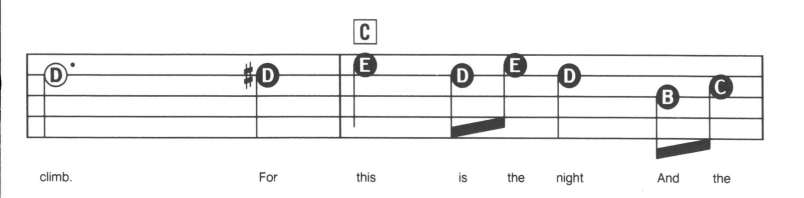

climb.   For   this   is   the   night   And   the

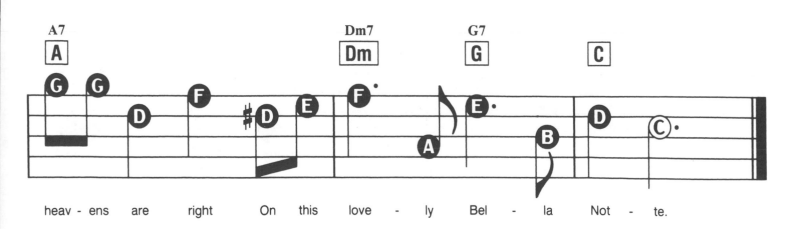

heav - ens   are   right   On   this   love - ly   Bel - la   Not - te.

Beyond the Sea
featured in the Walt Disney/Pixar film FINDING NEMO

Registration 7
Rhythm: Slow Rock or Ballad

Words and Music by Charles Trenet,
Albert Lasry and Jack Lawrence

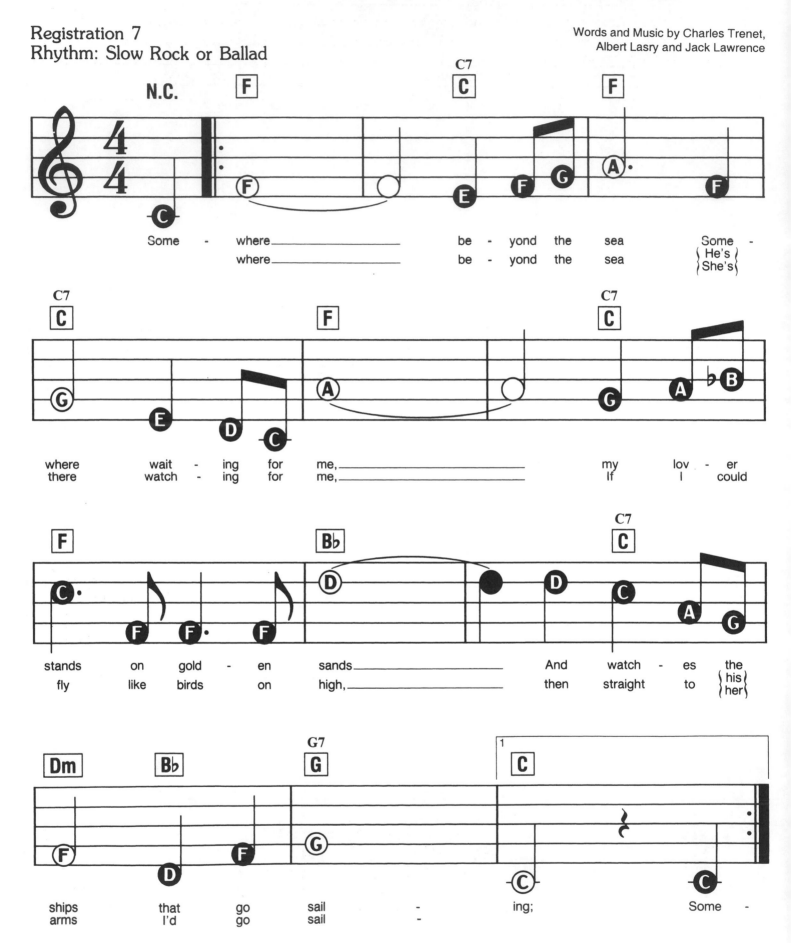

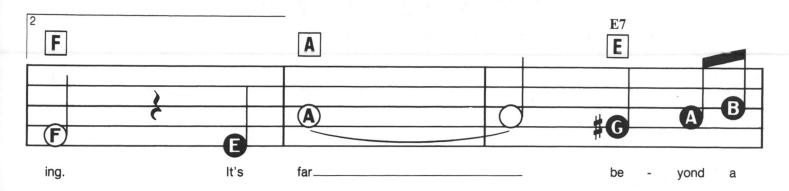

ing.   It's   far   be - yond a

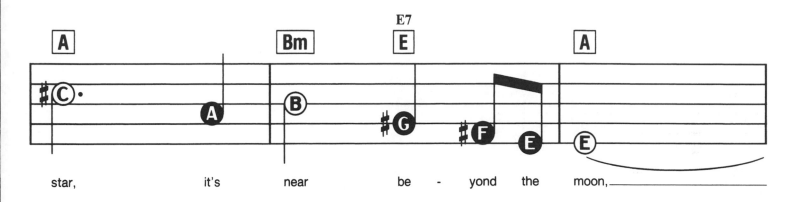

star,   it's   near   be - yond the moon,

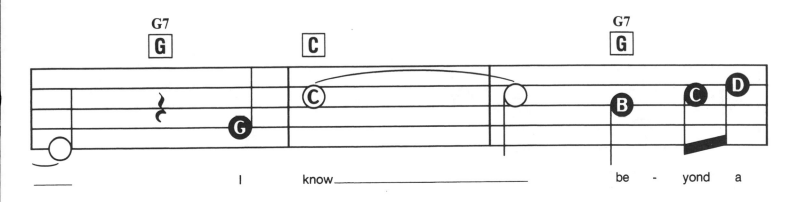

I   know   be - yond a

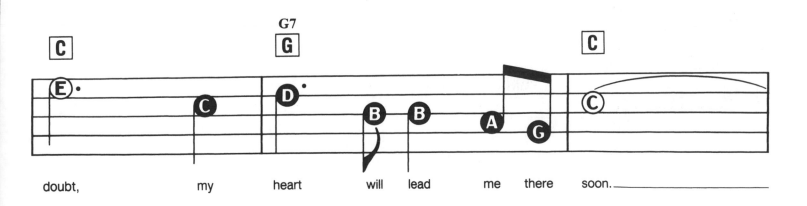

doubt,   my   heart will lead me there soon.

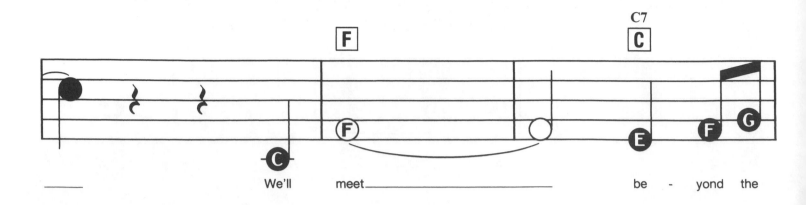

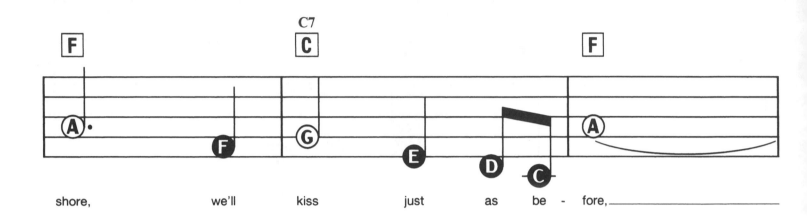

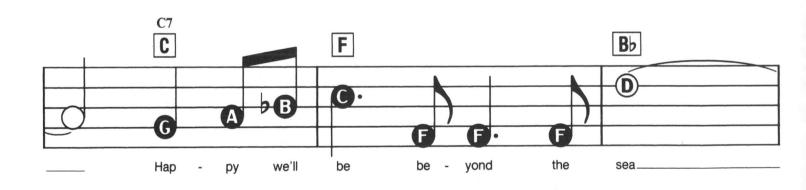

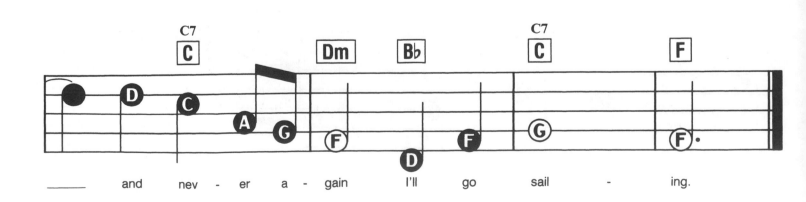

Can You Feel the Love Tonight
from Walt Disney Pictures' THE LION KING

Registration 2
Rhythm: Rock or 8 Beat

Music by Elton John
Lyrics by Tim Rice

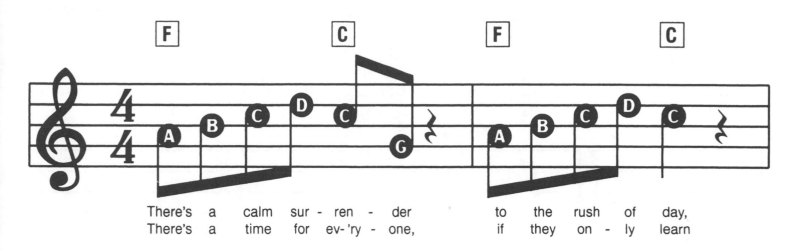

There's a calm sur - ren - der   to the rush of day,
There's a time for ev - 'ry - one,   if they on - ly learn

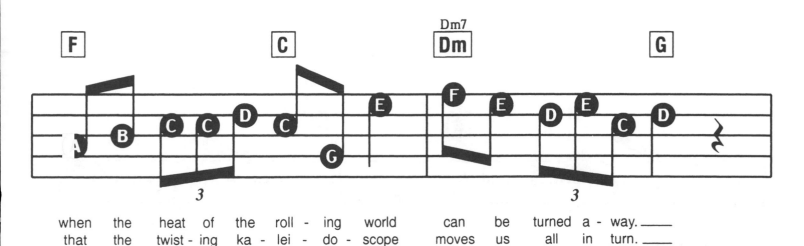

when the heat of the roll - ing world can be turned a - way. ____
that the twist - ing ka - lei - do - scope moves us all in turn. ____

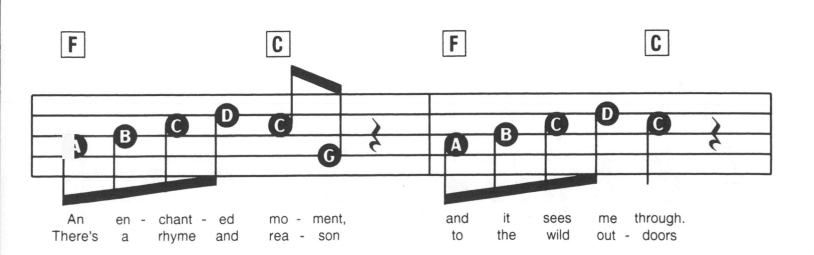

An en - chant - ed mo - ment,   and it sees me through.
There's a rhyme and rea - son   to the wild out - doors

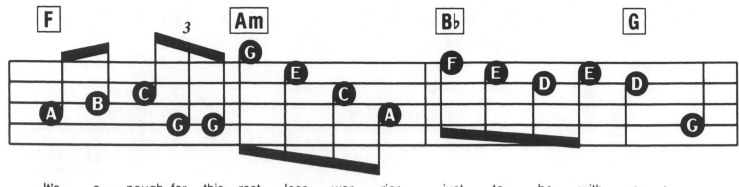

It's e - nough for this rest - less war - rior just to be with you.
when the heart of this star - crossed voy - ag - er beats in time with yours. } And

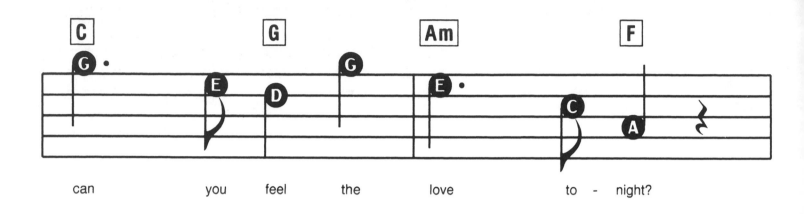

can you feel the love to - night?

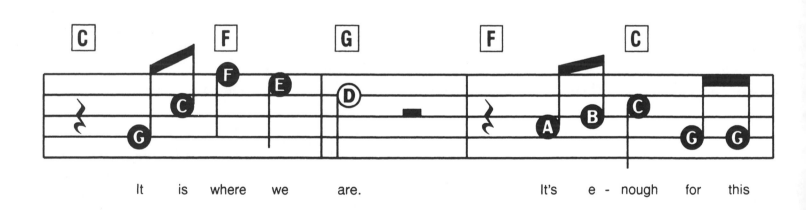

It is where we are. It's e - nough for this

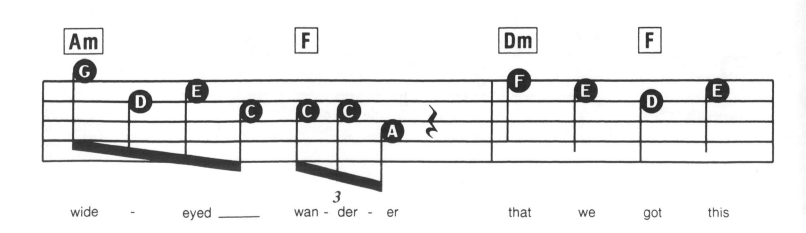

wide - eyed _____ wan - der - er that we got this

far. And can you feel the love to - night, _____

how it's laid to rest? It's e - nough to make

kings ____ and _____ vag - a - bonds be - lieve the ver - y

best. It's e - nough to make

kings ___ and ____ vag - a - bonds be - lieve the ver - y best.

Bibbidi-Bobbidi-Boo

(The Magic Song)
from Walt Disney's CINDERELLA

Registration 8
Rhythm: Swing

Words by Jerry Livingston
Music by Mack David and Al Hoffman

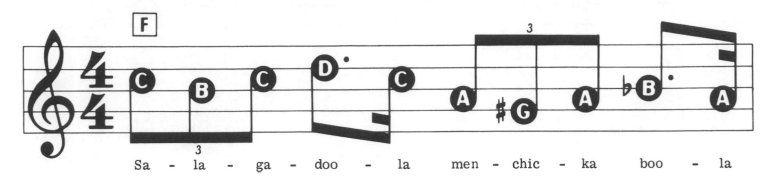

Sa - la - ga - doo - la men - chic - ka boo - la

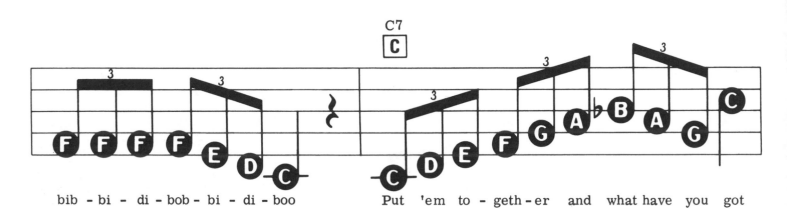

bib - bi - di - bob - bi - di - boo   Put 'em to - geth - er and what have you got

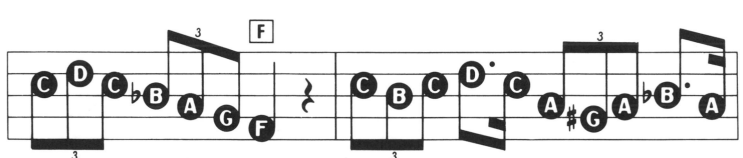

Bib - bi - di - bob - bi - di - boo.   Sa - la - ga - doo - la men - chic - ka boo - la

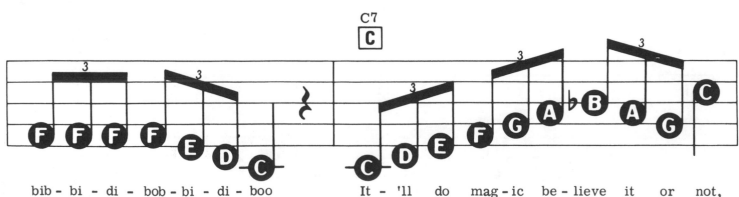

bib - bi - di - bob - bi - di - boo   It - 'll do mag - ic be - lieve it or not,

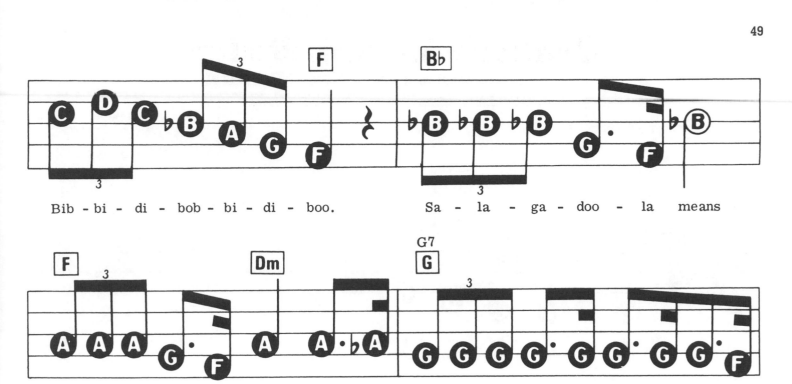

Bib - bi - di - bob - bi - di - boo.   Sa - la - ga - doo - la means

men – chic – ka boo – le – roo,   But   the   thing – a – ma – bob   that does   the   job   is

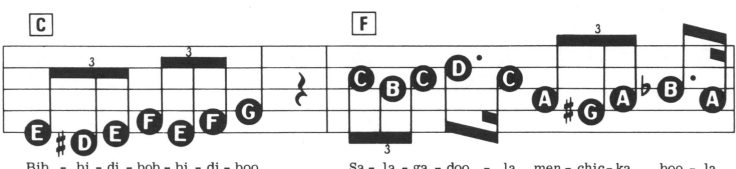

Bib - bi - di - bob - bi - di - boo.   Sa - la - ga - doo - la   men - chic - ka   boo - la

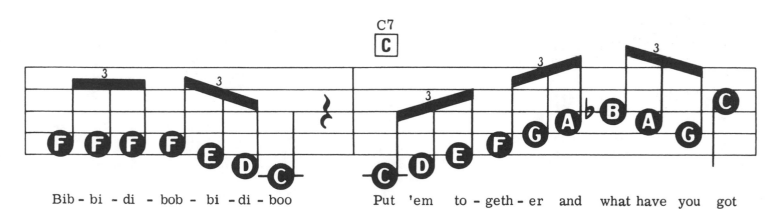

Bib - bi - di - bob - bi - di - boo   Put 'em   to - geth - er   and   what have you   got

Bib - bi - di - bob - bi - di - bib - bi - di - bob - bi - di   Bib - bi - di - bob - bi - di - boo.

Candle on the Water
from Walt Disney's PETE'S DRAGON

Registration 1
Rhythm: Fox Trot or Ballad

Words and Music by Al Kasha
and Joel Hirschhorn

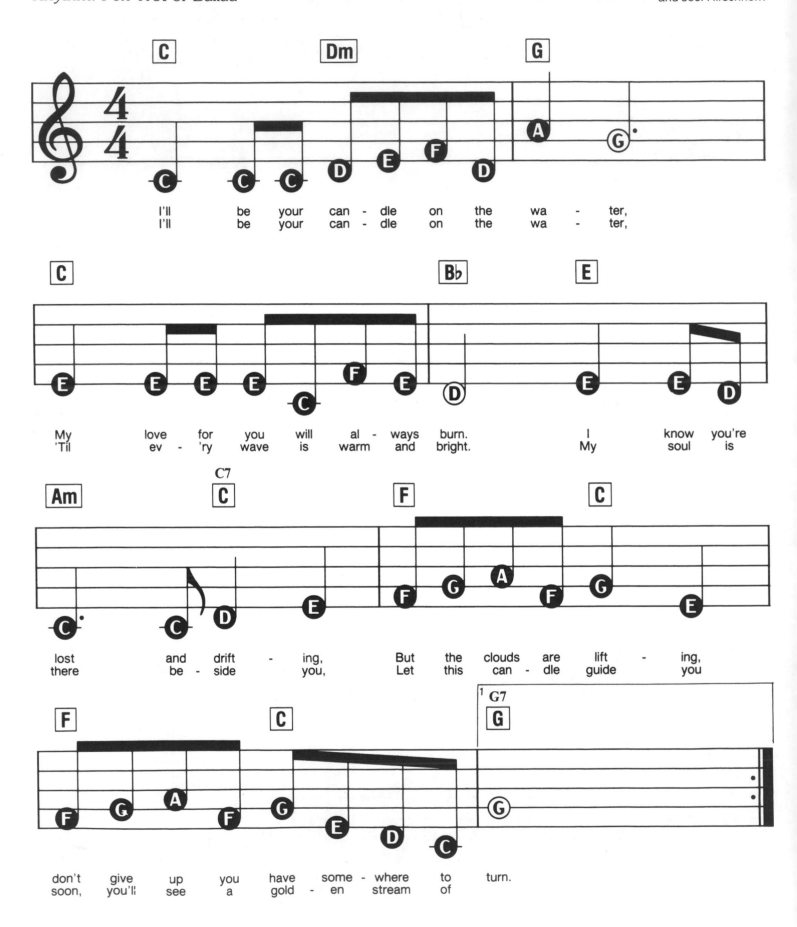

I'll be your can - dle on the wa - ter,
I'll be your can - dle on the wa - ter,

My love for you will al - ways burn. I know you're
'Til ev - 'ry wave is warm and bright. My soul is

lost and drift - ing, But the clouds are lift - ing,
there be - side you, Let this can - dle guide you

don't give up you have some - where to turn.
soon, you'll see a gold - en stream to of

Circle of Life
from Walt Disney Pictures' THE LION KING

Registration 2
Rhythm: Calypso or Reggae

Music by Elton John
Lyrics by Tim Rice

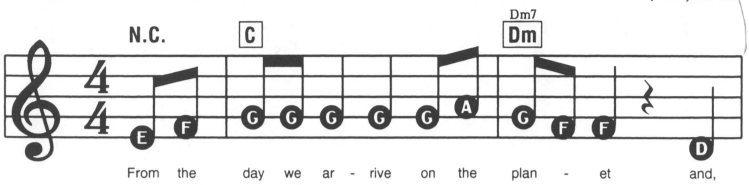

From the day we ar - rive on the plan - et and,

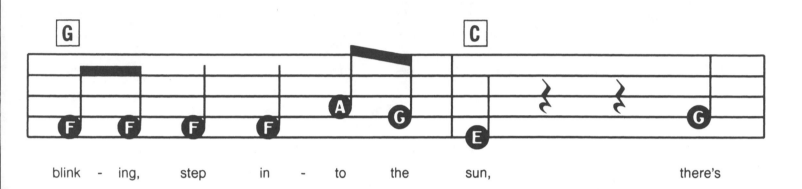

blink - ing, step in - to the sun, there's

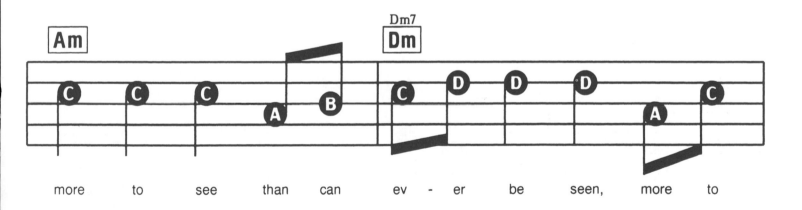

more to see than can ev - er be seen, more to

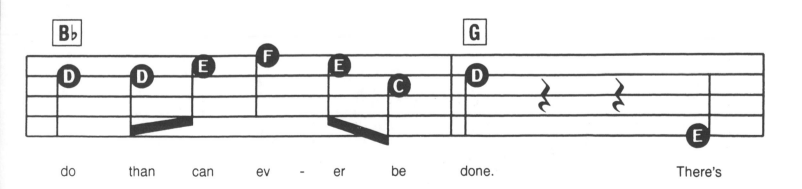

do than can ev - er be done. There's

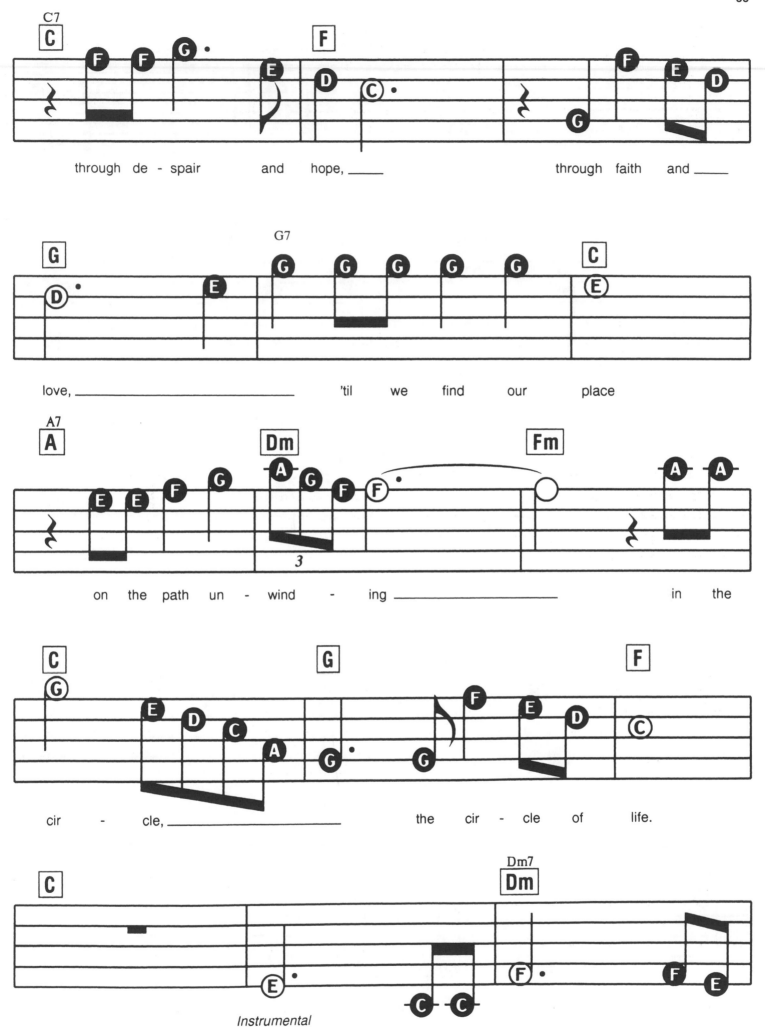

It's the cir - cle of life,

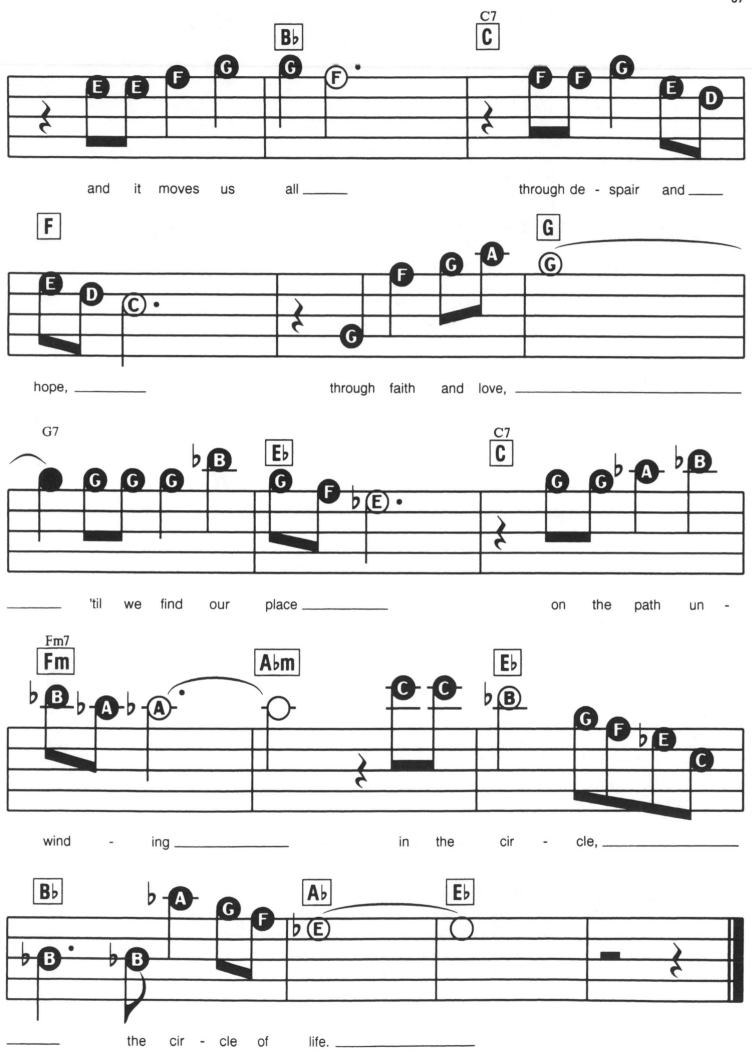

Chim Chim Cher-ee
from Walt Disney's MARY POPPINS

Registration 3
Rhythm: Waltz

Words and Music by Richard M. Sherman
and Robert B. Sherman

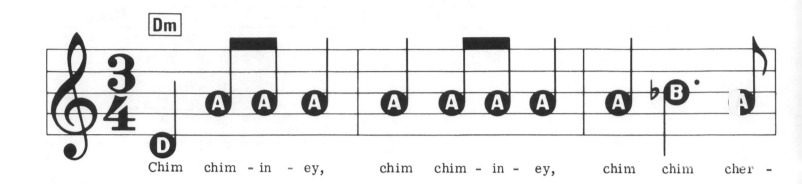

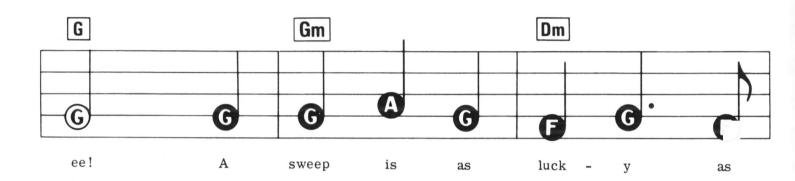

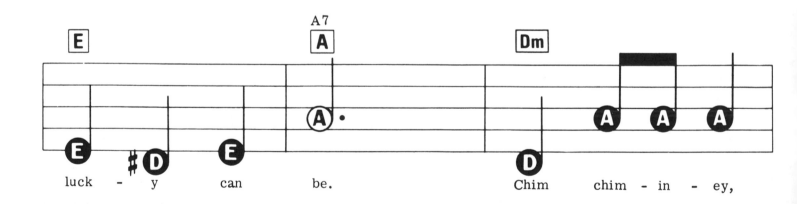

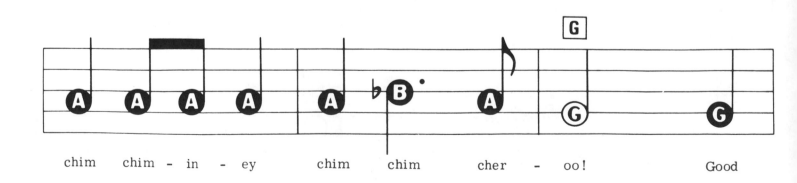

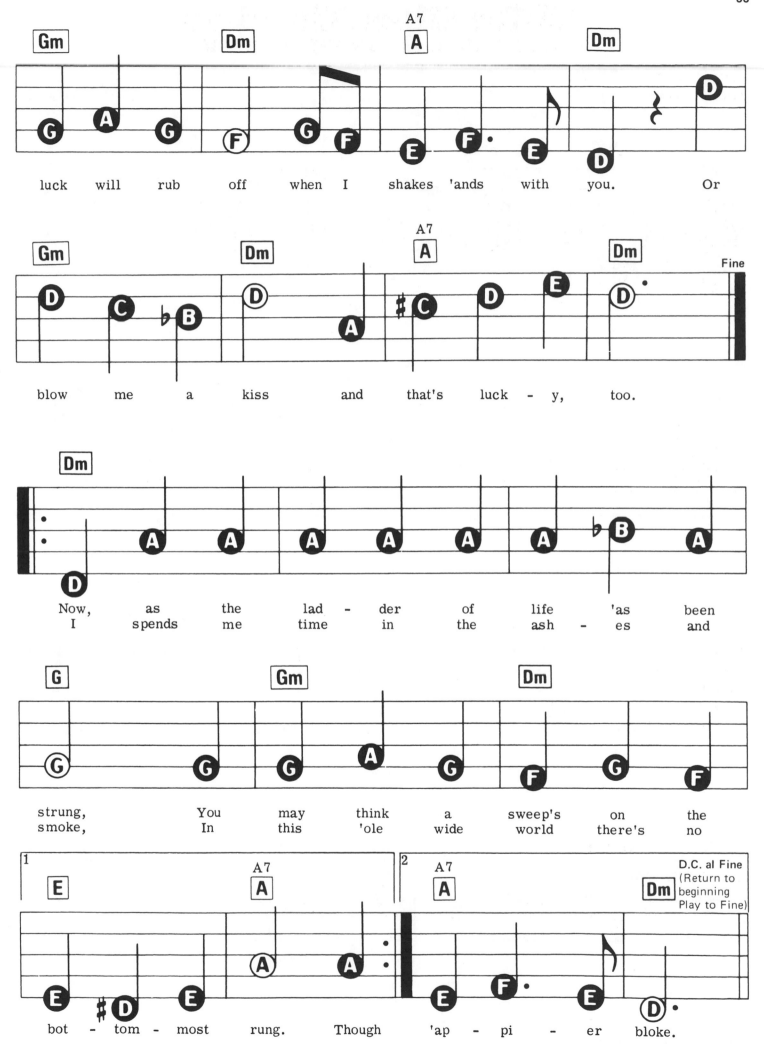

Cruella De Vil
from Walt Disney's 101 DALMATIANS

Registration 9
Rhythm: Swing

Words and Music by
Mel Leven

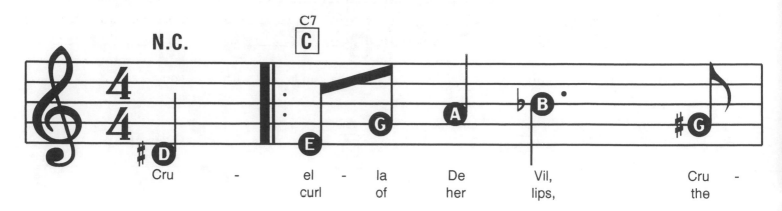

Cru - el - la De Vil, Cru -
curl of her lips,   the

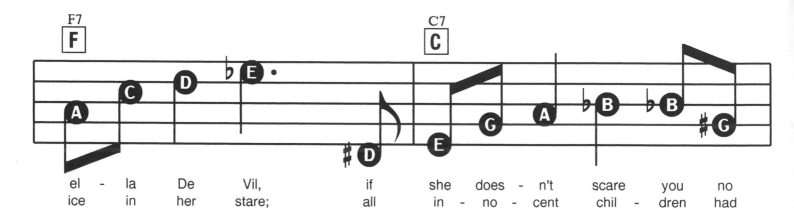

el - la De Vil, if she does - n't scare you no
ice in her stare; all in - no - cent chil - dren had

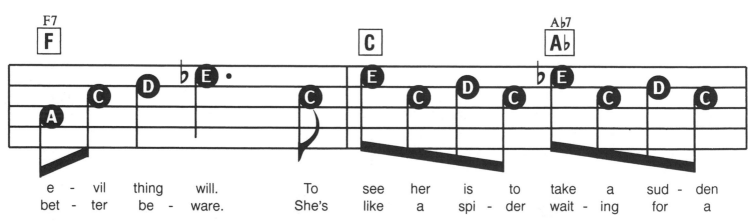

e - vil thing will. To see her is to take a sud - den
bet - ter be - ware. She's like a spi - der wait - ing for a

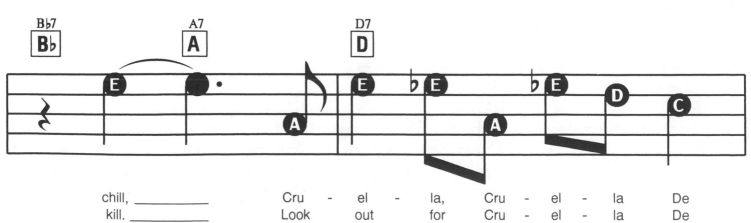

chill, _____ Cru - el - la, Cru - el - la De
kill. _____ Look out for Cru - el - la De

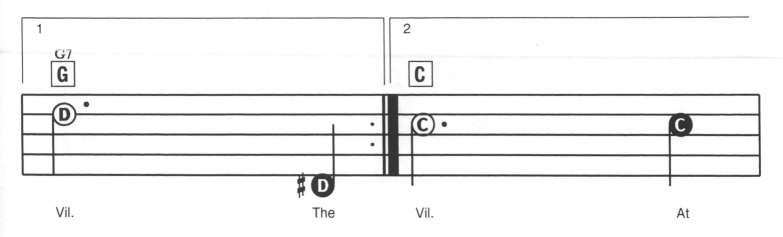

Vil.   The   Vil.   At

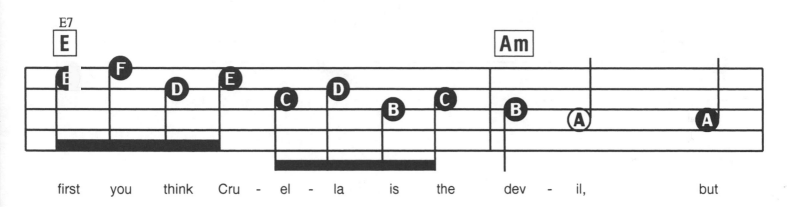

first   you   think   Cru - el - la   is   the   dev - il,   but

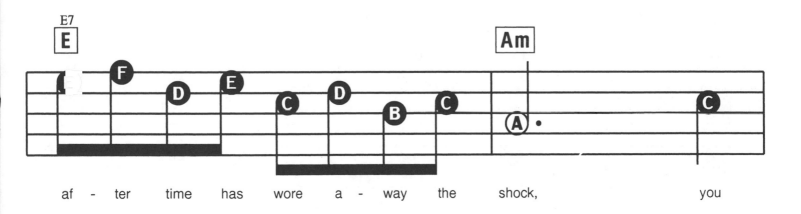

af - ter   time   has   wore   a - way   the   shock,   you

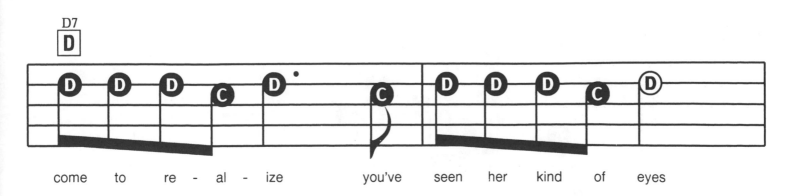

come   to   re - al - ize   you've   seen   her   kind   of   eyes

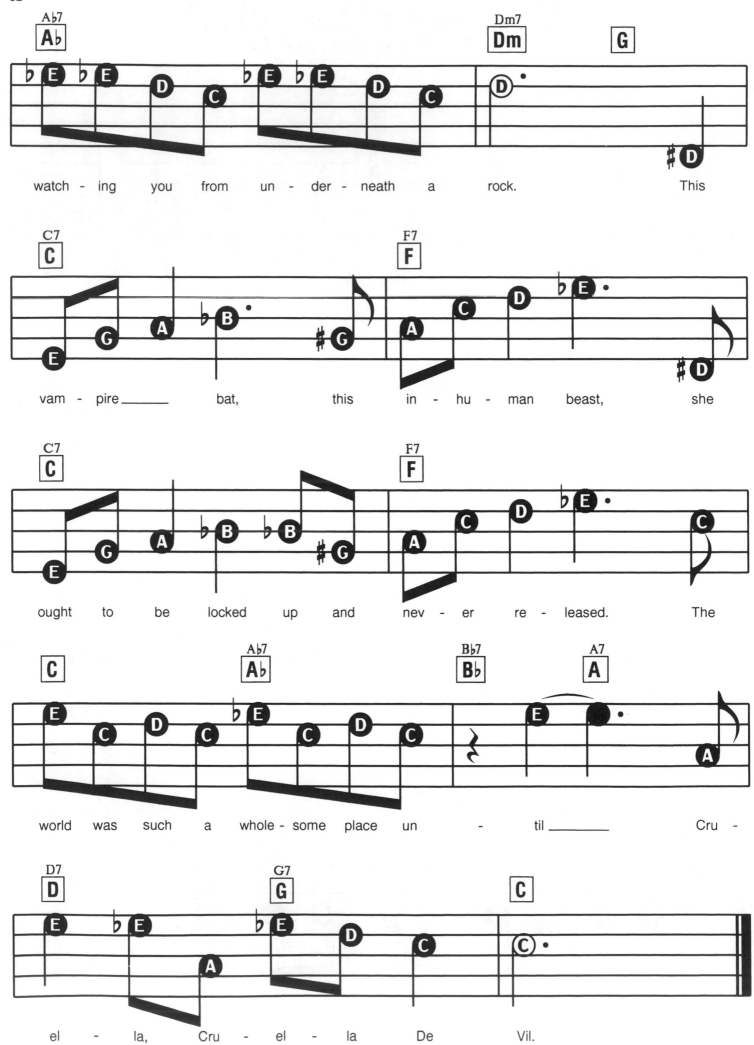

Colors of the Wind
from Walt Disney's POCAHONTAS

Registration 5
Rhythm: None

Music by Alan Menken
Lyrics by Stephen Schwartz

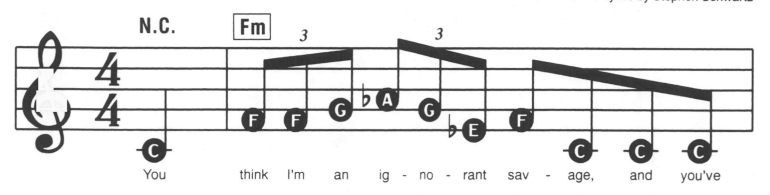

You think I'm an ig - no - rant sav - age, and you've

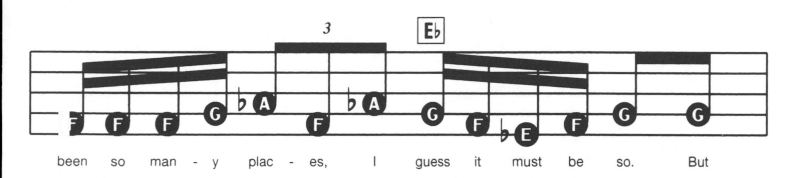

been so man - y plac - es, I guess it must be so. But

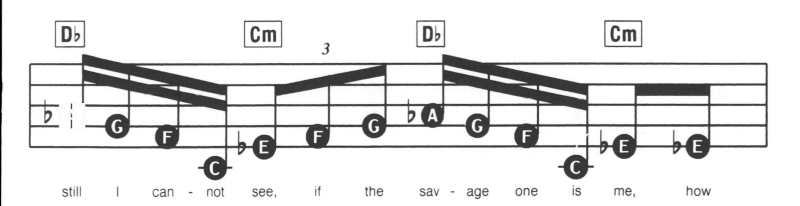

still I can - not see, if the sav - age one is me, how

Rhythm: Rock or 8-Beat

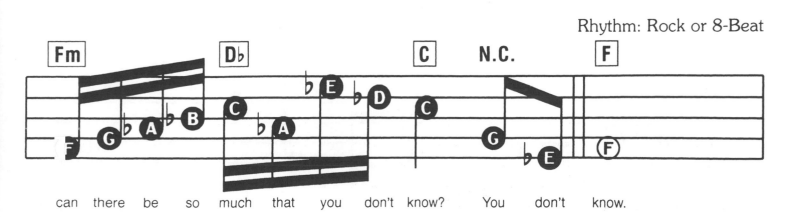

can there be so much that you don't know? You don't know.

64

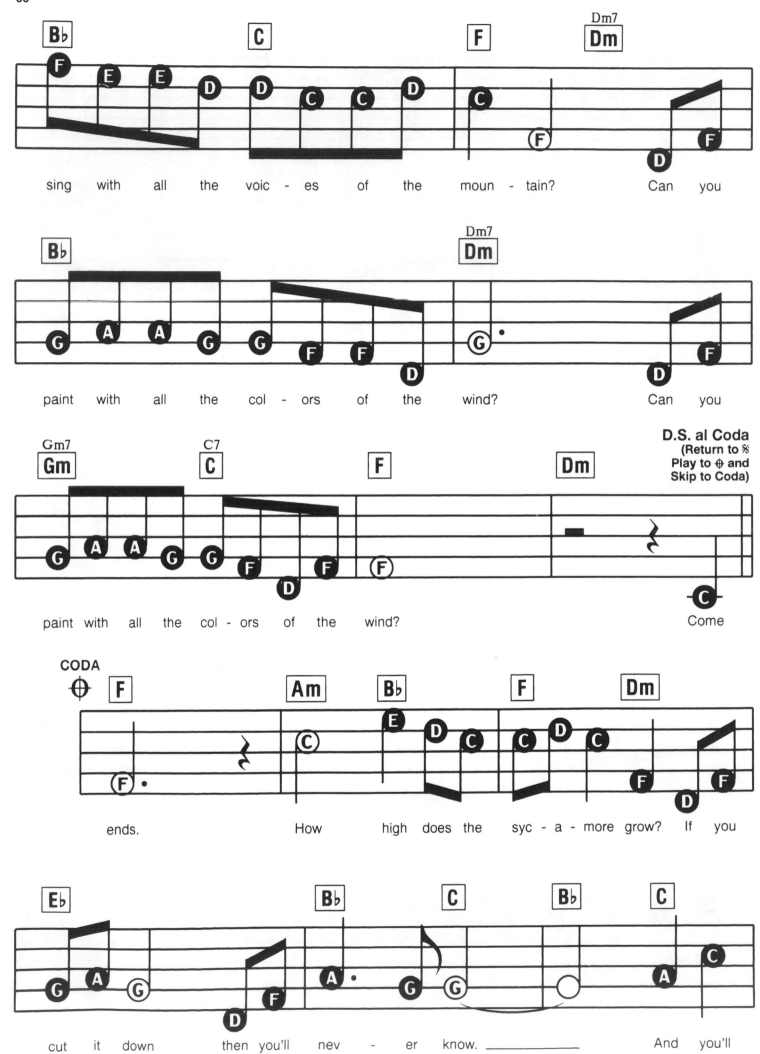

67

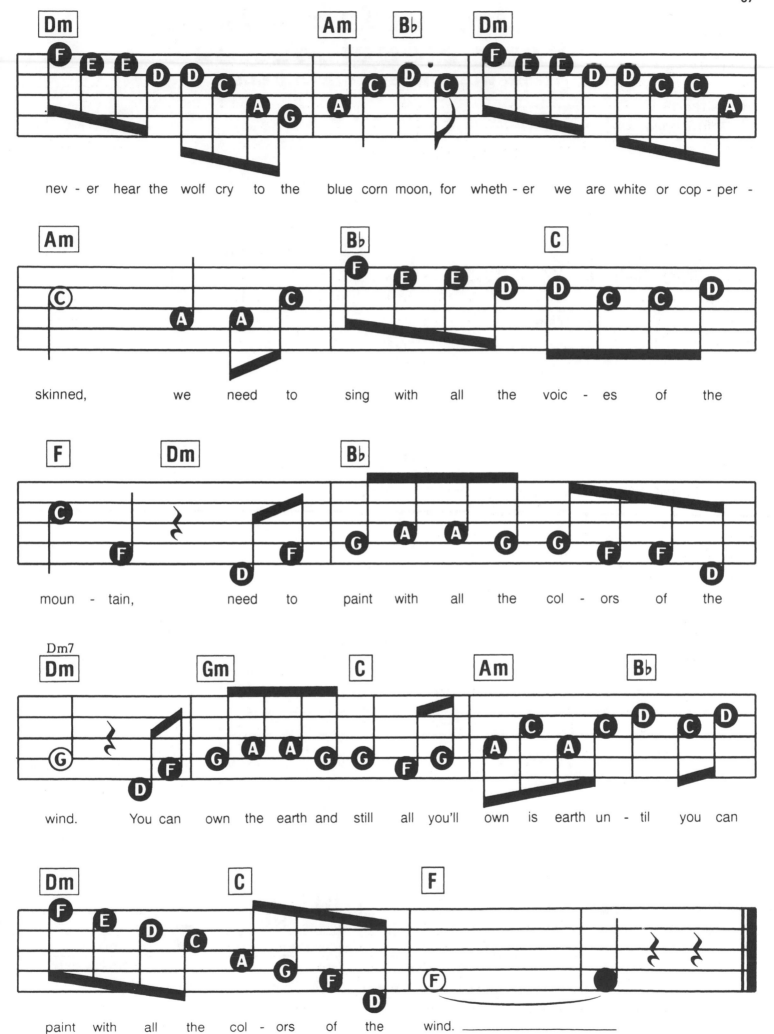

A Dream Is a Wish Your Heart Makes

from Walt Disney's CINDERELLA

Registration 1
Rhythm: Ballad or Fox Trot

Words and Music by Mack David,
Al Hoffman and Jerry Livingston

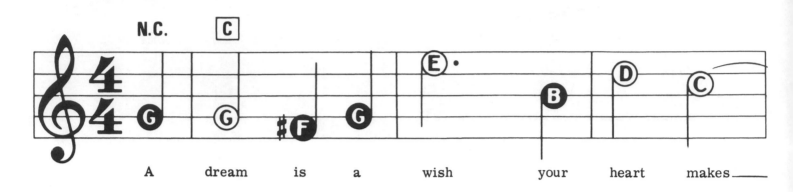

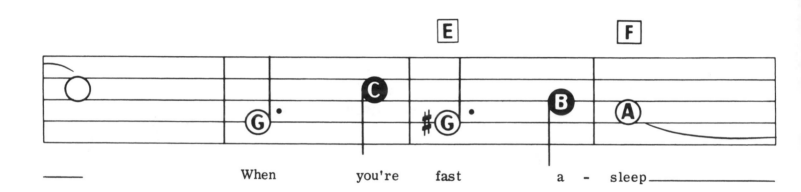

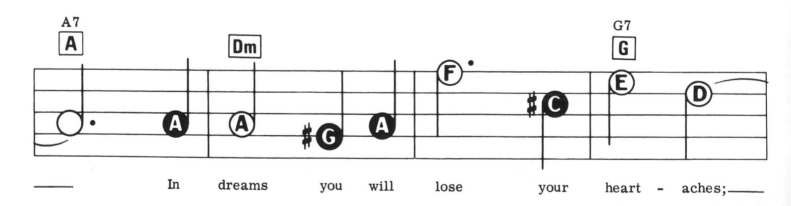

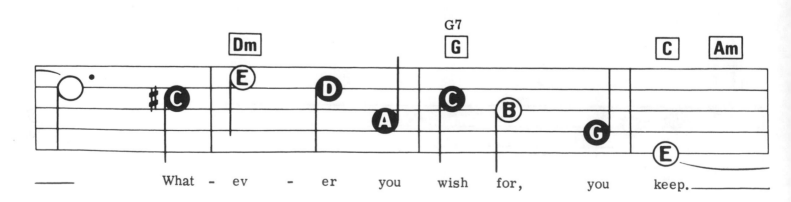

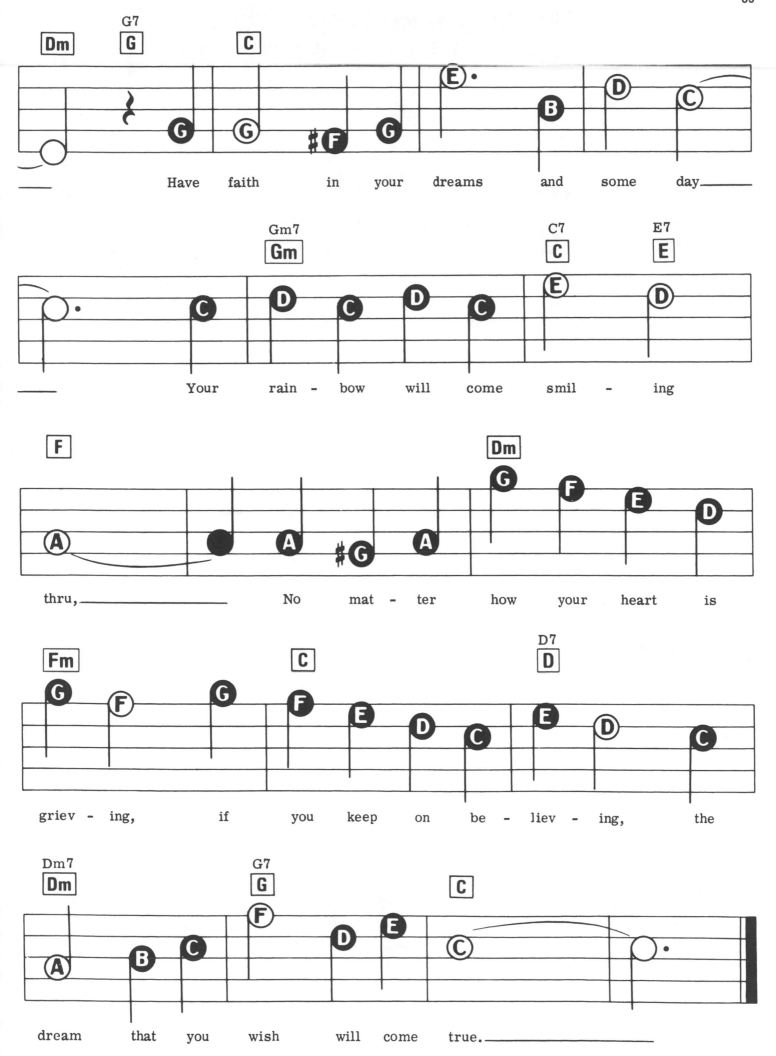

Ev'rybody Wants to Be a Cat
from Walt Disney's THE ARISTOCATS

Registration 10
Rhythm: Fox Trot

Words by Floyd Huddleston
Music by Al Rinker

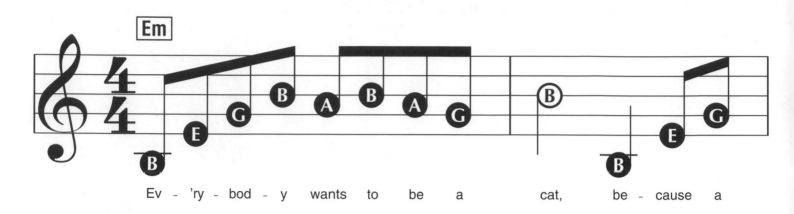

Ev – 'ry – bod – y wants to be a cat, be – cause a

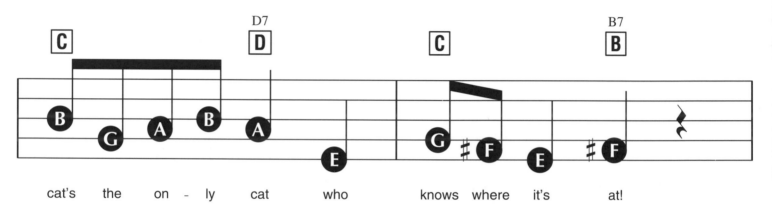

cat's the on – ly cat who knows where it's at!

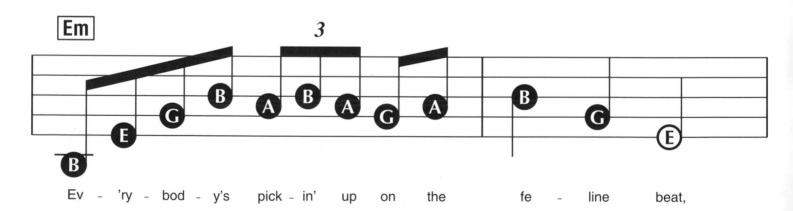

Ev – 'ry – bod – y's pick – in' up on the fe – line beat,

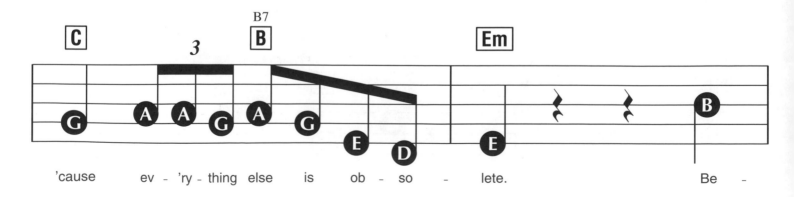

'cause ev – 'ry – thing else is ob – so – lete. Be –

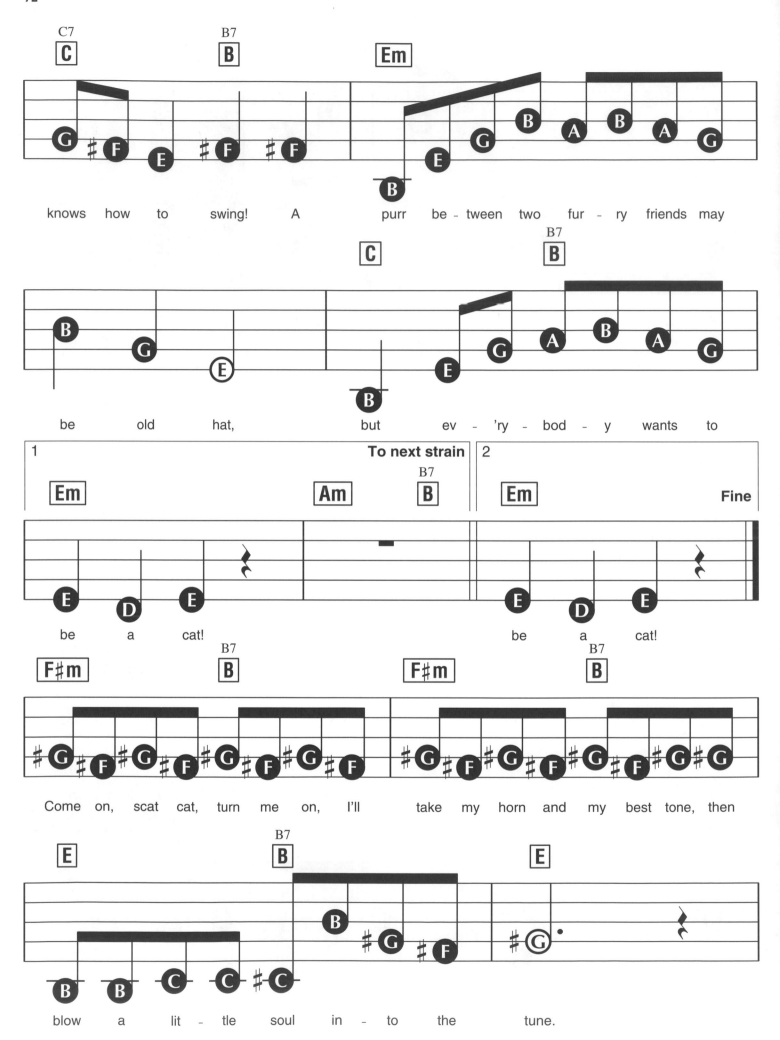

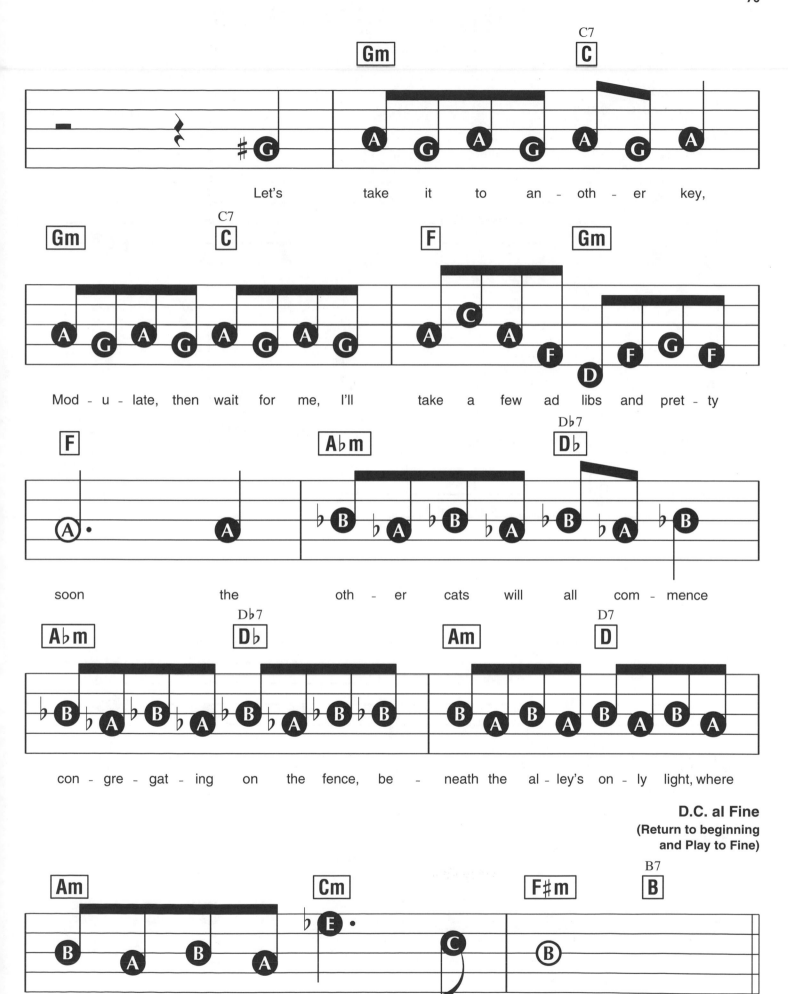

D.C. al Fine
(Return to beginning
and Play to Fine)

Friend Like Me
from Walt Disney's ALADDIN

Registration 1
Rhythm: Polka or March

Lyrics by Howard Ashman
Music by Alan Menken

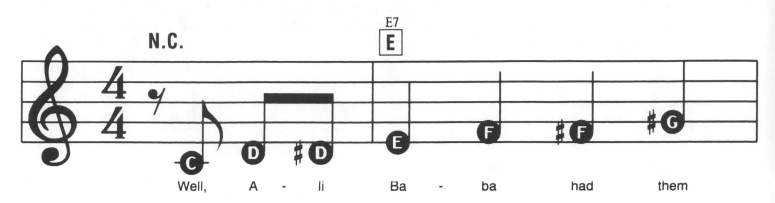

Well, A - li Ba - ba had them

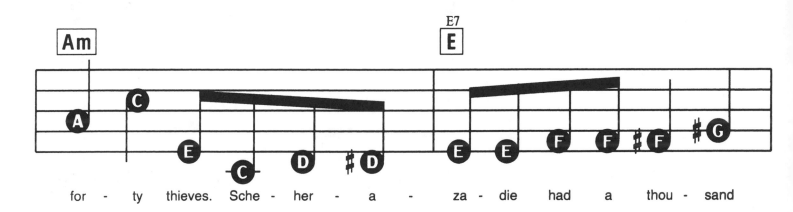

for - ty thieves. Sche - her - a - za - die had a thou - sand

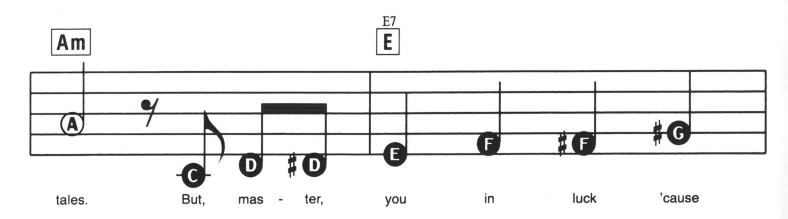

tales. But, mas - ter, you in luck 'cause

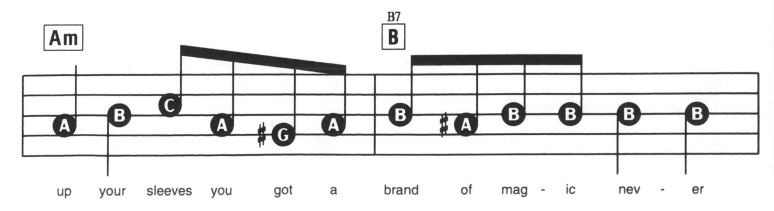

up your sleeves you got a brand of mag - ic nev - er

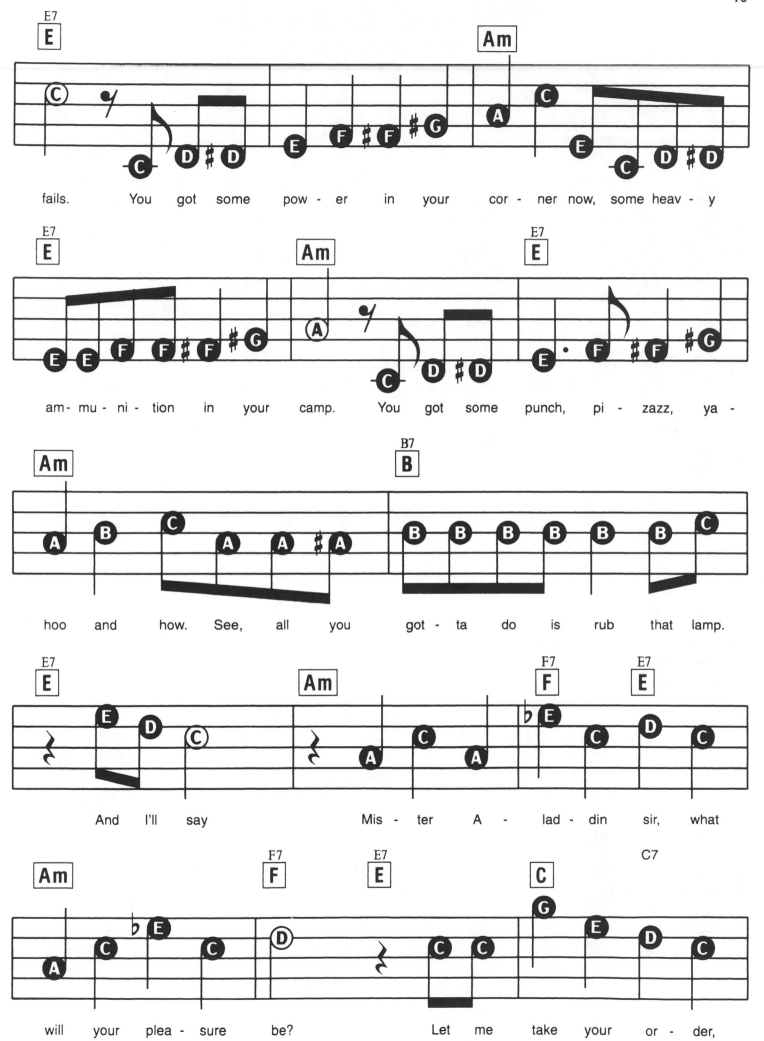

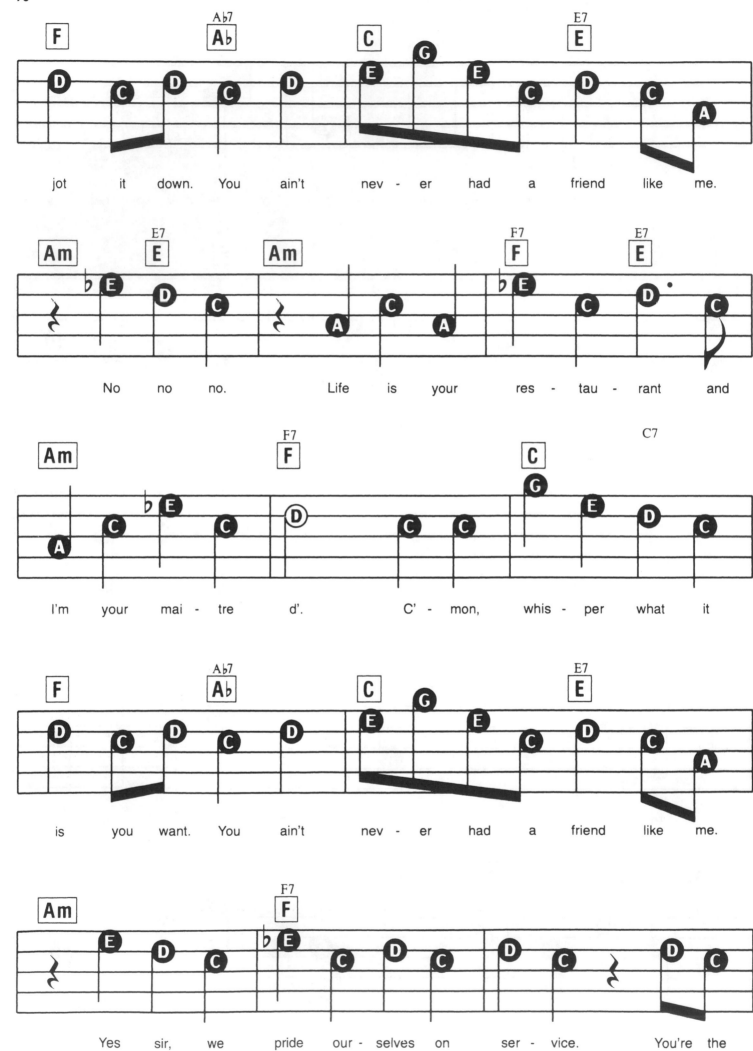

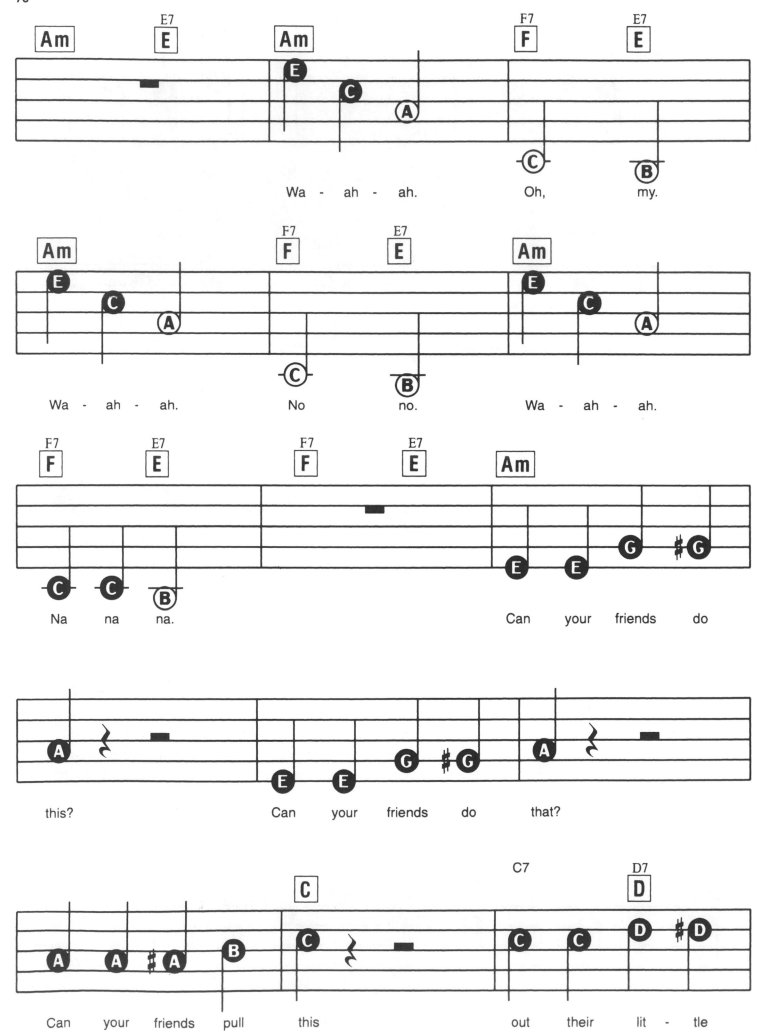

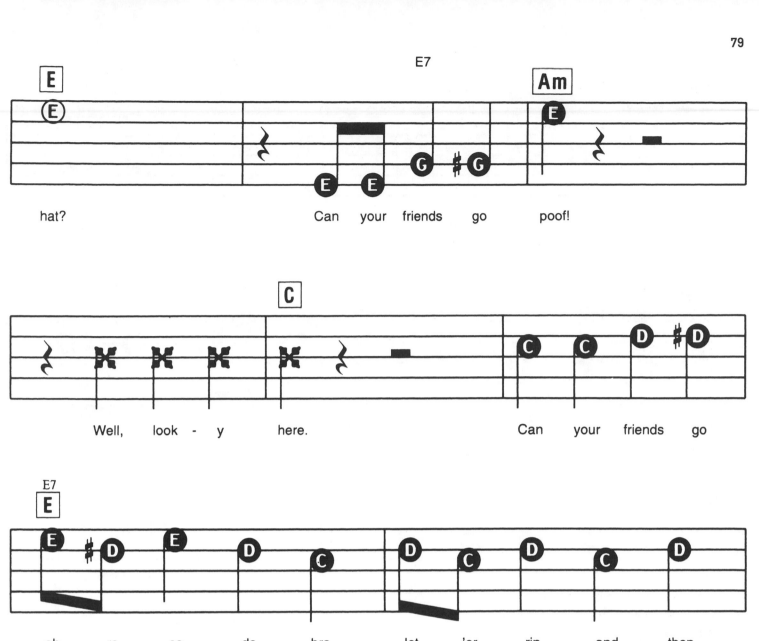

hat?   Can your friends go poof!

Well, look - y here.   Can your friends go

ab - ra - ca - da - bra,   let 'er rip and then

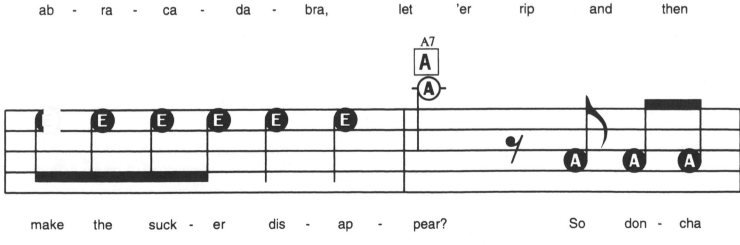

make the suck - er dis - ap - pear?   So don - cha

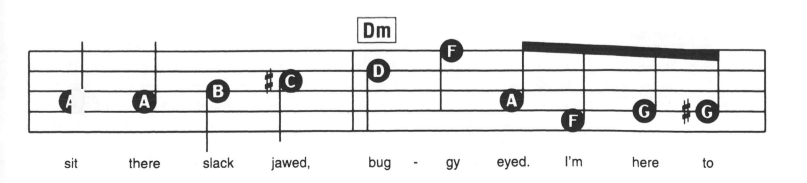

sit there slack jawed, bug - gy eyed. I'm here to

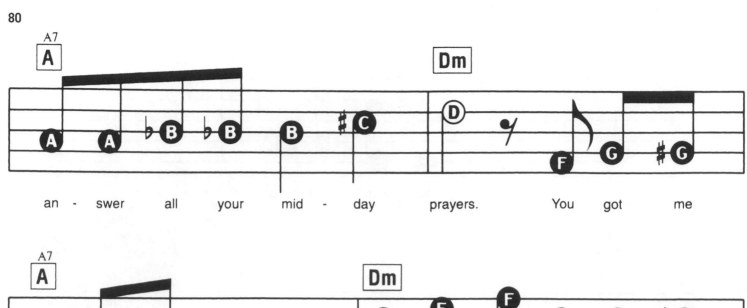

an - swer all your mid - day prayers. You got me

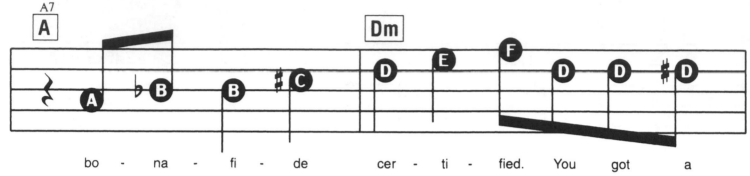

bo - na - fi - de cer - ti - fied. You got a

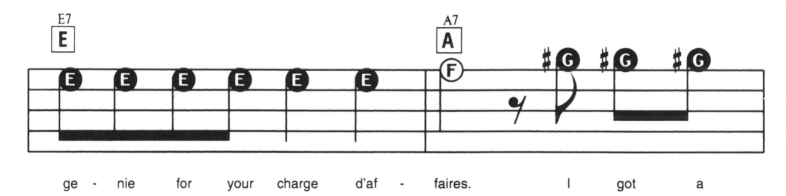

ge - nie for your charge d'af - faires. I got a

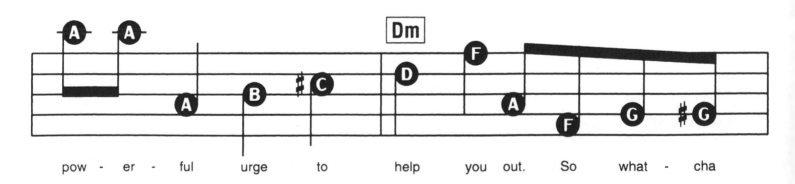

pow - er - ful urge to help you out. So what - cha

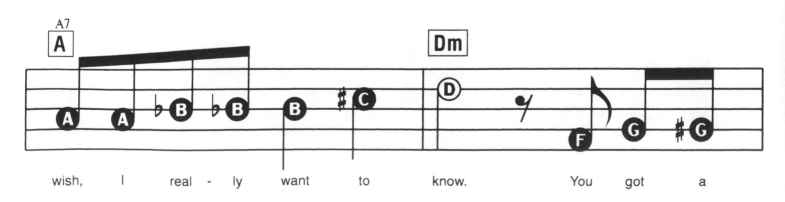

wish, I real - ly want to know. You got a

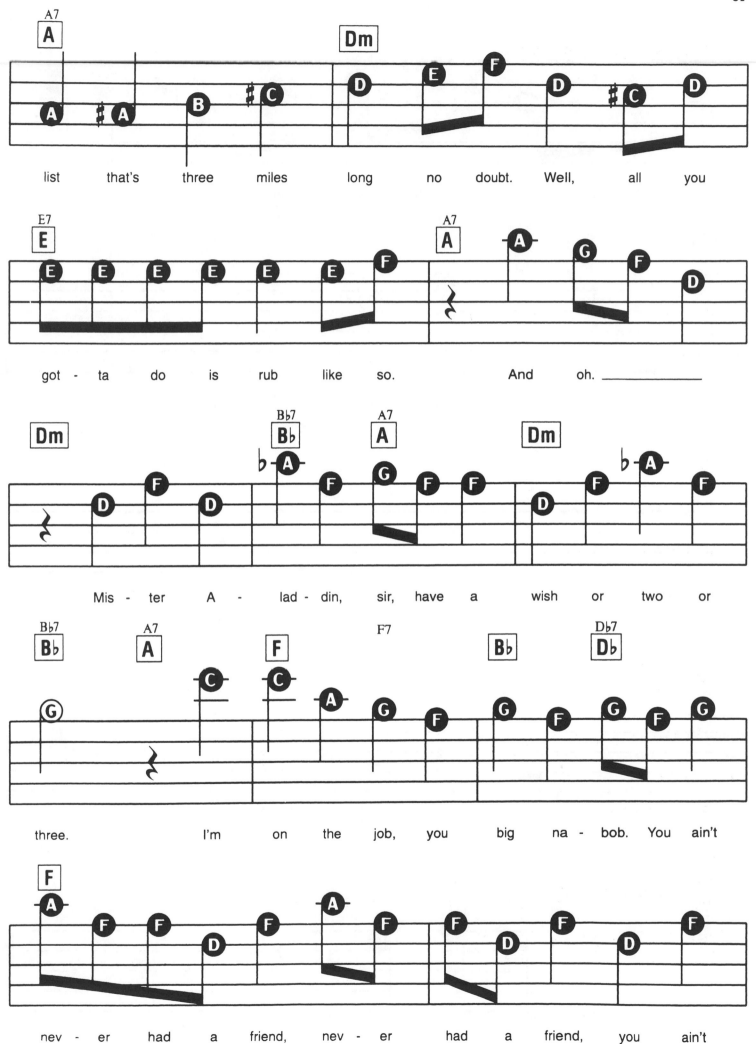

Hakuna Matata
from Walt Disney Pictures' THE LION KING

Registration 5
Rhythm: Swing

Music by Elton John
Lyrics by Tim Rice

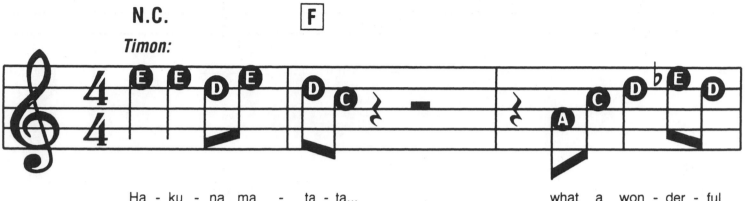

Ha - ku - na ma - ta - ta... what a won - der - ful

phrase! Ha - ku - na ma - ta - ta...

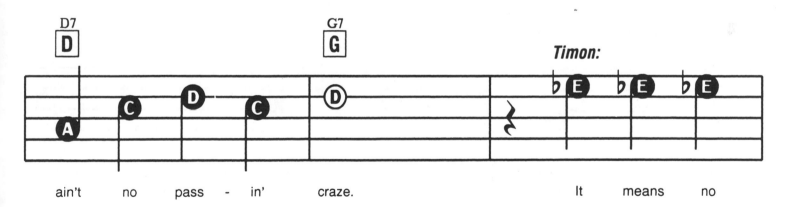

ain't no pass - in' craze. It means no

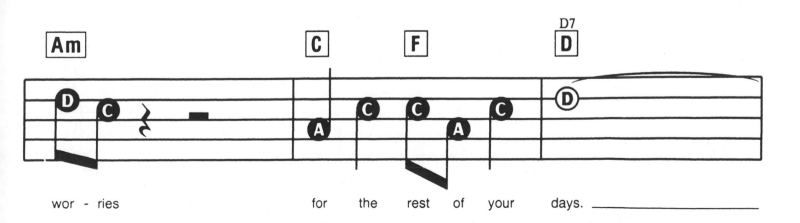

wor - ries for the rest of your days. _____

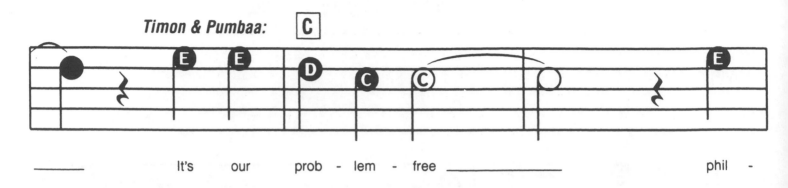

Timon & Pumbaa:

It's our prob - lem - free _____ phil -

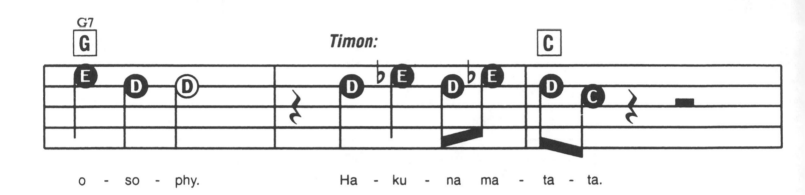

o - so - phy. Ha - ku - na ma - ta - ta.

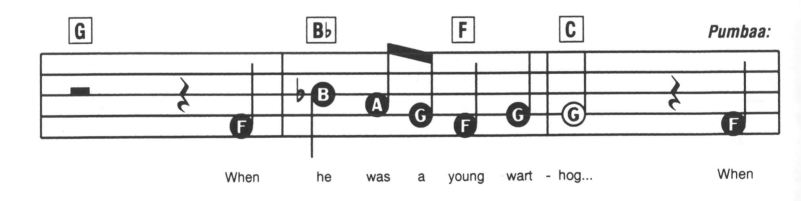

When he was a young wart - hog... When

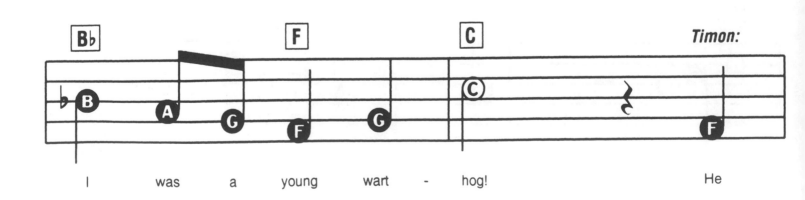

I was a young wart - hog! He

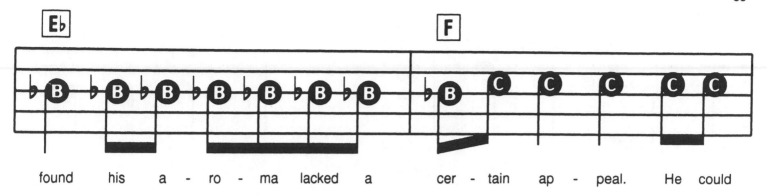

found his a - ro - ma lacked a cer - tain ap - peal. He could

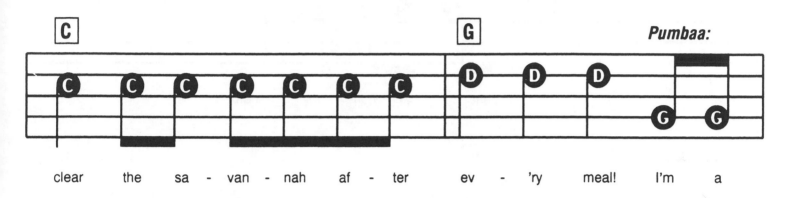

clear the sa - van - nah af - ter ev - 'ry meal! I'm a

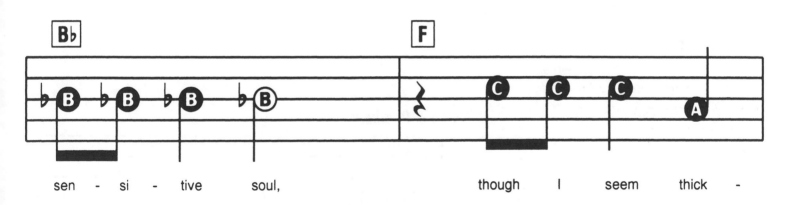

sen - si - tive soul, though I seem thick -

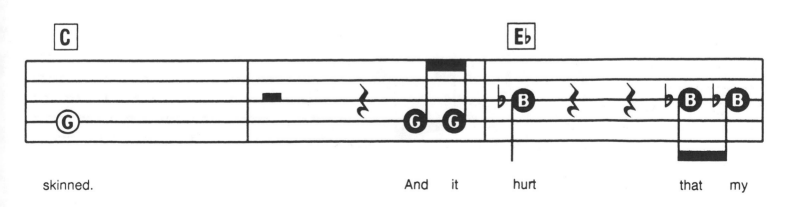

skinned. And it hurt that my

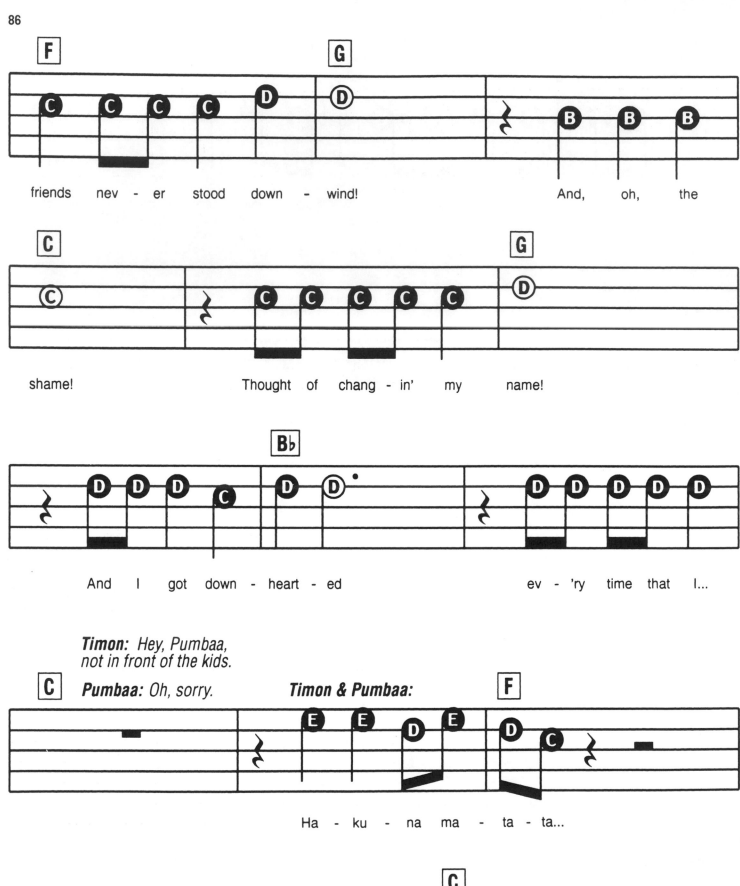

friends nev - er stood down - wind!   And, oh, the

shame!   Thought of chang - in' my   name!

And I got down - heart - ed   ev - 'ry time that I...

Timon: *Hey, Pumbaa,*
not in front of the kids.

Pumbaa: *Oh, sorry.*   **Timon & Pumbaa:**

Ha - ku - na ma - ta - ta...

what a won - der - ful phrase.

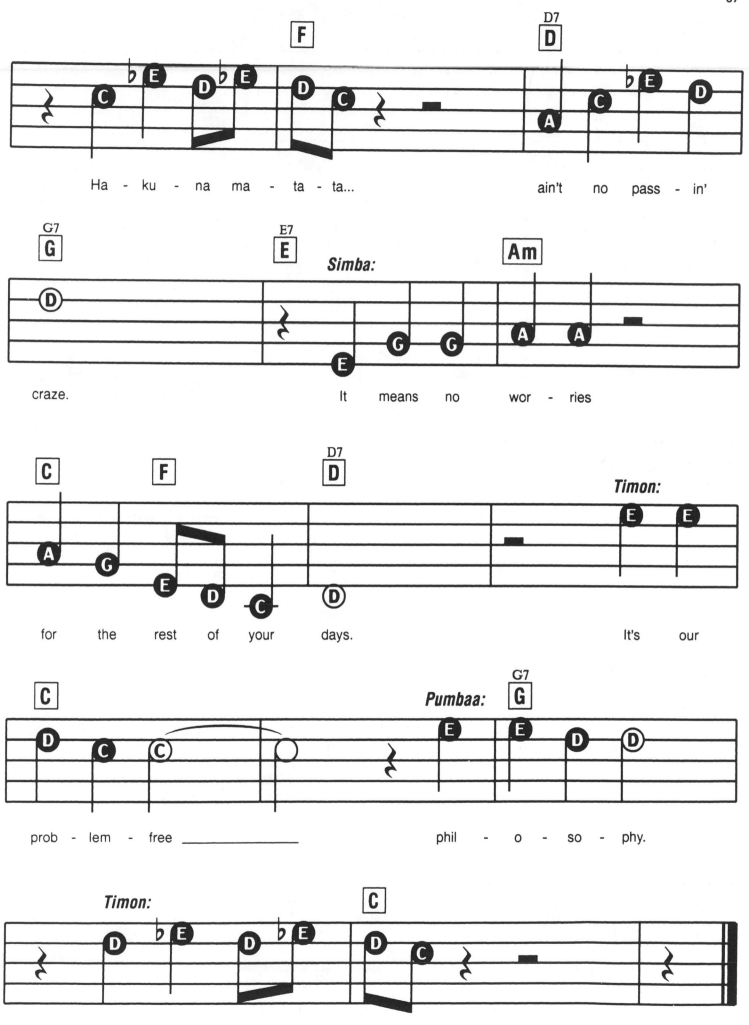

Go the Distance
from Walt Disney Pictures' HERCULES

Registration 3
Rhythm: 16 Beat or Pop

Music by Alan Menken
Lyrics by David Zippel

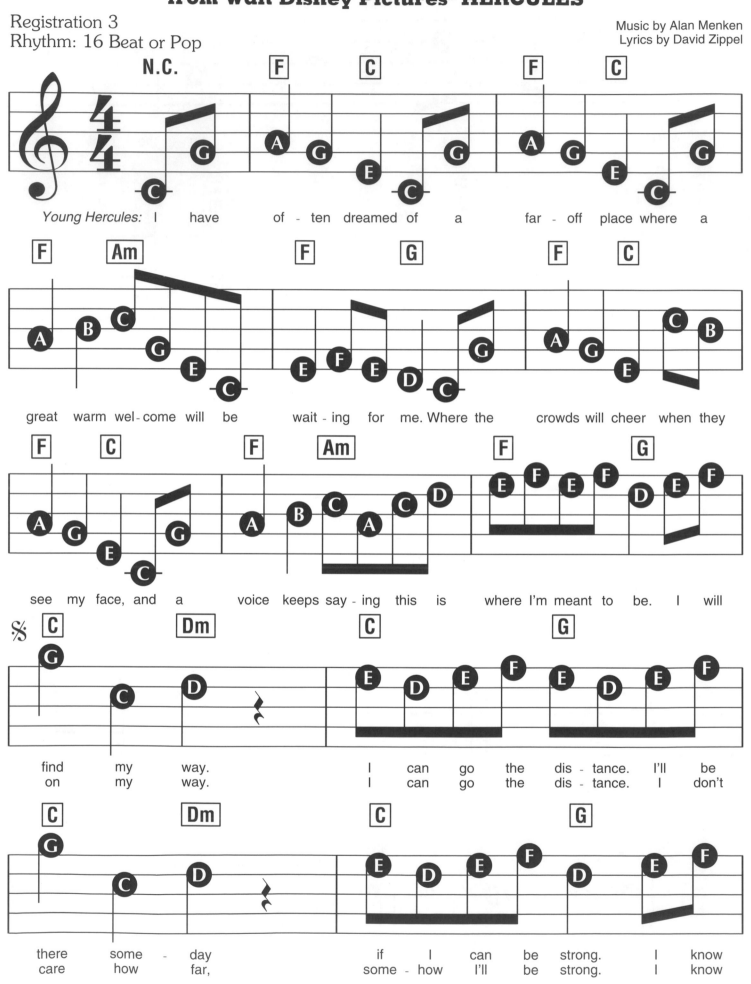

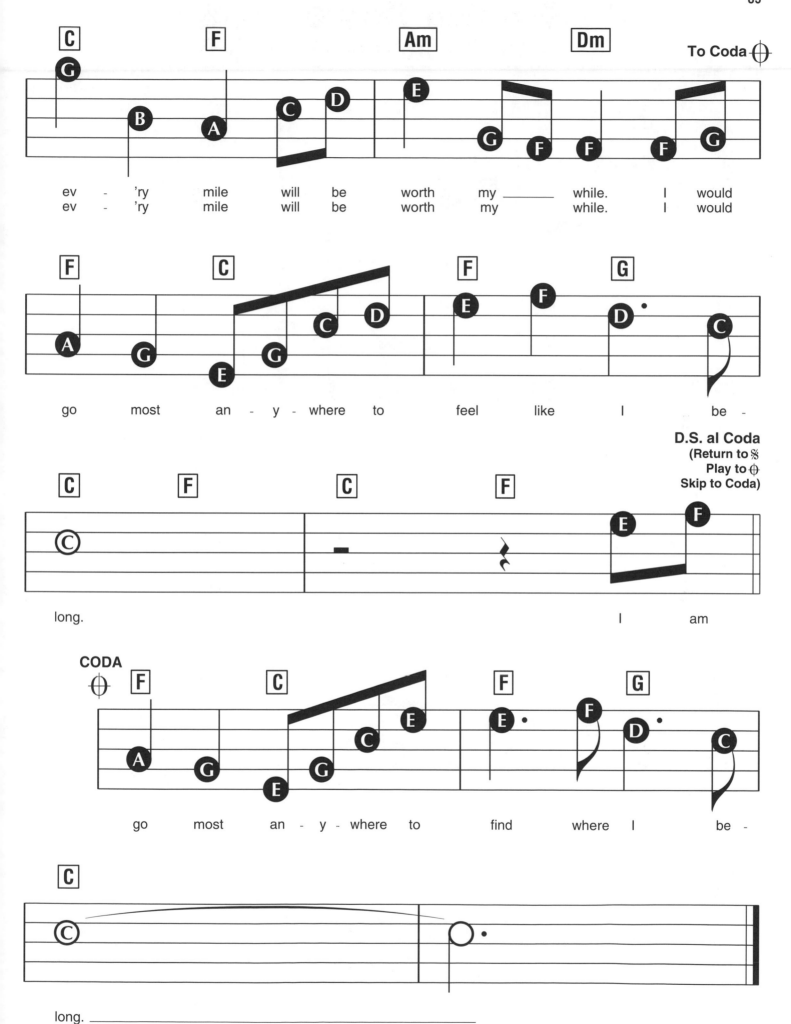

God Help the Outcasts

from Walt Disney's THE HUNCHBACK OF NOTRE DAME

Registration 10
Rhythm: Waltz

Music by Alan Menken
Lyrics by Stephen Schwartz

(Esmeralda:) I don't know if You can hear me or if You're e - ven

there. I don't know if You would lis - ten

to a gyp - sy's prayer. Yes, I know I'm just an

out - cast, I should - n't speak to You.

Still I see Your face and won - der were You once an out - cast

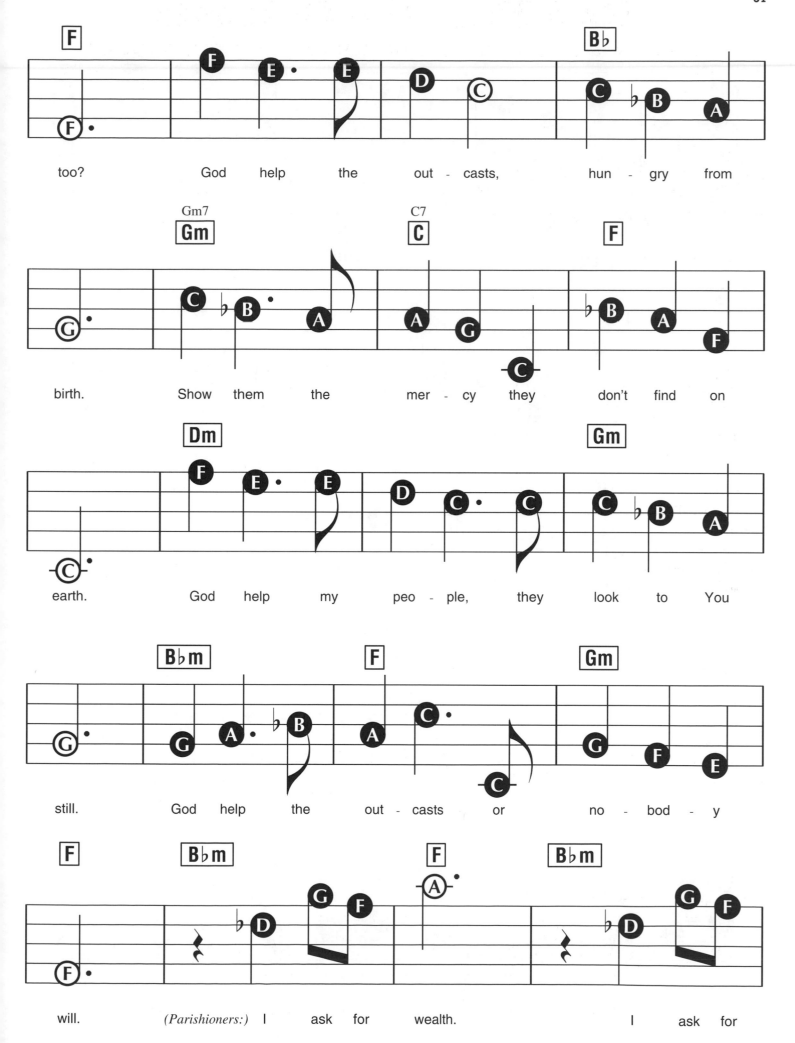

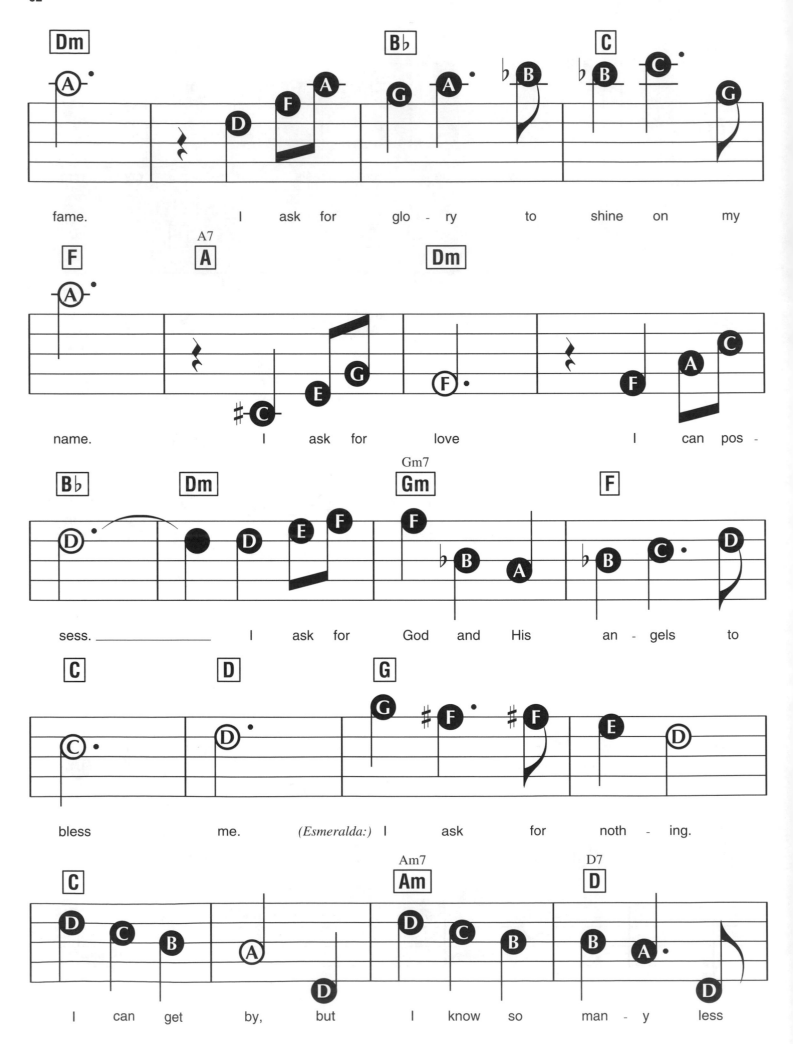

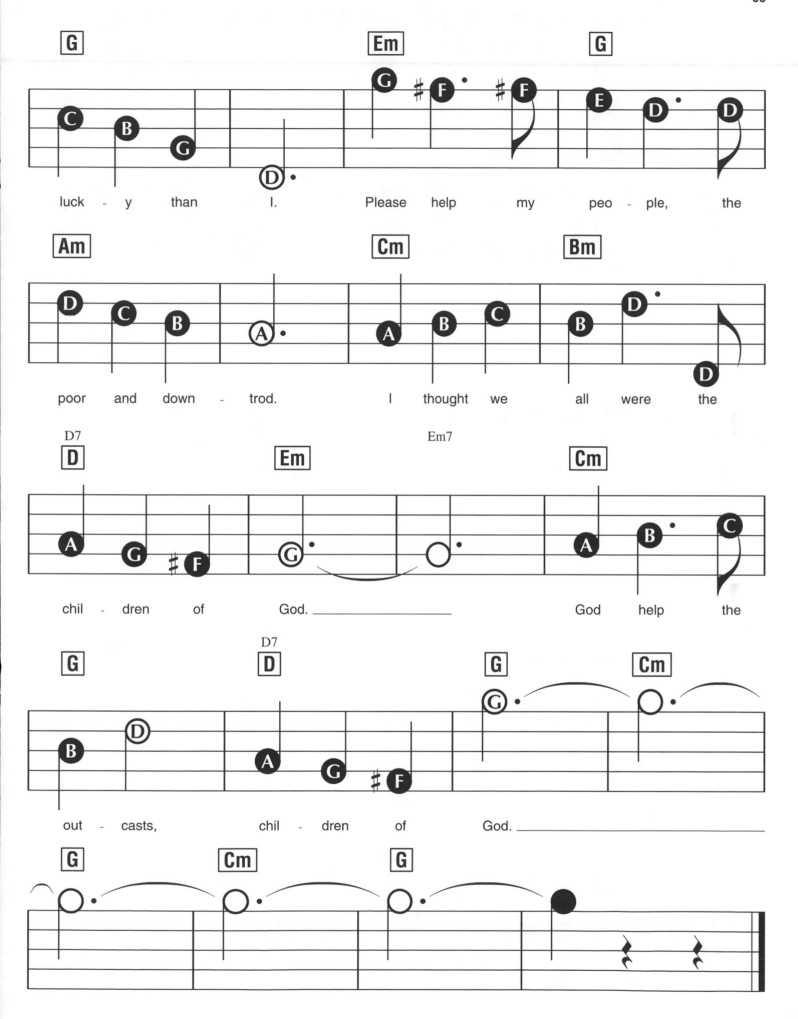

Hawaiian Roller Coaster Ride
from Walt Disney's LILO & STITCH

Registration 2
Rhythm: None

Words and Music by Alan Silvestri
and Mark Keali'i Ho'omalu

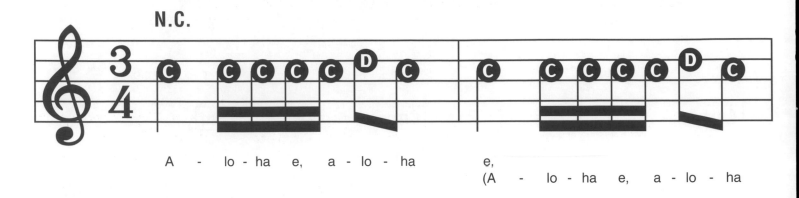

A - lo - ha e, a - lo - ha   e,
(A - lo - ha e, a - lo - ha

'an - o'ai ke a - lo - ha   e.
e,)   ('an - o'ai ke a - lo - ha e.)

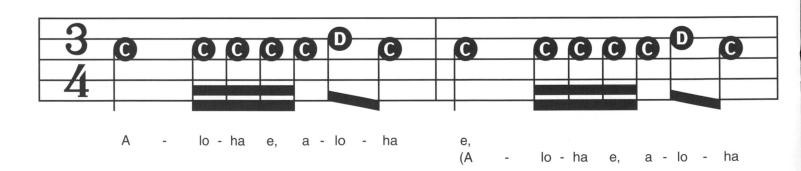

A - lo - ha e, a - lo - ha   e,
(A - lo - ha e, a - lo - ha

'an - o'ai ke a - lo - ha   e.
e,)   ('an - o'ai ka a - lo - ha e.) _____

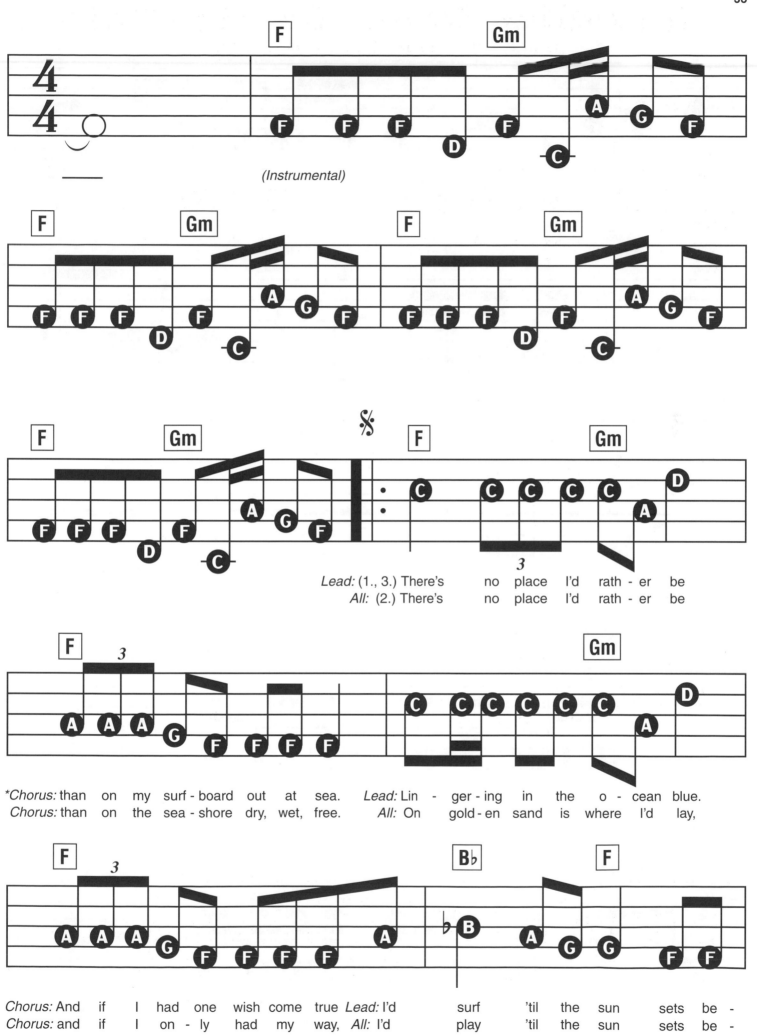

*Chorus: than on my surf - board out at sea. Lead: Lin - ger - ing in the o - cean blue.
Chorus: than on the sea - shore dry, wet, free. All: On gold - en sand is where I'd lay,

Chorus: And if I had one wish come true Lead: I'd surf 'til the sun sets be -
Chorus: and if I on - ly had my way, All: I'd play 'til the sun sets be -

* Childrens' chorus

96

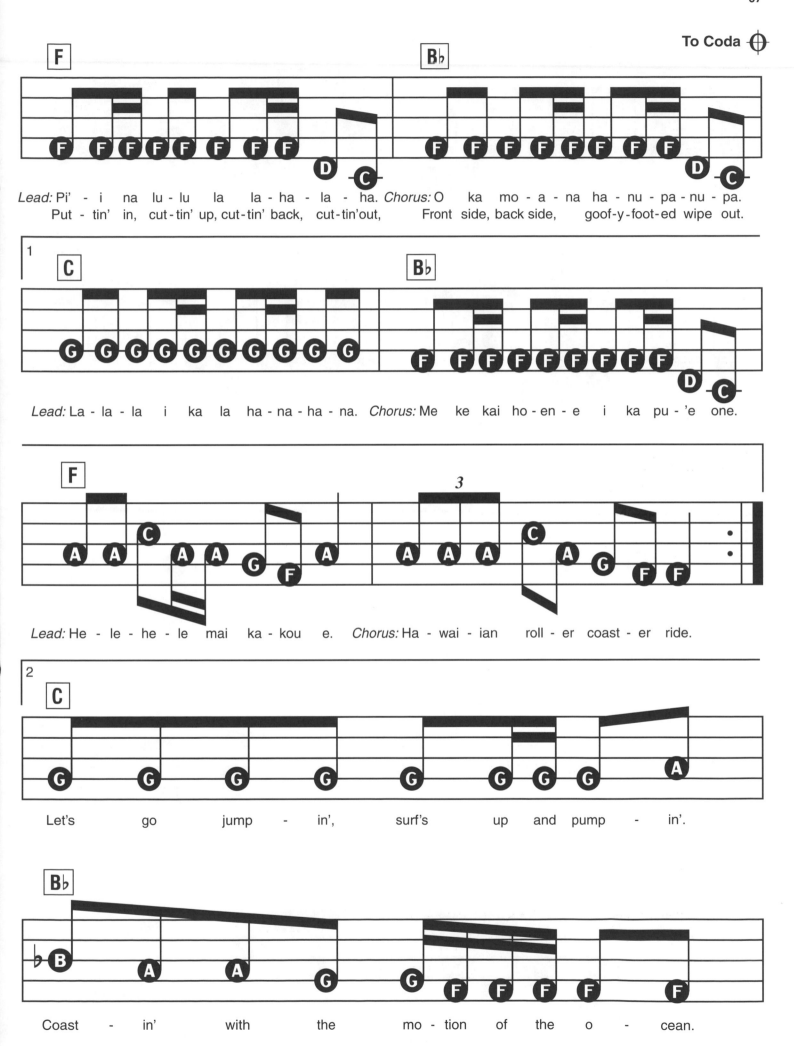

98

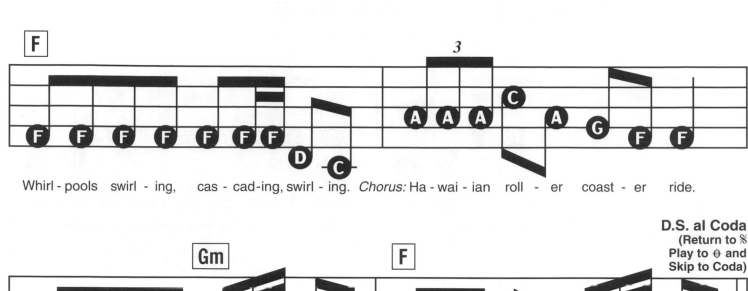

Whirl - pools swirl - ing, cas - cad-ing, swirl - ing. *Chorus:* Ha - wai - ian roll - er coast - er ride.

D.S. al Coda
(Return to 𝄋
Play to ⊕ and
Skip to Coda)

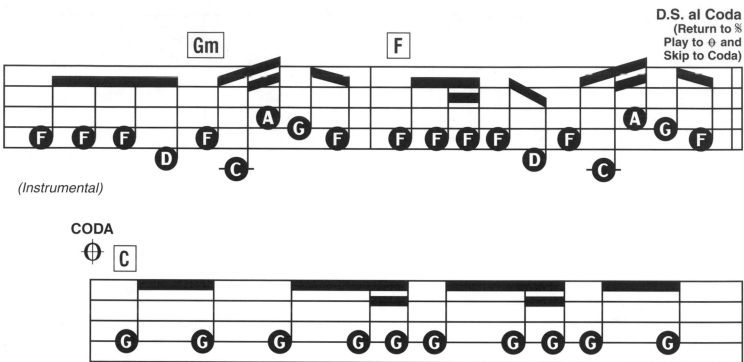

(Instrumental)

CODA

Lead: La - la - la i ka la ha - na - ha - na.

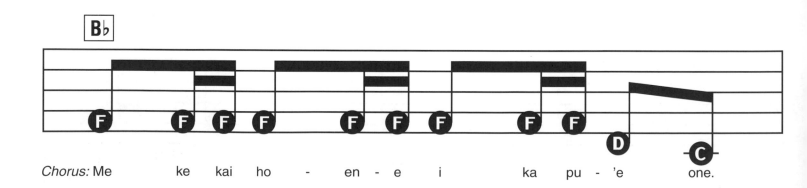

Chorus: Me ke kai ho - en - e i ka pu - 'e one.

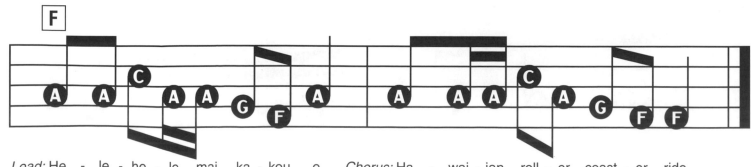

Lead: He - le - he - le mai ka-kou e. *Chorus:* Ha - wai - ian roll - er coast - er ride.

I Wan'na Be Like You
(The Monkey Song)
from Walt Disney's THE JUNGLE BOOK

Registration 2
Rhythm: Fox Trot

Words and Music by Richard M. Sherman
and Robert B. Sherman

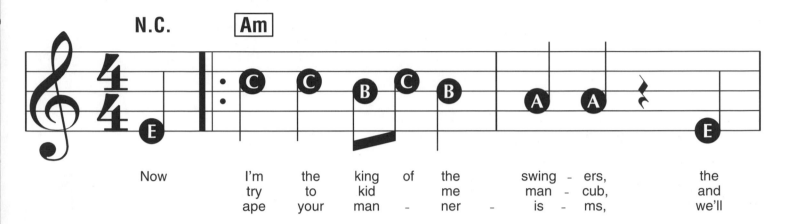

Now I'm the king of the swing-ers, the
try to kid me man - cub, and
ape your man - ner - is - ms, we'll

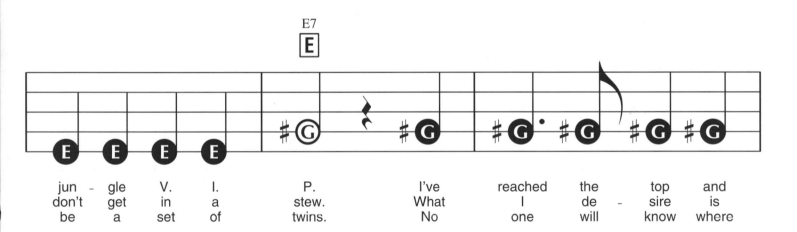

jun - gle V. I. P. I've reached the top and
don't get in a stew. What I de - sire is
be a set of twins. No one will know where

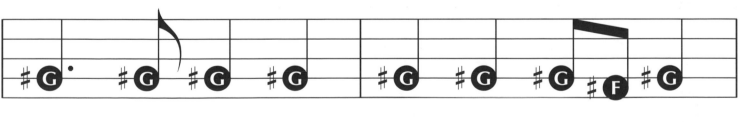

had to stop and that's what's both - er - in'
man's red fire, so I can be _____ like
man - cub ends and o - rang - u - tan _____ be -

100

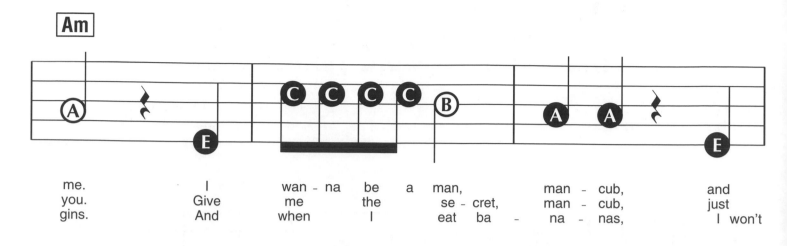

me.   I   wan - na   be   a   man,   man - cub,   and
you.   Give   me   the   se - cret,   man - cub,   just
gins.   And   when   I   eat ba - na - nas,   I won't

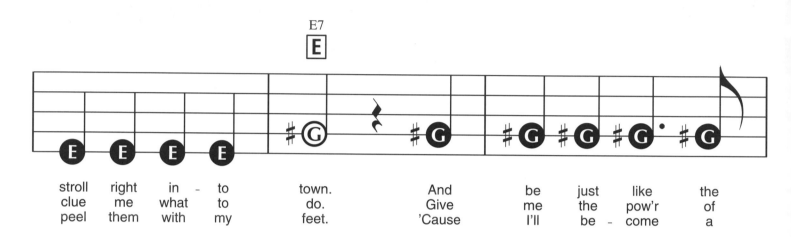

stroll   right   in - to   town.   And   be   just   like   the
clue   me   what   to   do.   Give   me   the   pow'r   of
peel   them   with   my   feet.   'Cause   I'll   be - come   a

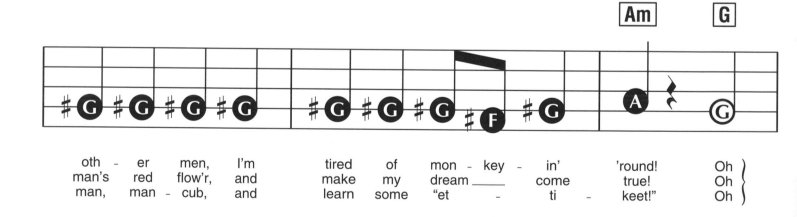

oth - er   men,   I'm   tired   of   mon - key - in'   'round!   Oh
man's   red   flow'r,   and   make   my   dream ____ come   true!   Oh
man,   man - cub,   and   learn   some   "et - ti - keet!"   Oh

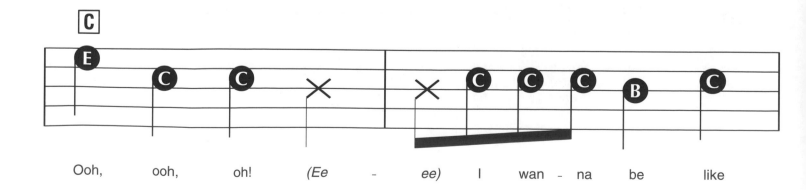

Ooh,   ooh,   oh!   (Ee - ee)   I   wan - na   be   like

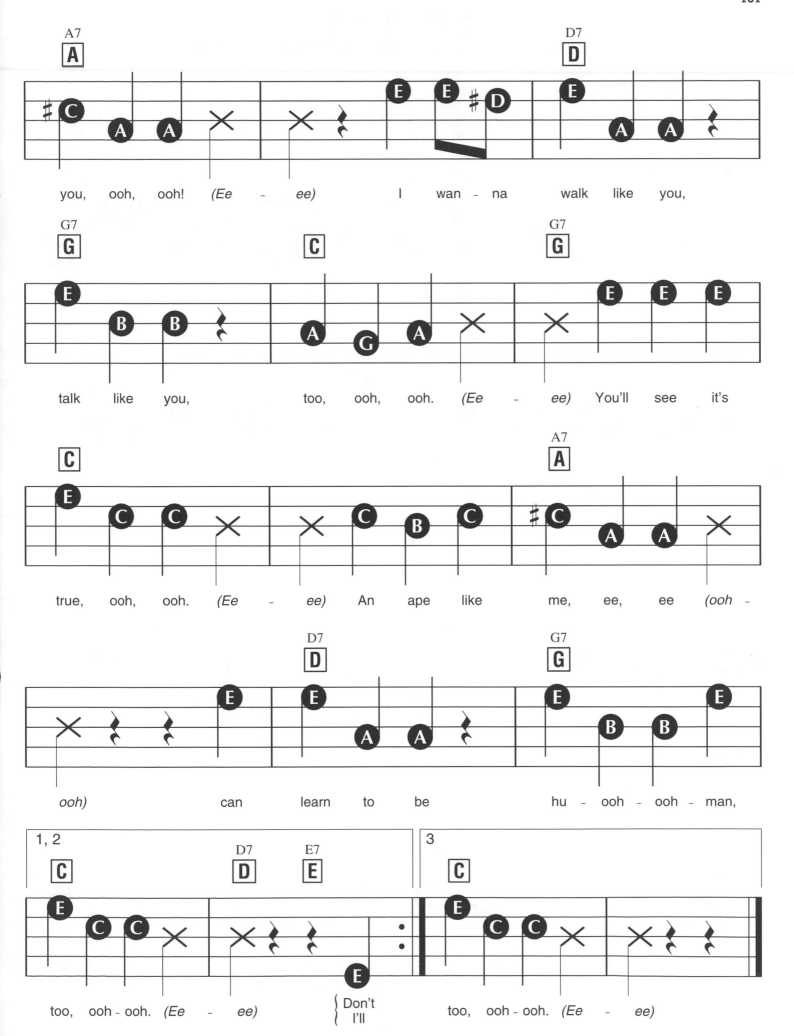

I'm Late
from Walt Disney's ALICE IN WONDERLAND

Registration 1
Rhythm: Fox Trot or Swing

Words by Bob Hilliard
Music by Sammy Fain

I'm   late,   I'm   late   for a   ver - y   im - por - tant

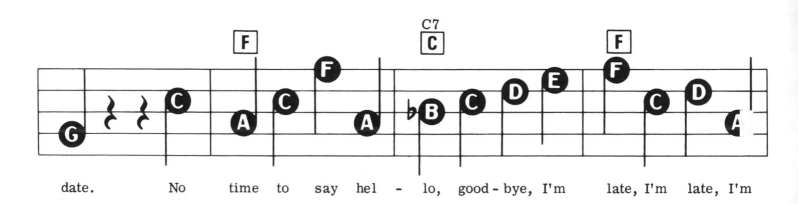

date.   No   time to   say hel - lo, good - bye, I'm   late, I'm   late, I'm

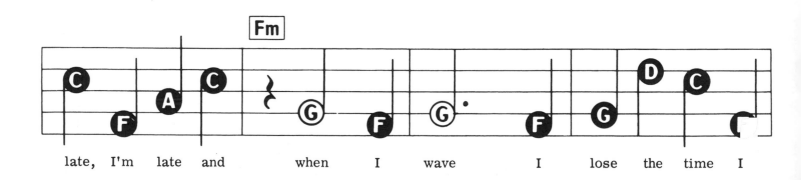

late, I'm   late and   when   I   wave   I   lose   the   time   I

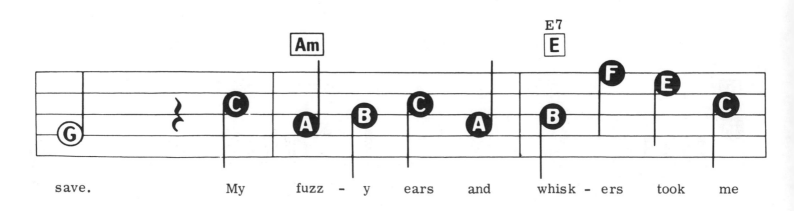

save.   My   fuzz - y   ears   and   whisk - ers   took   me

103

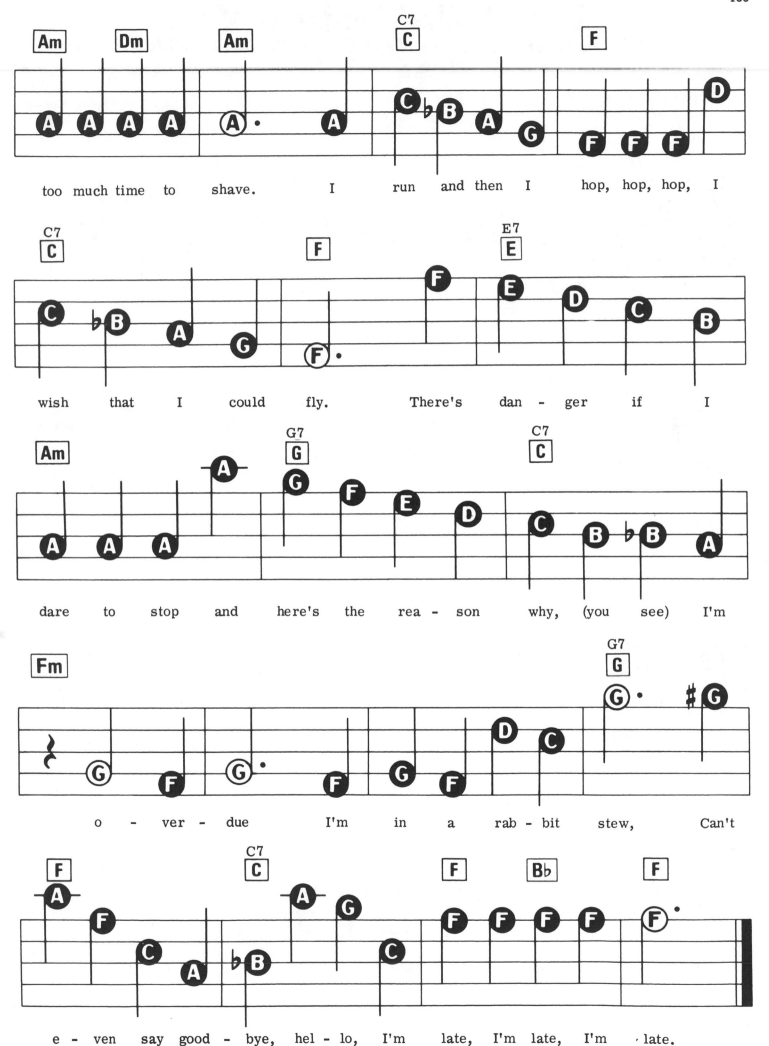

If I Didn't Have You
Walt Disney Pictures Presents A Pixar Animation Studio Film
MONSTERS, INC.

Registration 7
Rhythm: Fox Trot or Swing

Music and Lyrics by
Randy Newman

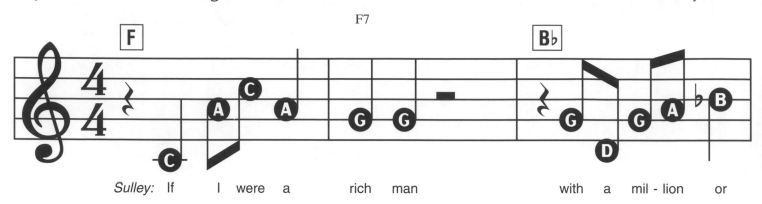

Sulley: If I were a rich man with a mil - lion or

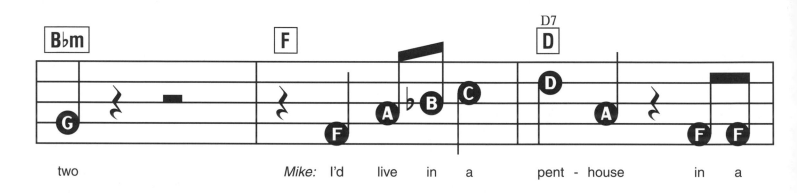

two Mike: I'd live in a pent - house in a

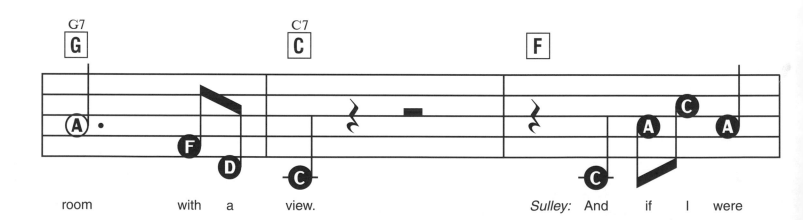

room with a view. Sulley: And if I were

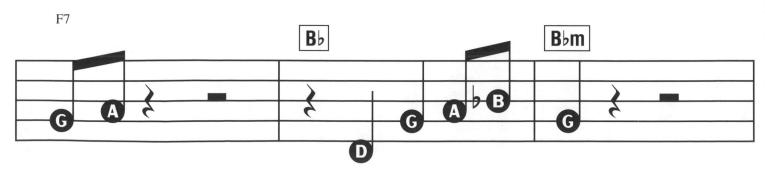

hand - some, (It could happen,) Sulley: 'cause dreams do come true,
(Spoken:) Mike: No way!

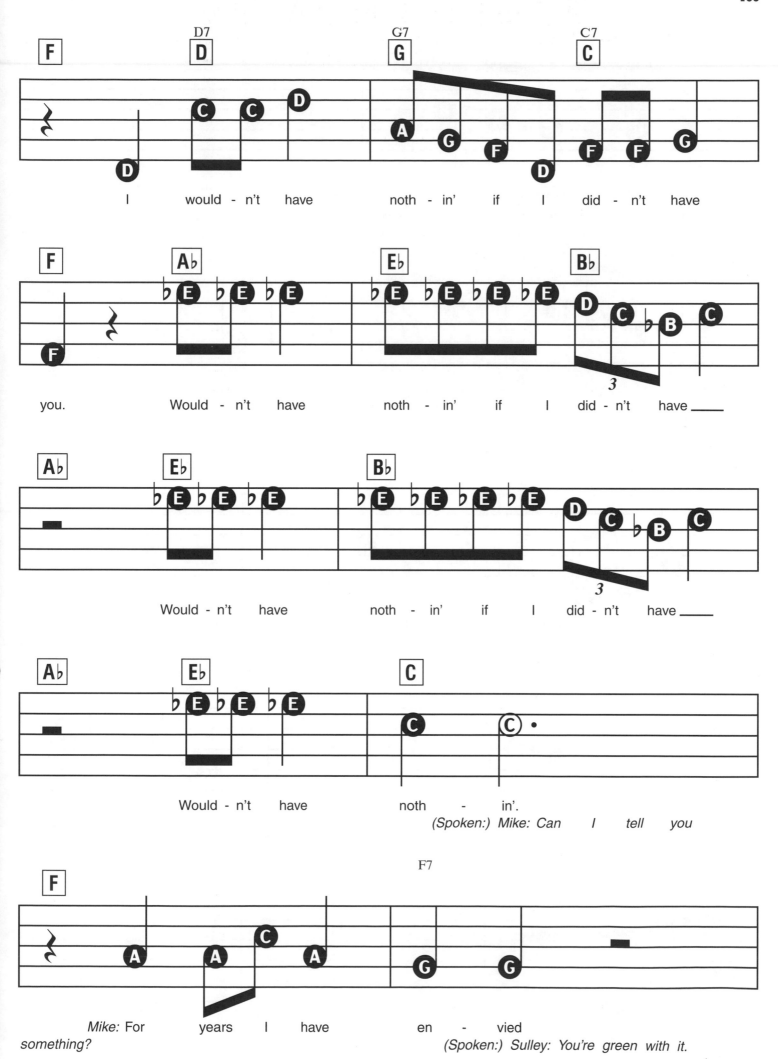

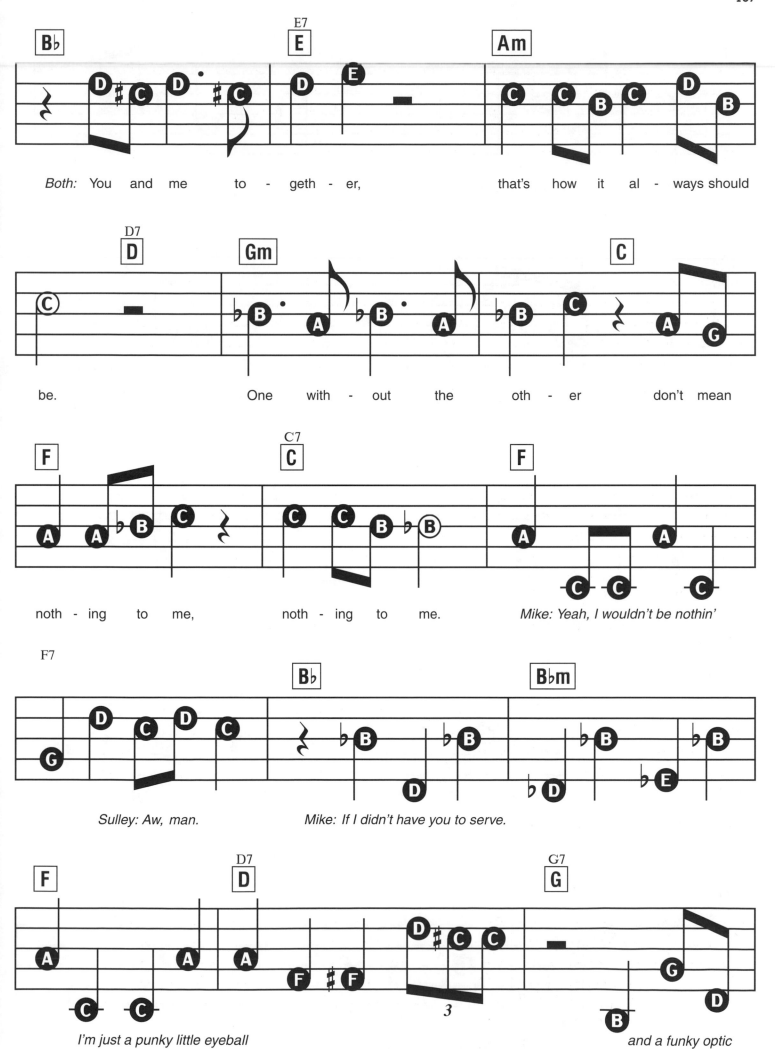

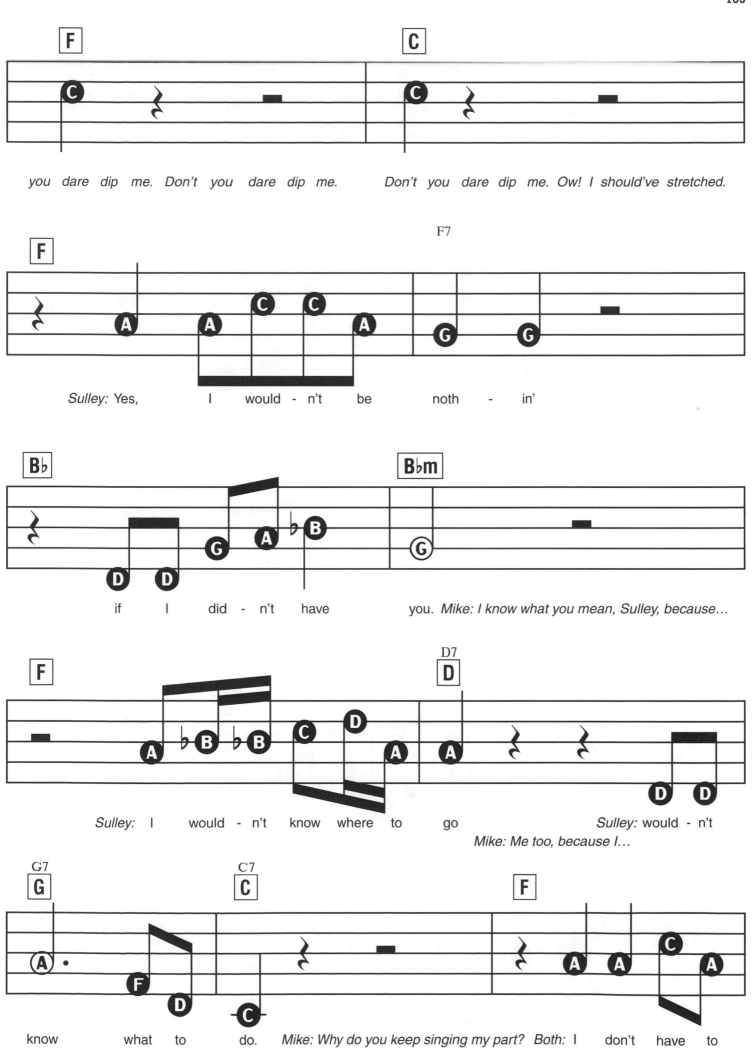

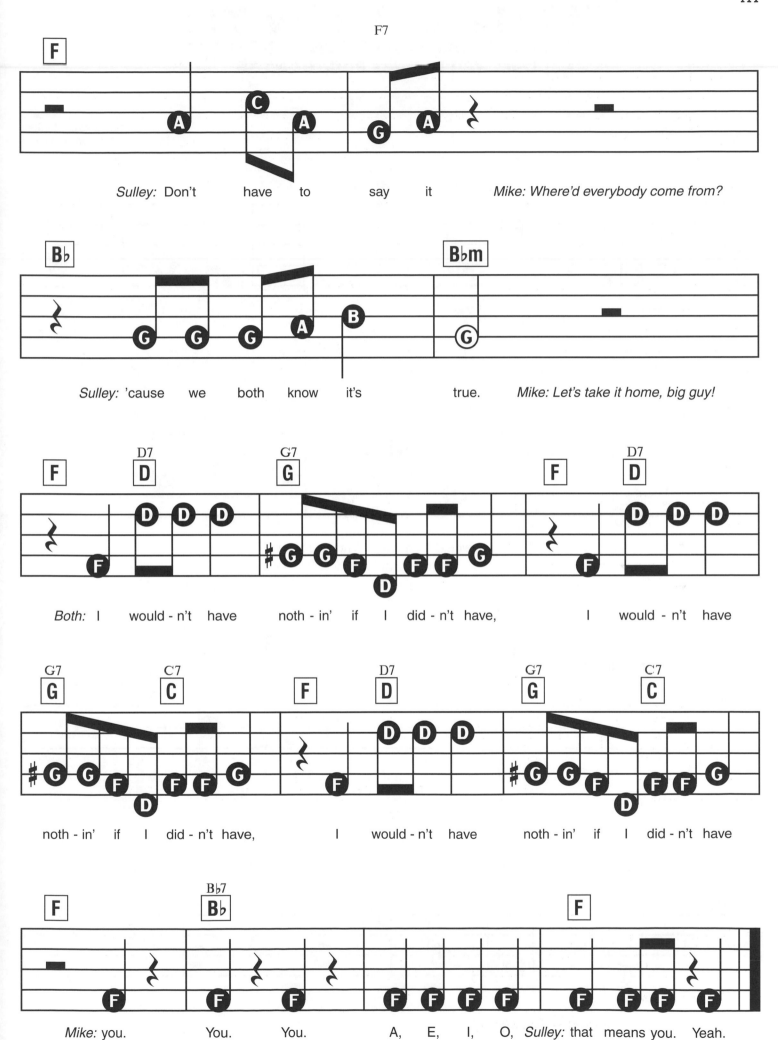

If I Never Knew You
(Love Theme from POCAHONTAS)
from Walt Disney's POCAHONTAS

Registration 3
Rhythm: Ballad or 8 Beat

Music by Alan Menken
Lyrics by Stephen Schwartz

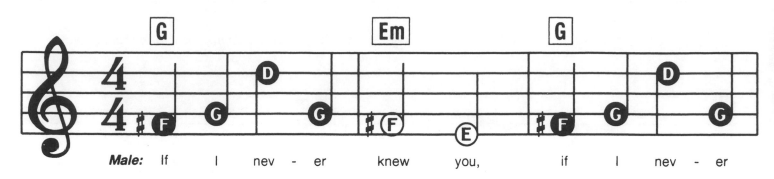

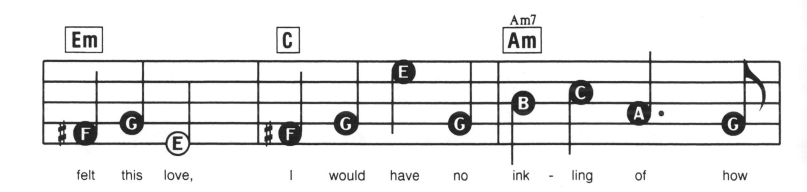

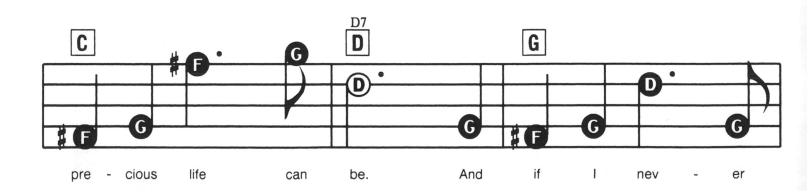

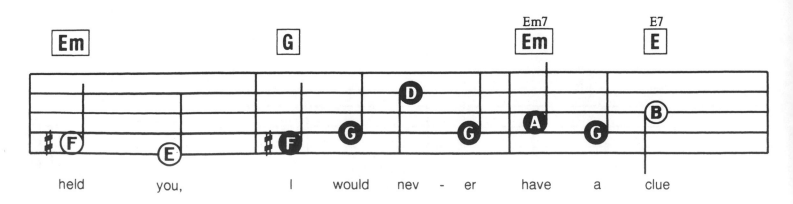

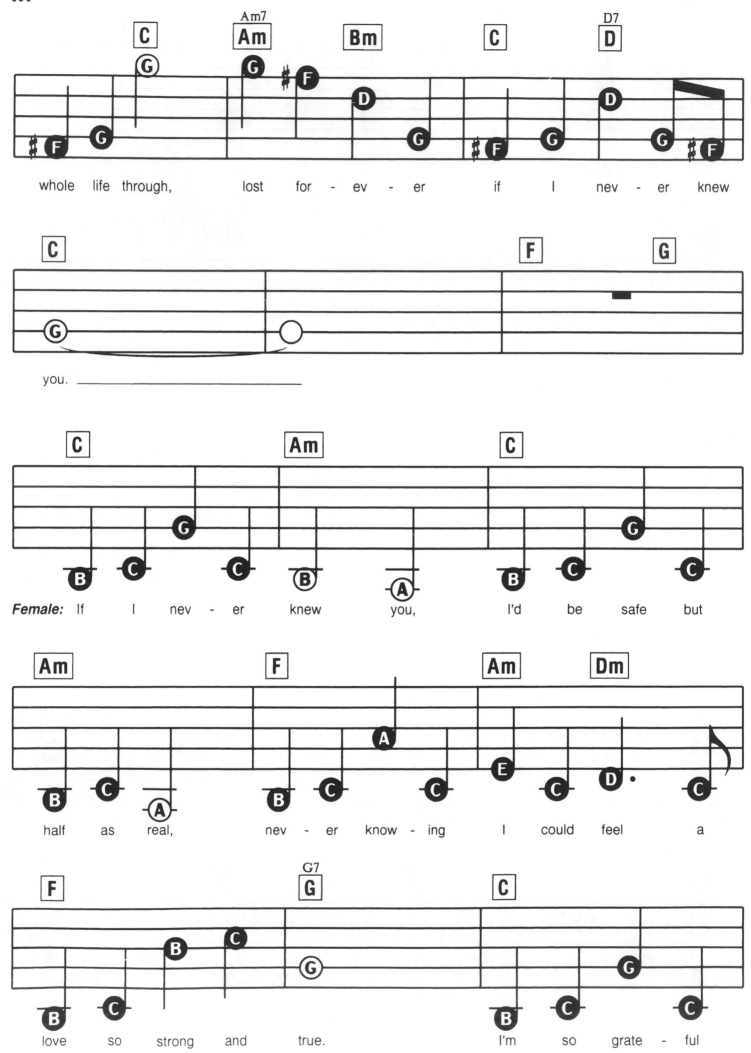

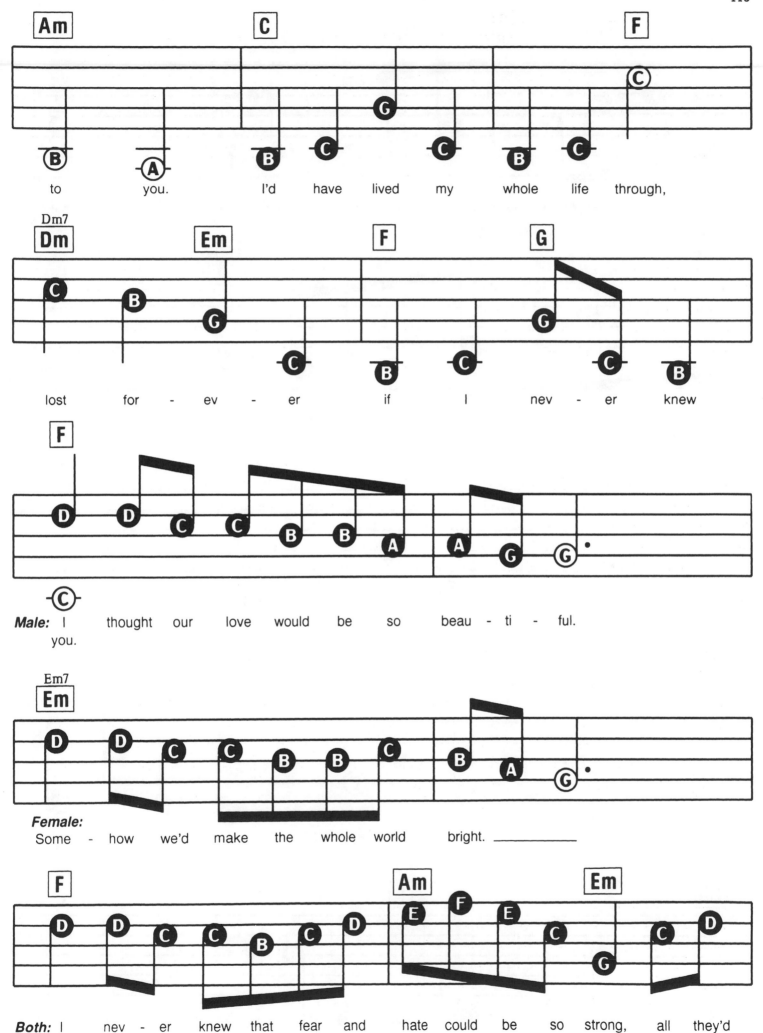

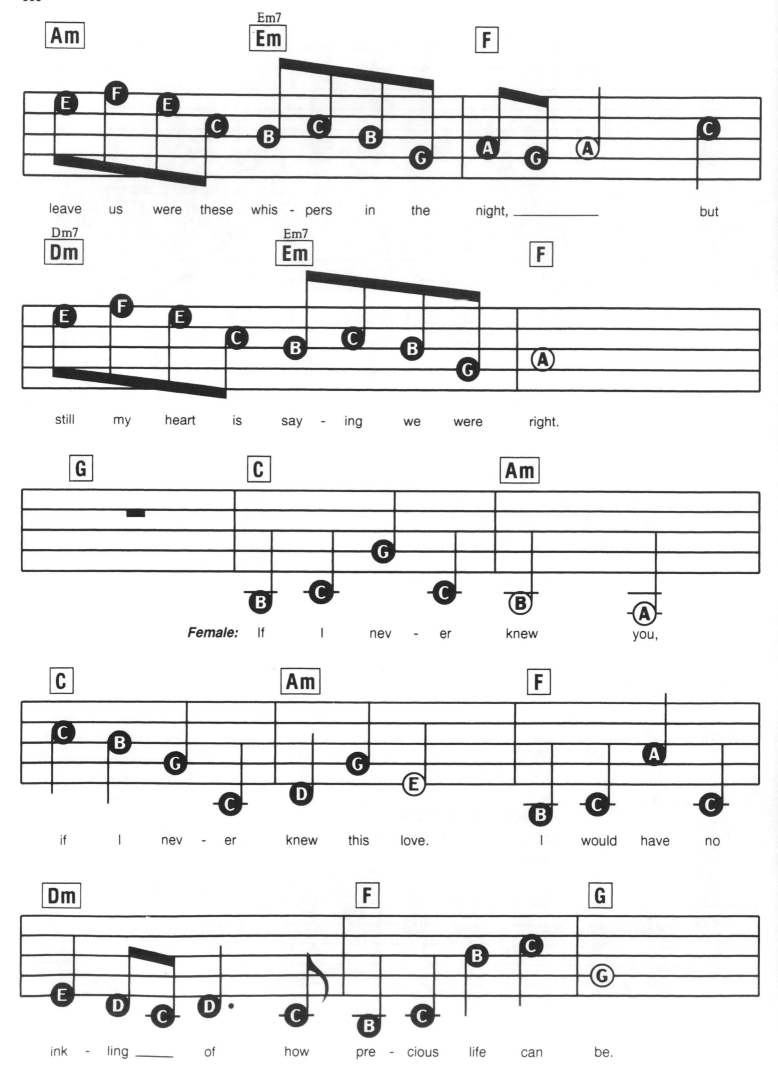

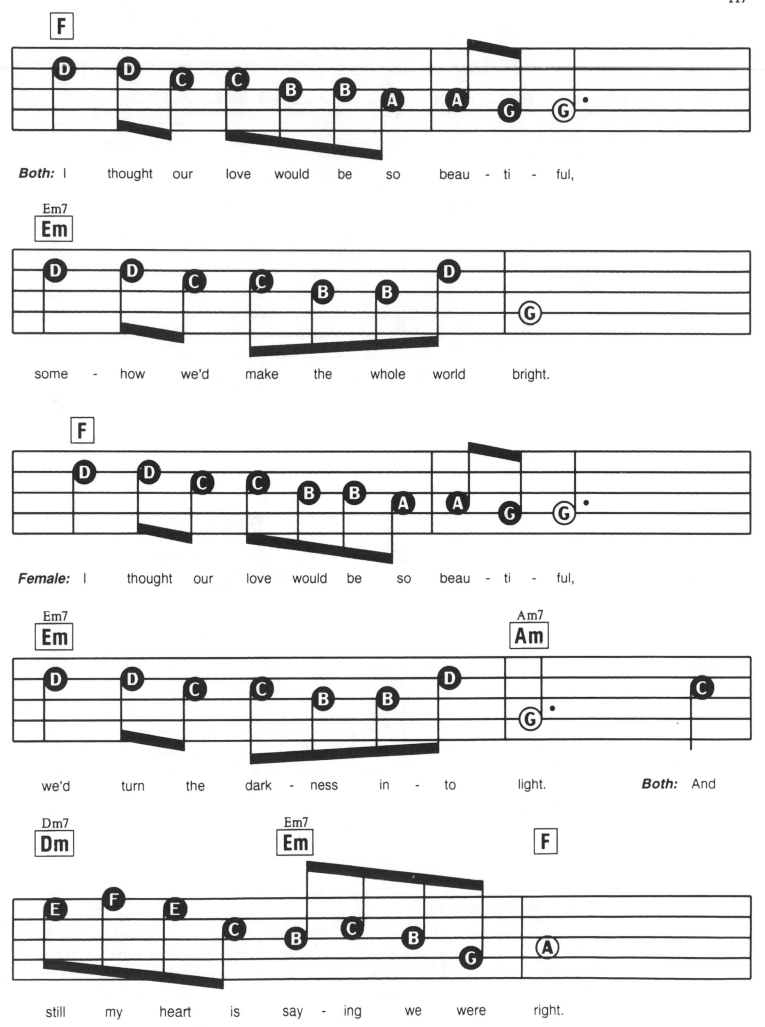

117

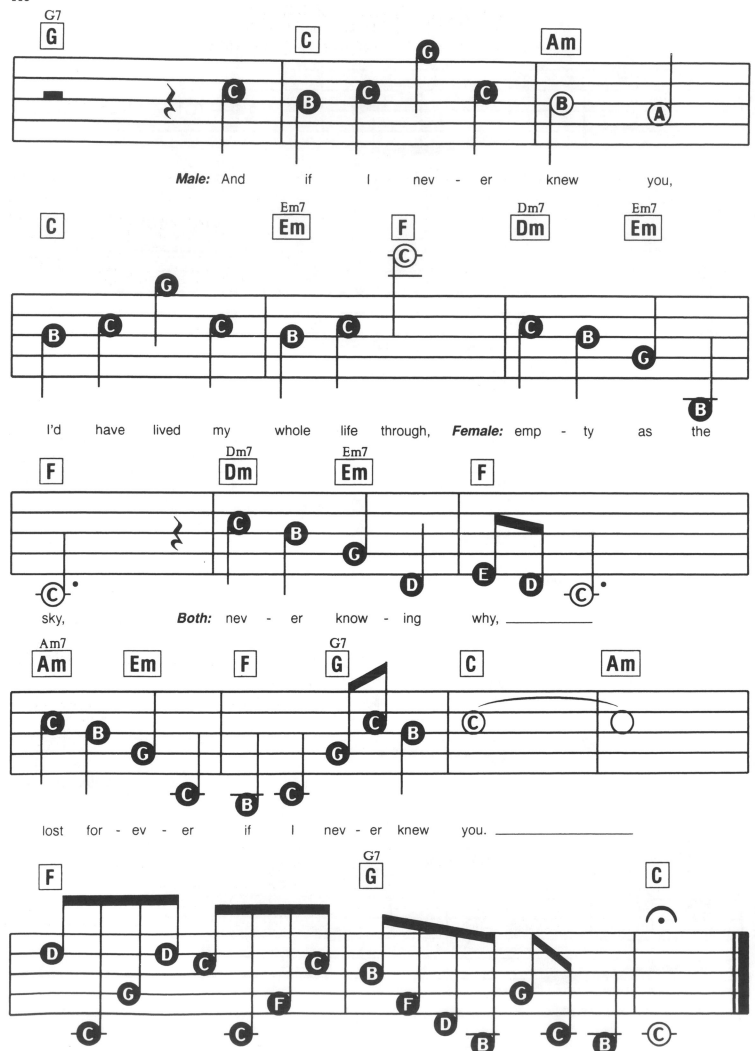

Male: And if I nev - er knew you,

I'd have lived my whole life through, *Female:* emp - ty as the

sky, *Both:* nev - er know - ing why, _____

lost for - ev - er if I nev - er knew you. _____

Kiss the Girl
from Walt Disney's THE LITTLE MERMAID

Registration 7
Rhythm: Bossa Nova or Latin

Lyrics by Howard Ashman
Music by Alan Menken

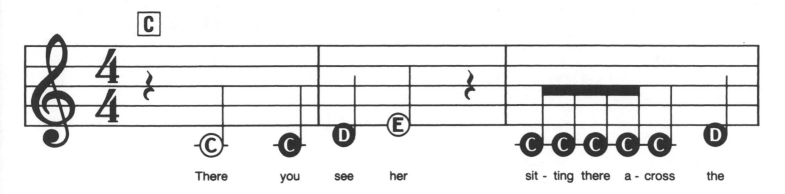

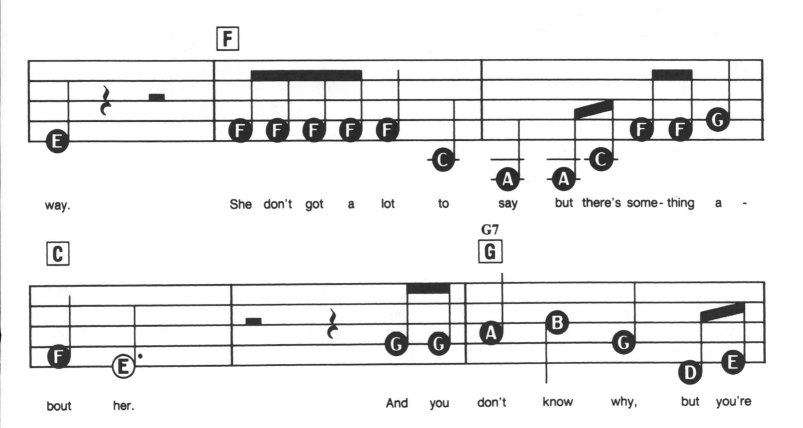

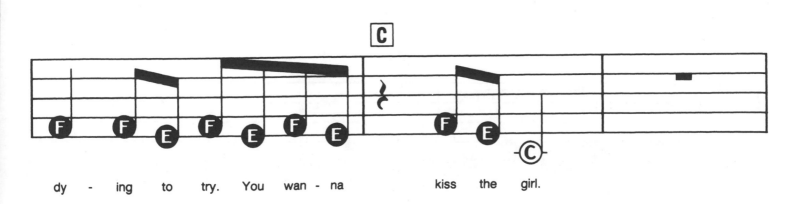

Yes, you want her. Look at her, you know you

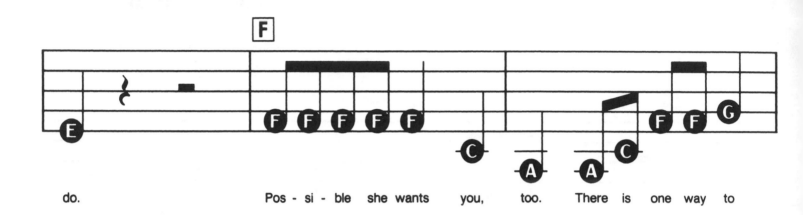

do. Pos - si - ble she wants you, too. There is one way to

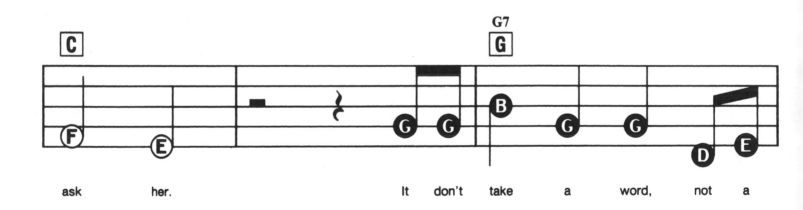

ask her. It don't take a word, not a

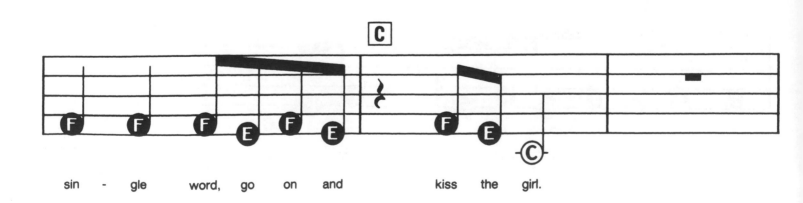

sin - gle word, go on and kiss the girl.

Sha la la la la la, my oh my. Look like the
boy too shy. Ain't gon - na kiss the girl
Sha la la la la la, ain't that sad. Ain't it a
shame, too bad. He gon - na miss the girl.

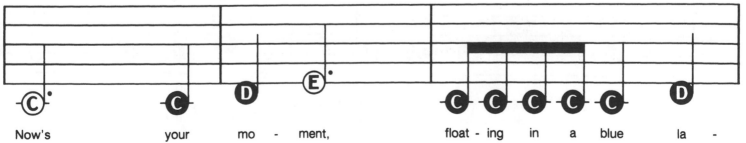

Now's your mo - ment, float - ing in a blue la -

It's a Small World

from "it's a small world" at Disneyland Park and Magic Kingdom Park

Registration 2
Rhythm: March

Words and Music by Richard M. Sherman
and Robert B. Sherman

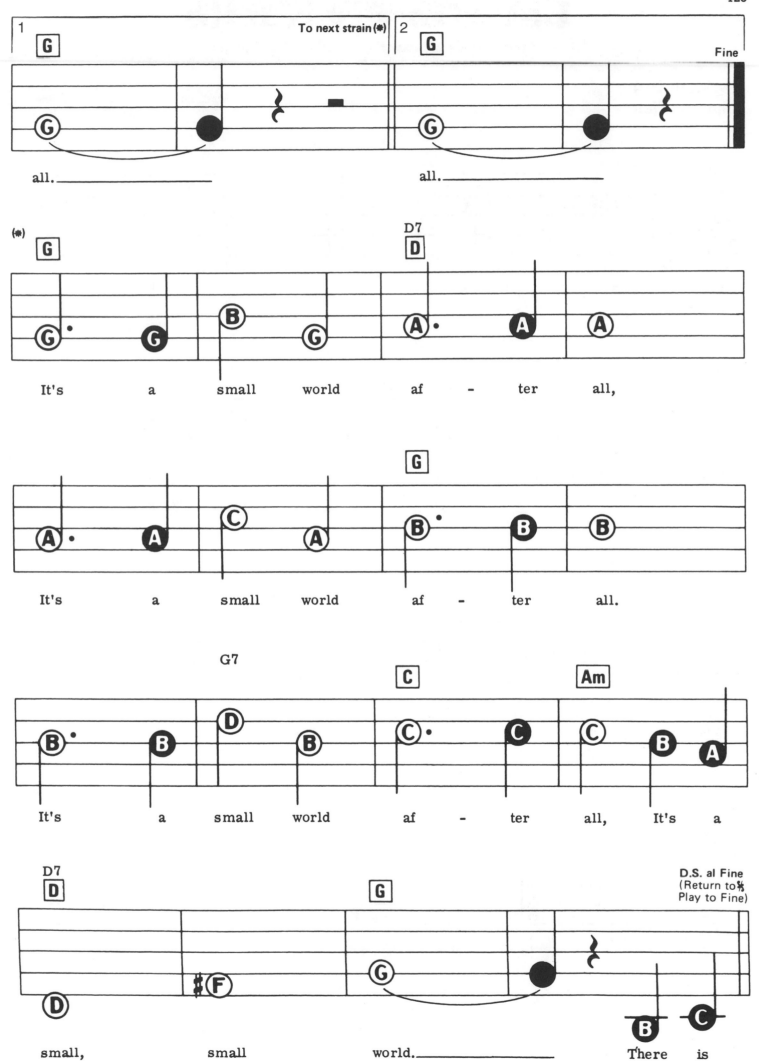

Let's Go Fly a Kite
from Walt Disney's MARY POPPINS

Registration 4
Rhythm: Waltz

Words and Music by Richard M. Sherman
and Robert B. Sherman

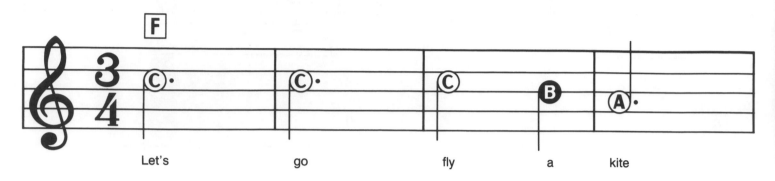

Let's go fly a kite

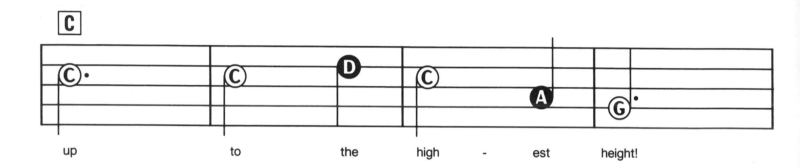

up to the high - est height!

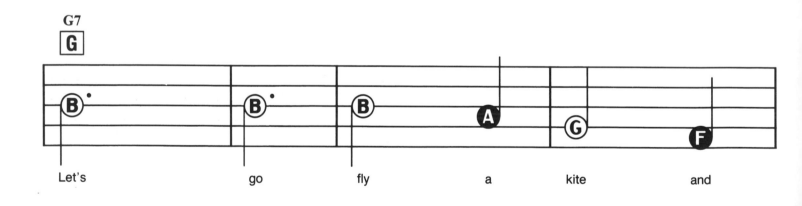

Let's go fly a kite and

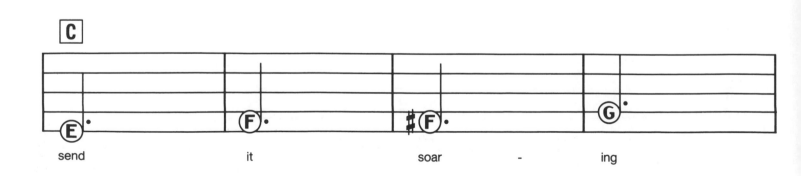

send it soar - ing

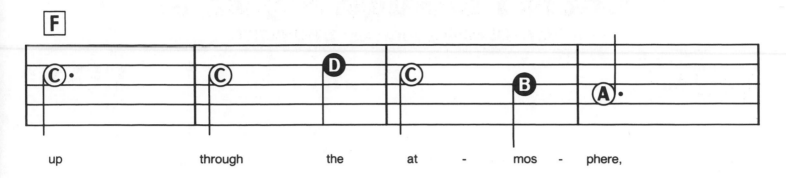

F

up   through   the   at - mos - phere,

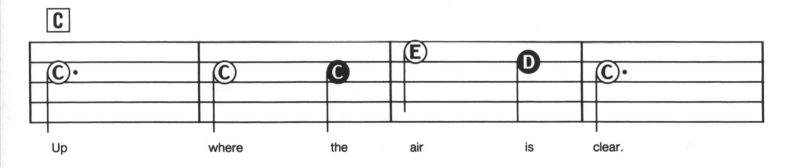

C

Up   where   the   air   is   clear.

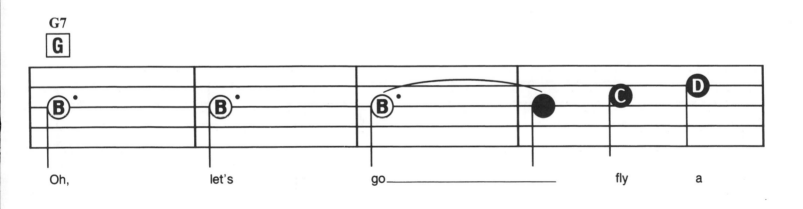

G7
G

Oh,   let's   go_____ fly   a

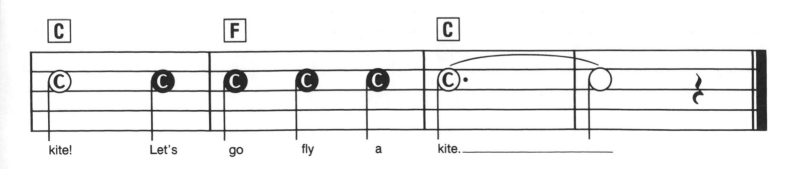

C   F   C

kite!   Let's   go   fly   a   kite._____

Look Through My Eyes
from Walt Disney Pictures' BROTHER BEAR

Registration 8
Rhythm: Waltz

Words and Music by
Phil Collins

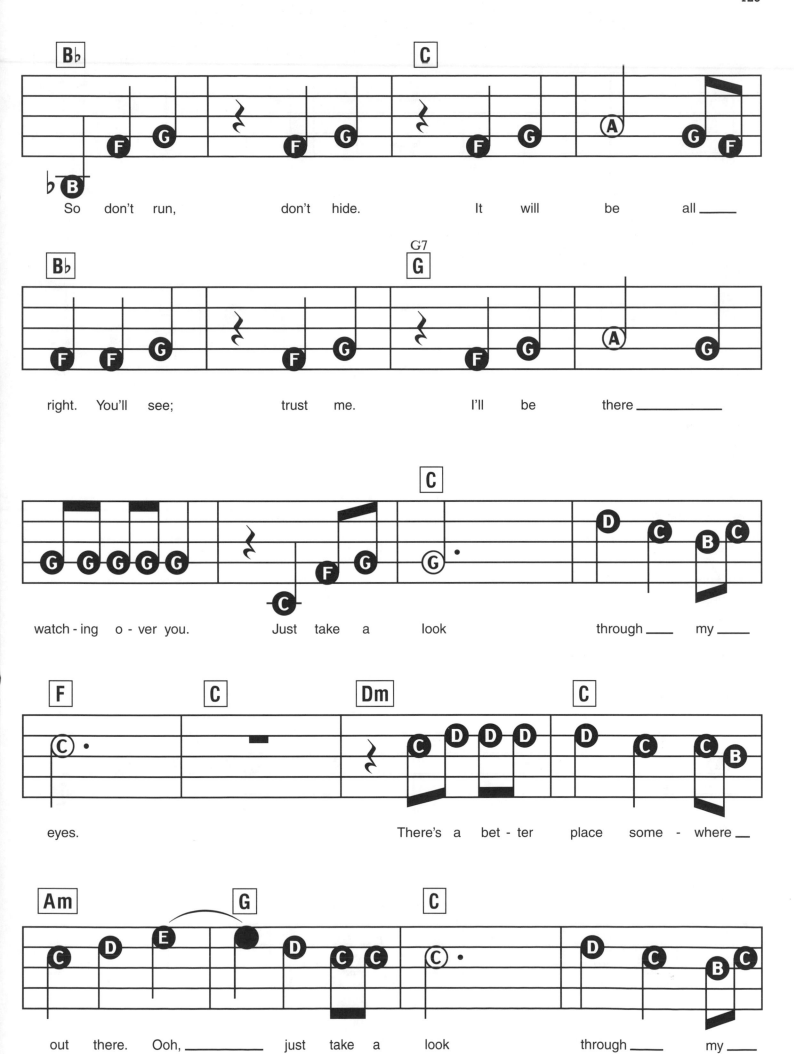

130

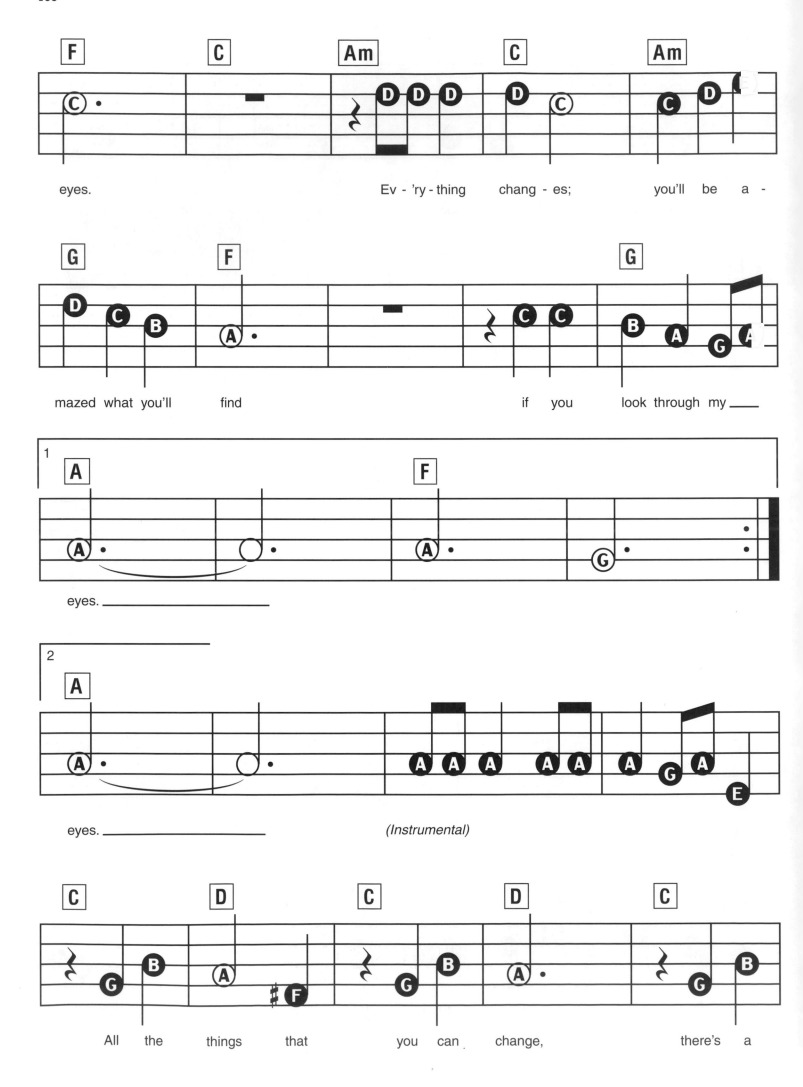

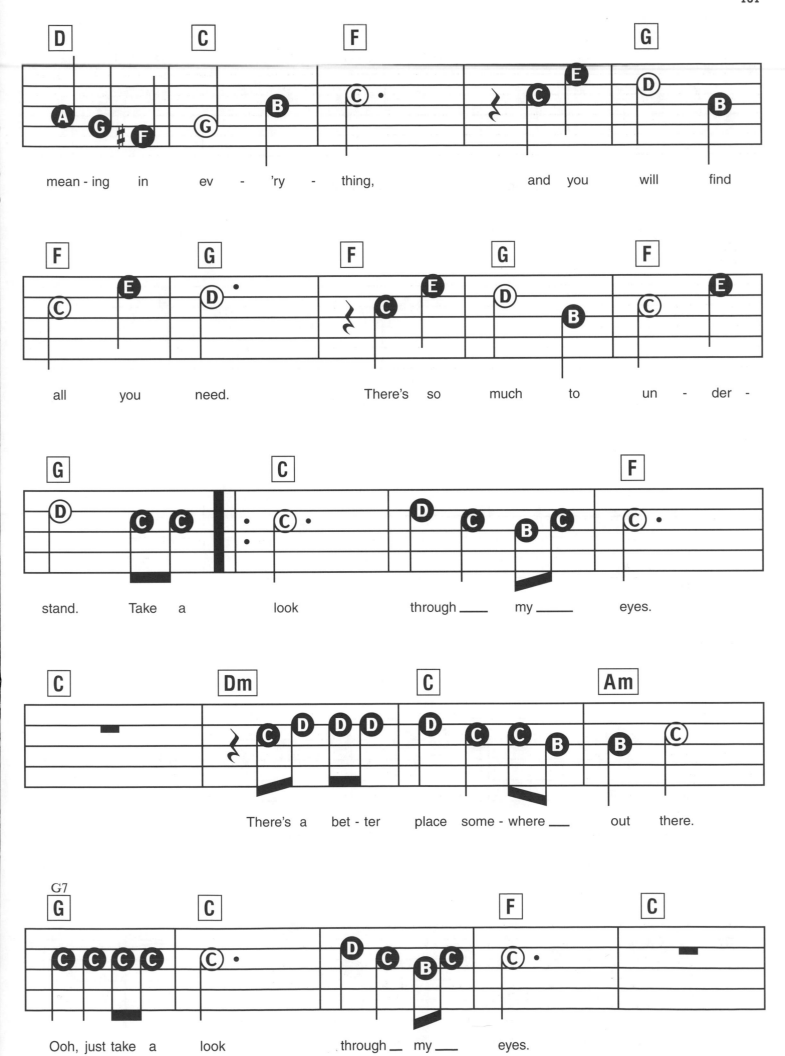

132

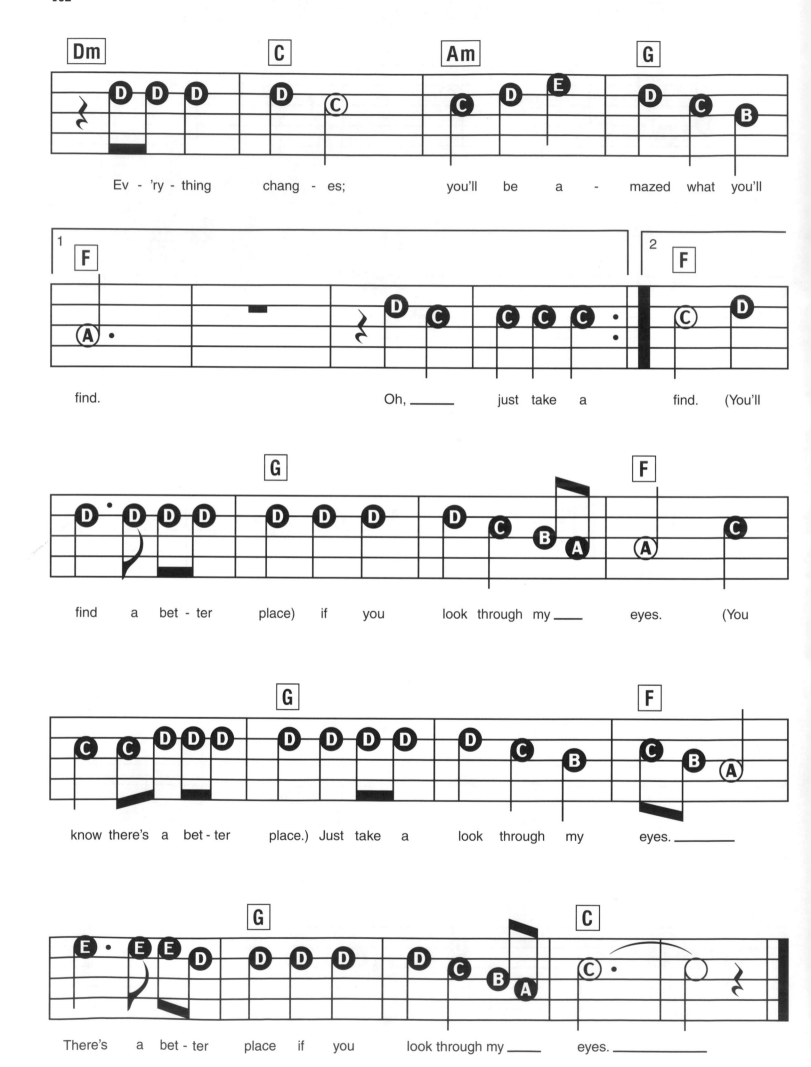

The Lord Is Good to Me
from Walt Disney's MELODY TIME
from Walt Disney's JOHNNY APPLESEED

Registration 1
Rhythm: Fox Trot

Words and Music by Kim Gannon
and Walter Kent

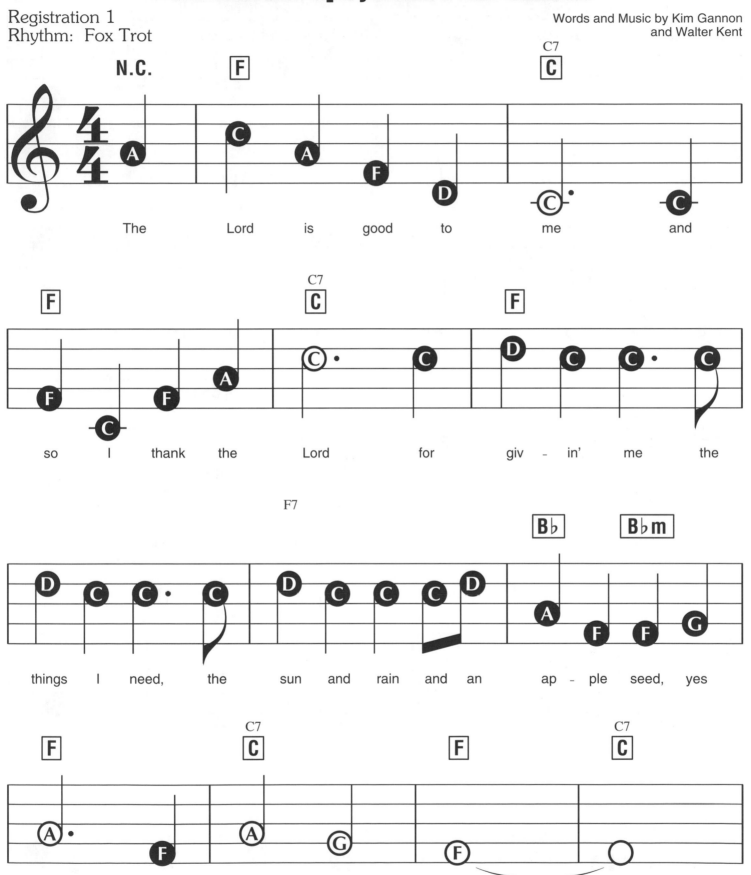

134

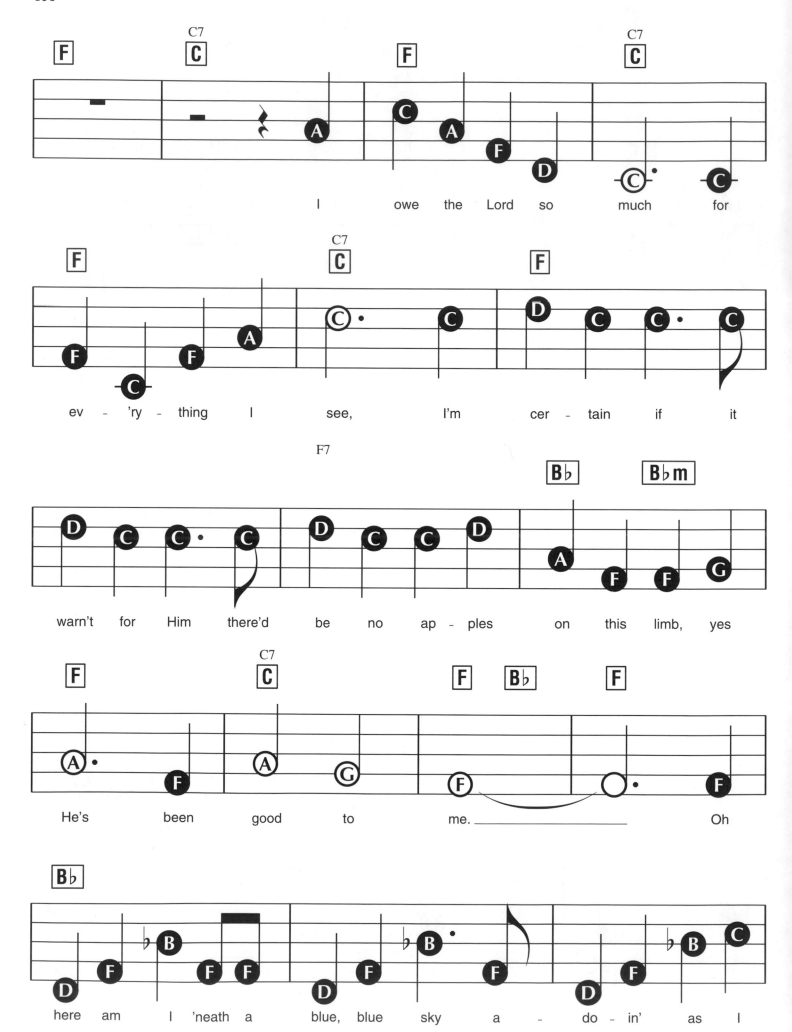

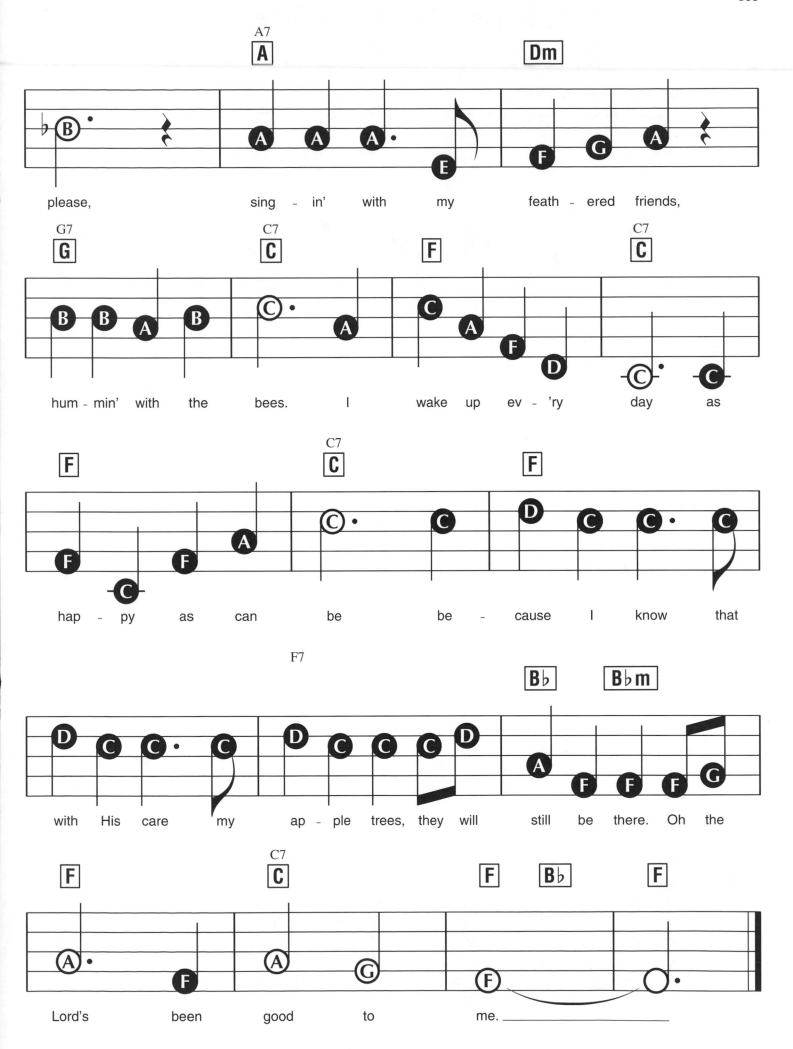

Mickey Mouse March
from Walt Disney's THE MICKEY MOUSE CLUB

Registration 5
Rhythm: 6/8 March

Words and Music by
Jimmie Dodd

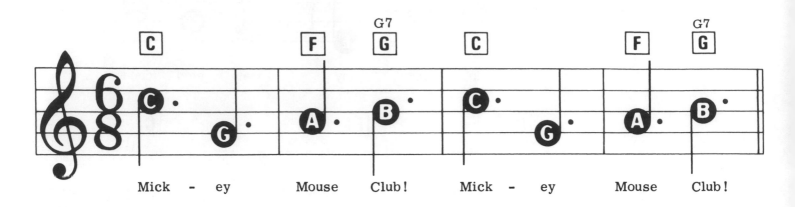

Mick - ey Mouse Club! Mick - ey Mouse Club!

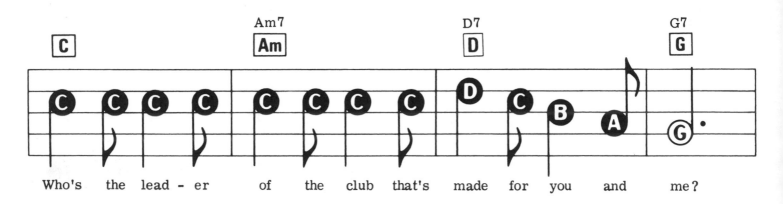

Who's the lead - er of the club that's made for you and me?

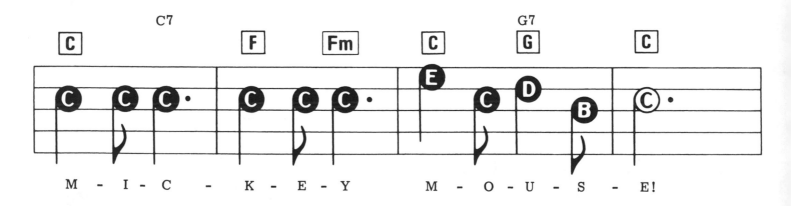

M - I - C - K - E - Y M - O - U - S - E!

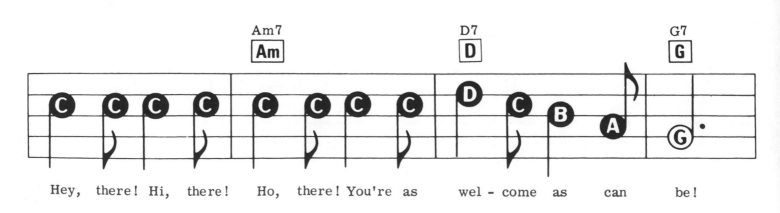

Hey, there! Hi, there! Ho, there! You're as wel - come as can be!

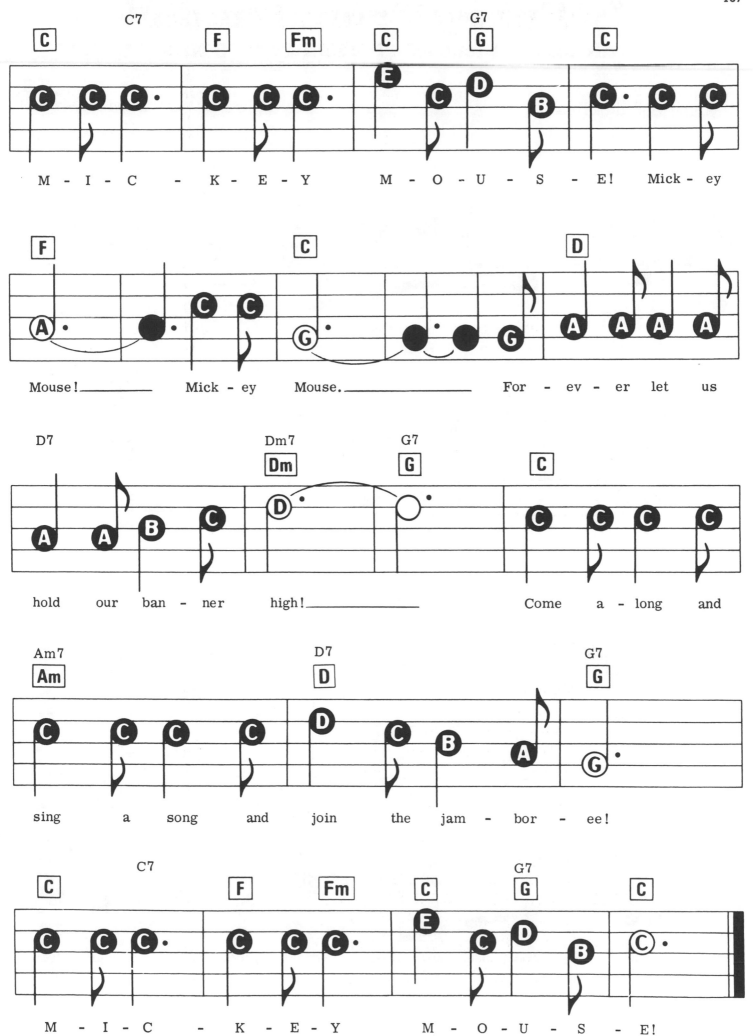

My Funny Friend and Me

from Walt Disney Pictures' THE EMPEROR'S NEW GROOVE

Registration 2
Rhythm: Ballad or Rock

Lyrics by Sting
Music by Sting and David Hartley

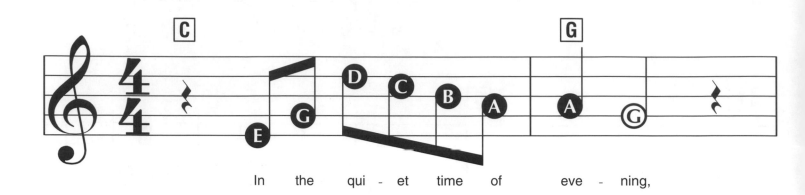

In the qui - et time of eve - ning,

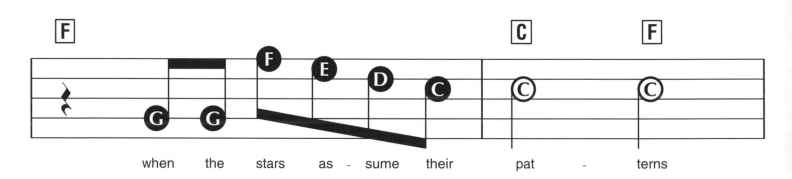

when the stars as - sume their pat - terns

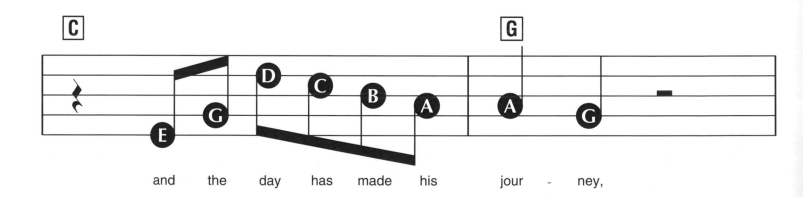

and the day has made his jour - ney,

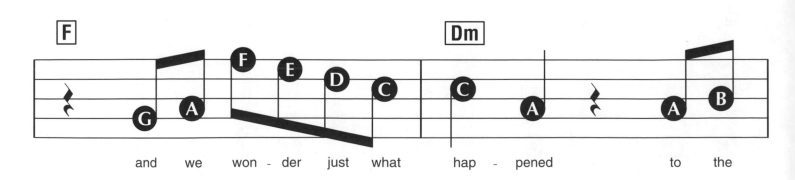

and we won - der just what hap - pened to the

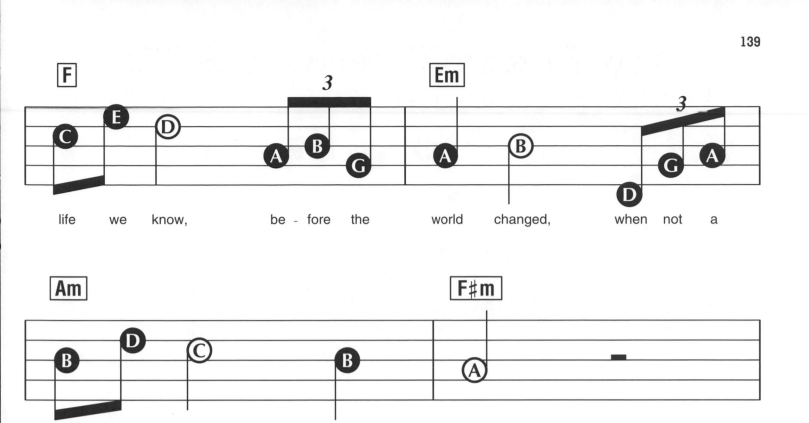

life we know, be - fore the world changed, when not a

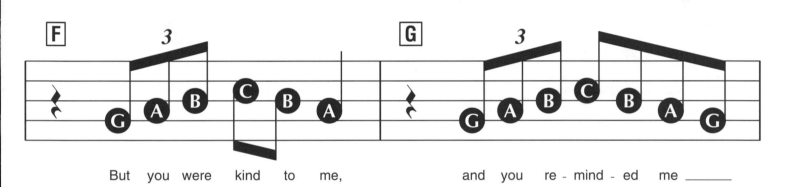

thing I held was true.

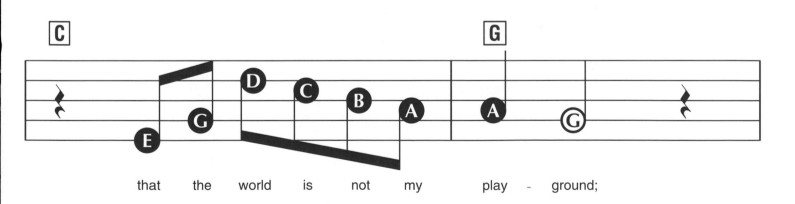

But you were kind to me, and you re - mind - ed me _____

that the world is not my play - ground;

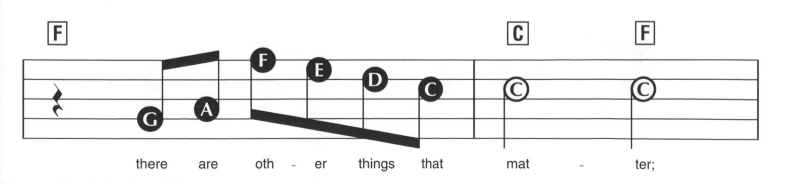

there are oth - er things that mat - ter;

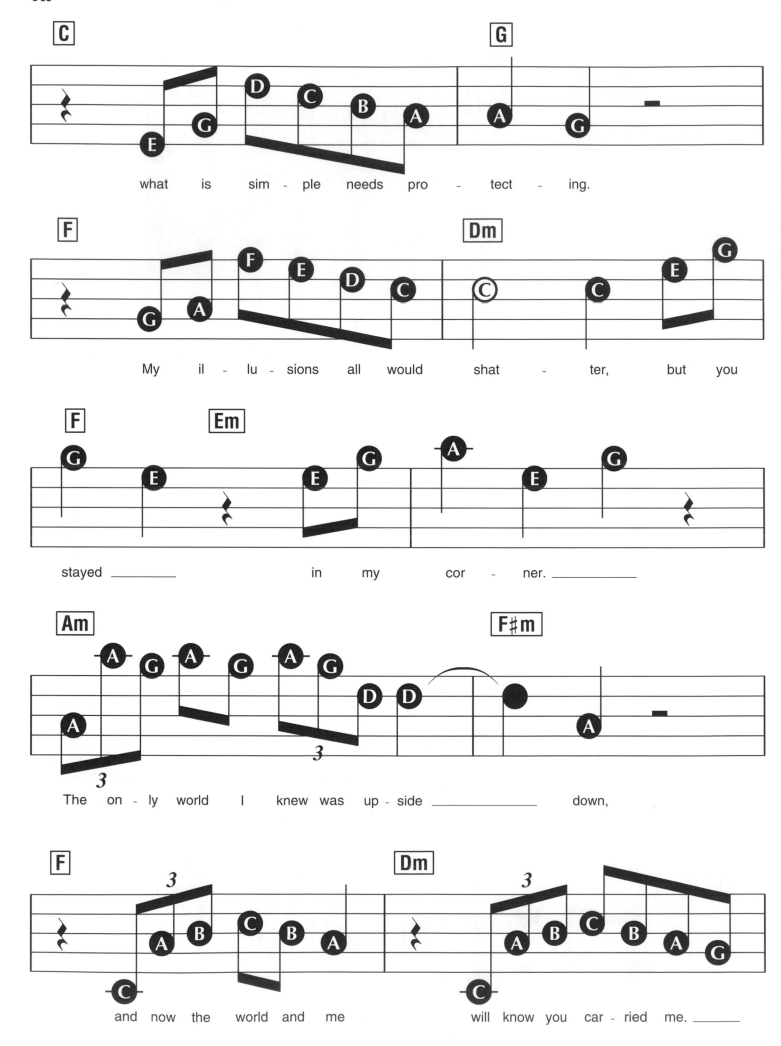

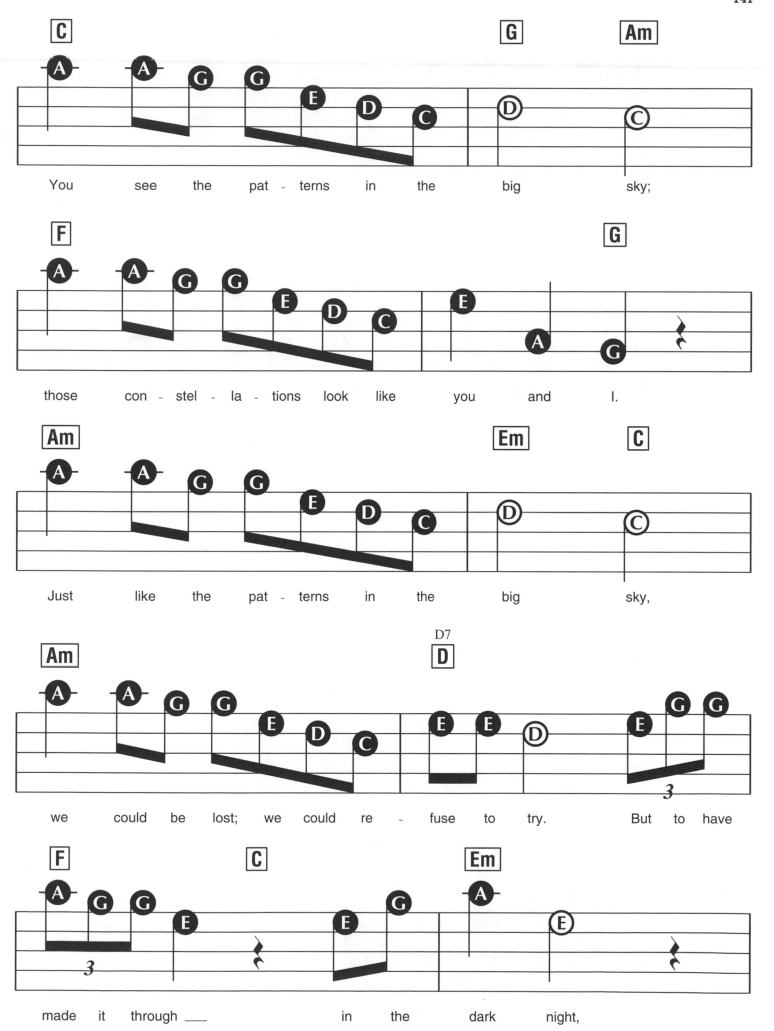

142

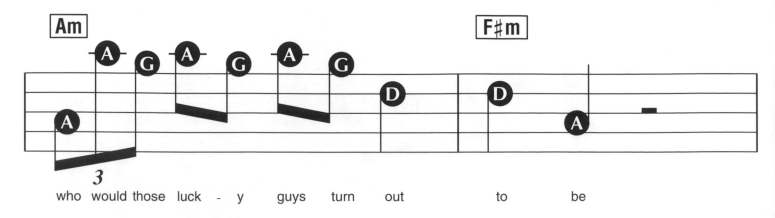

who would those luck - y guys turn out to be

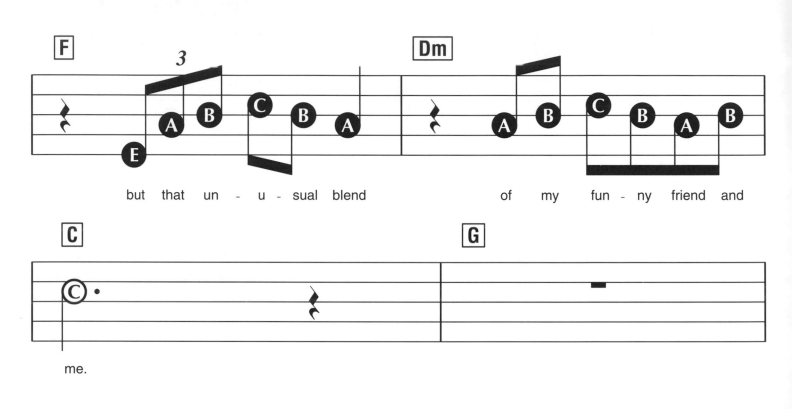

but that un - u - sual blend of my fun - ny friend and

me.

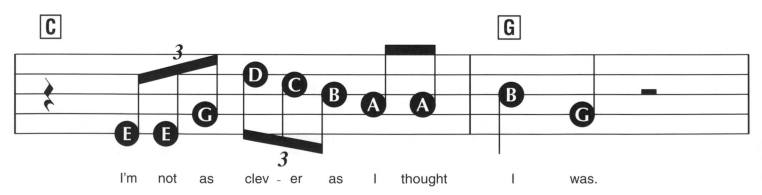

I'm not as clev - er as I thought I was.

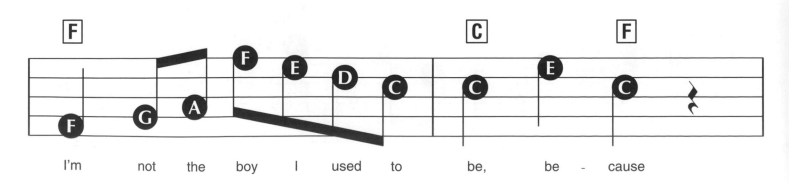

I'm not the boy I used to be, be - cause

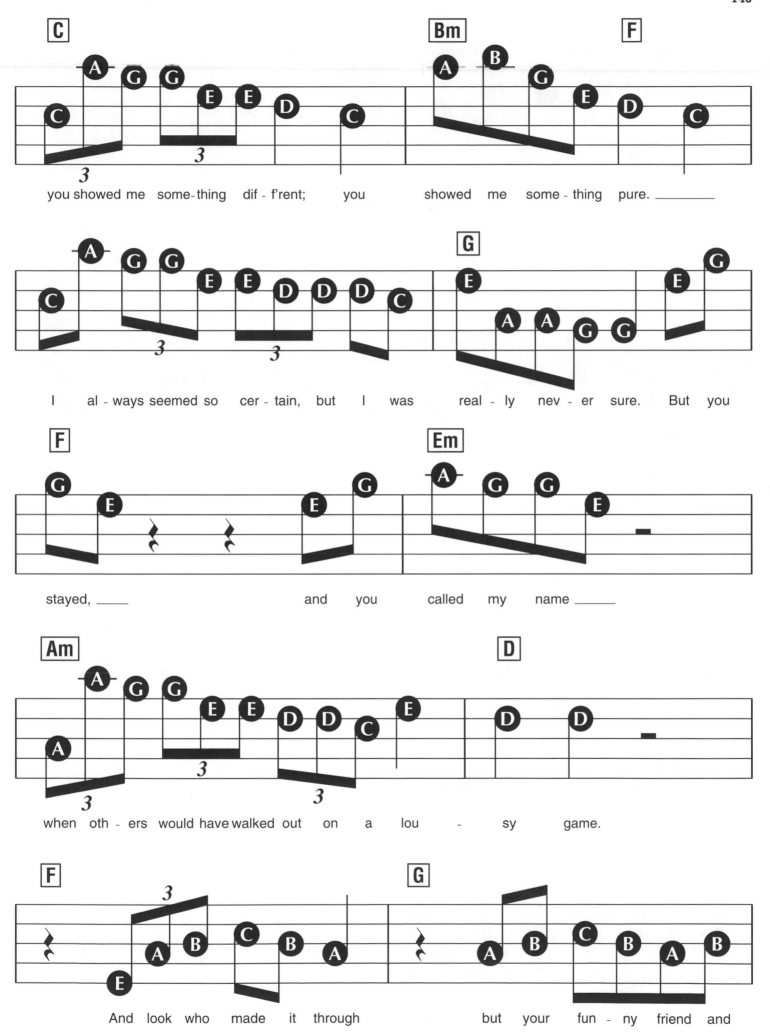

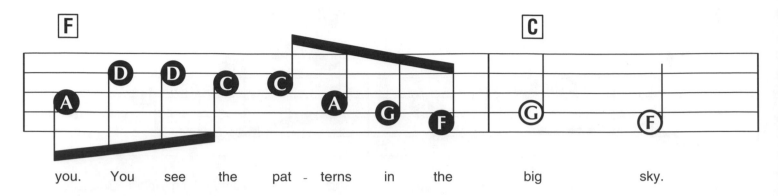

you. You see the pat - terns in the big sky.

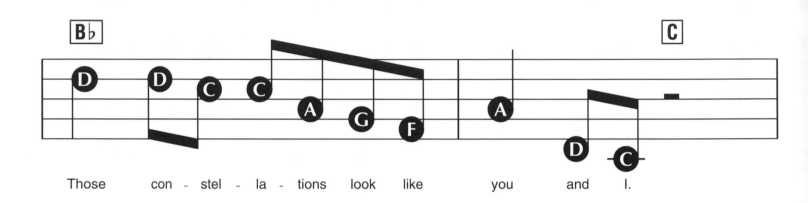

Those con - stel - la - tions look like you and I.

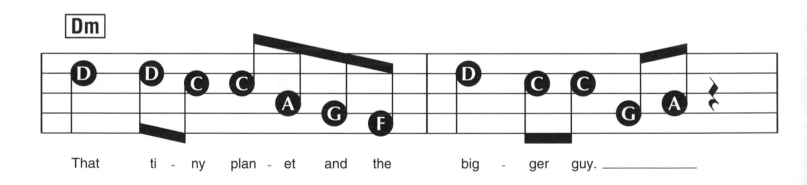

That ti - ny plan - et and the big - ger guy. _____

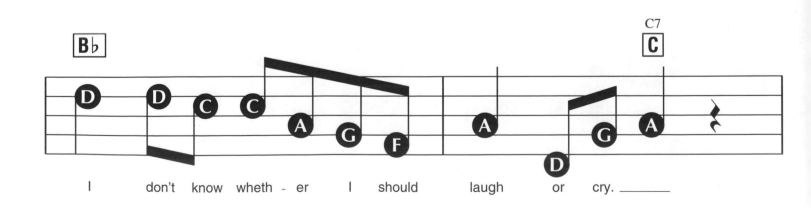

I don't know wheth - er I should laugh or cry. _____

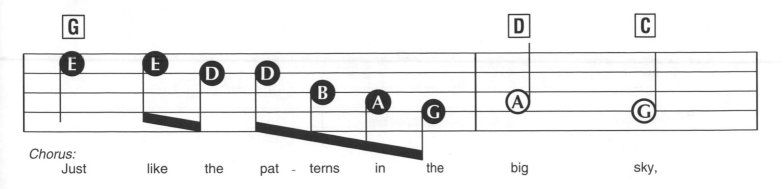

Chorus:
Just like the pat - terns in the big sky,

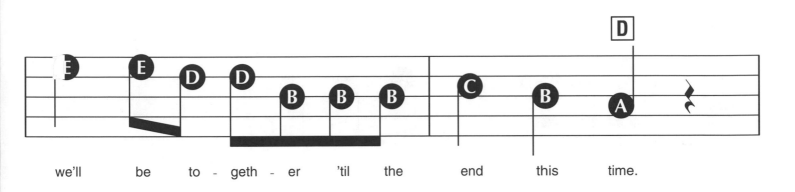

we'll be to - geth - er 'til the end this time.

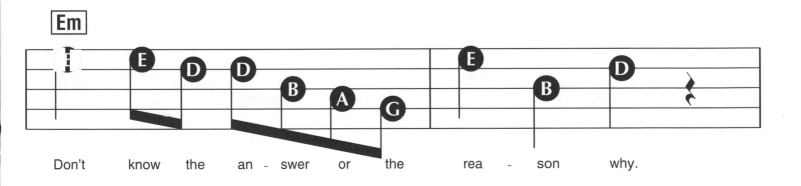

Don't know the an - swer or the rea - son why.

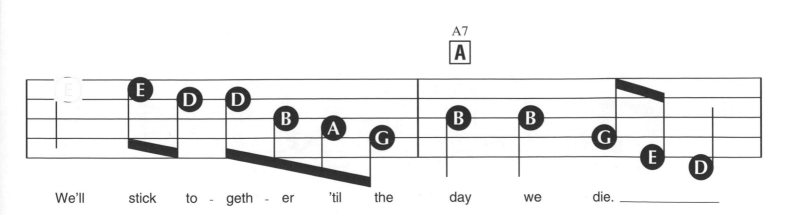

We'll stick to - geth - er 'til the day we die. _____

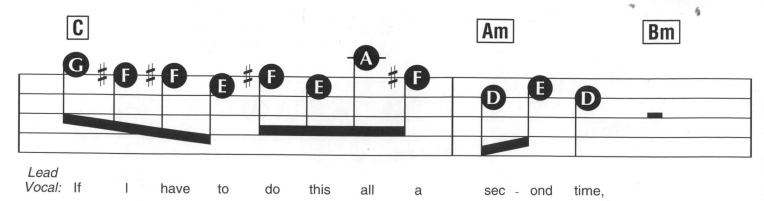

Lead
Vocal: If I have to do this all a sec - ond time,

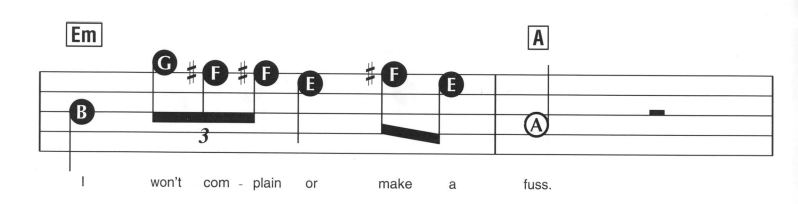

I won't com - plain or make a fuss.

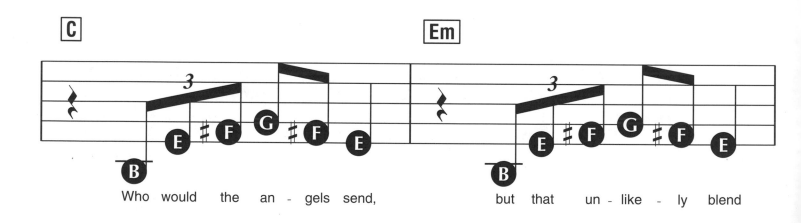

Who would the an - gels send, but that un - like - ly blend

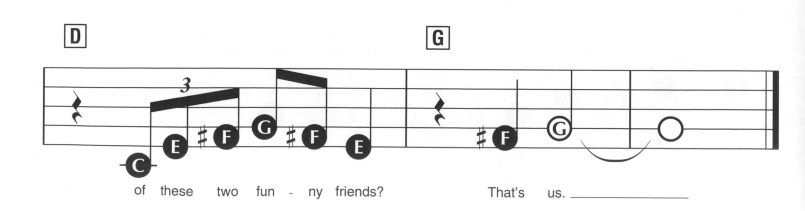

of these two fun - ny friends? That's us. _____

Part of Your World
from Walt Disney's THE LITTLE MERMAID

Registration 1
Rhythm: Pops or 8 Beat

Lyrics by Howard Ashman
Music by Alan Menken

148

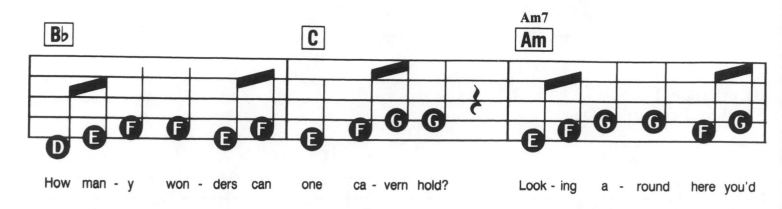

How man-y won-ders can one ca-vern hold? Look-ing a-round here you'd

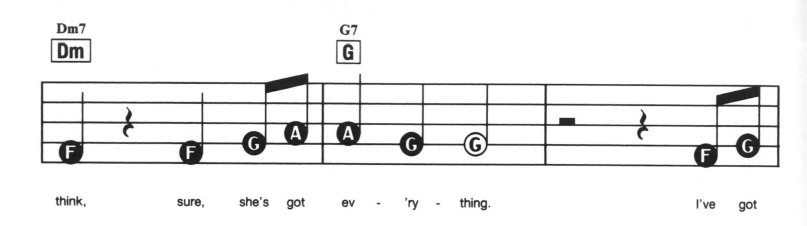

think, sure, she's got ev - 'ry - thing. I've got

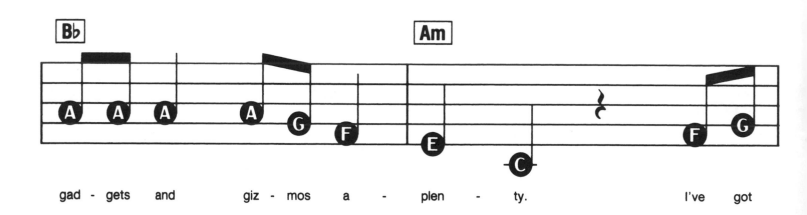

gad - gets and giz - mos a - plen - ty. I've got

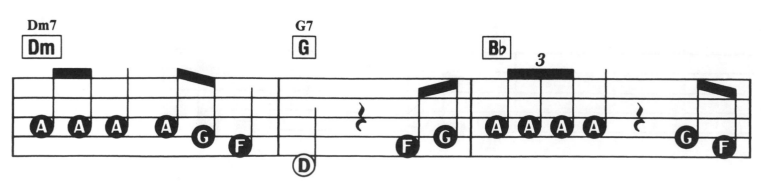

who - zits and what - zits ga - lore. You want thing - a - ma- bobs, I've got

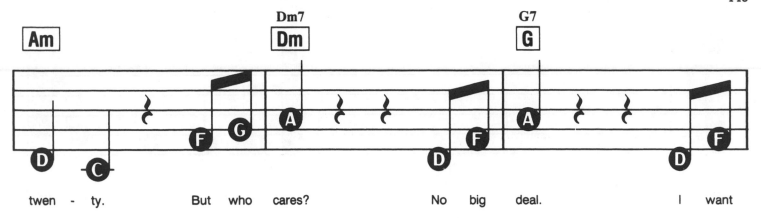

twen - ty. But who cares? No big deal. I want

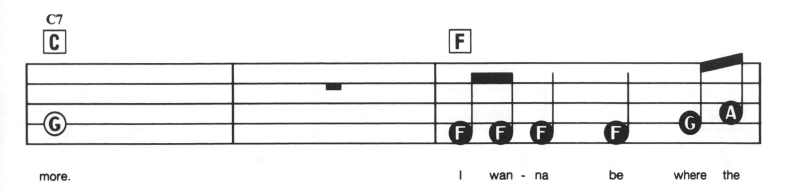

more. I wan - na be where the

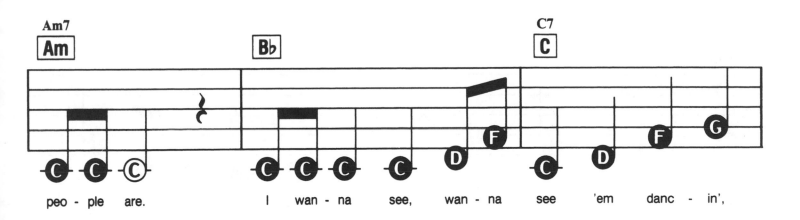

peo - ple are. I wan - na see, wan - na see 'em danc - in',

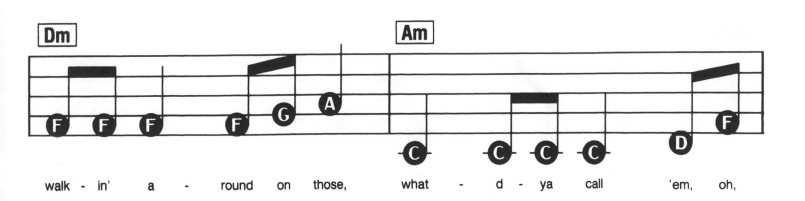

walk - in' a - round on those, what - d - ya call 'em, oh,

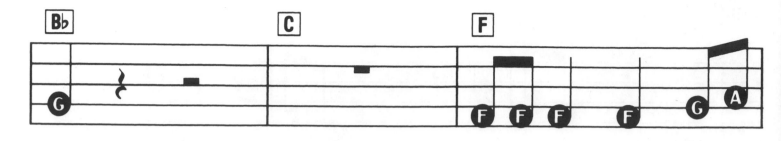

feet.   Flip - pin' your   fins   you don't

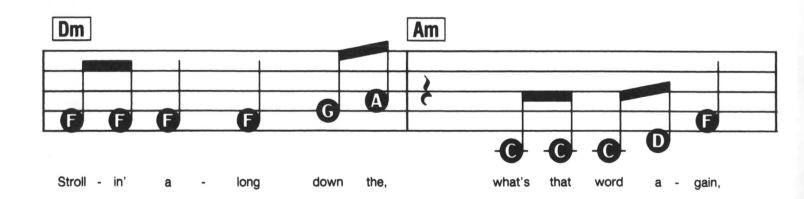

get   too   far.   Legs are re - quired___ for   jump - in',   danc - in'.

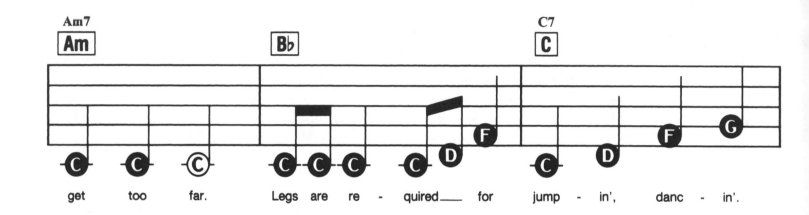

Stroll - in' a - long   down the,   what's that word a - gain,

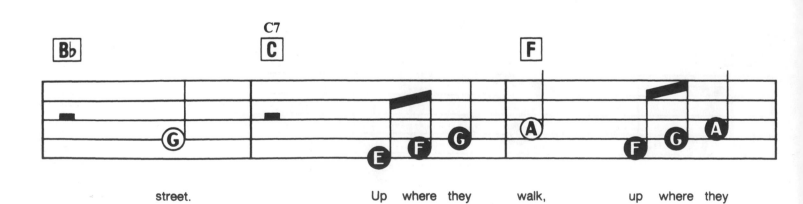

street.   Up where they   walk,   up where they

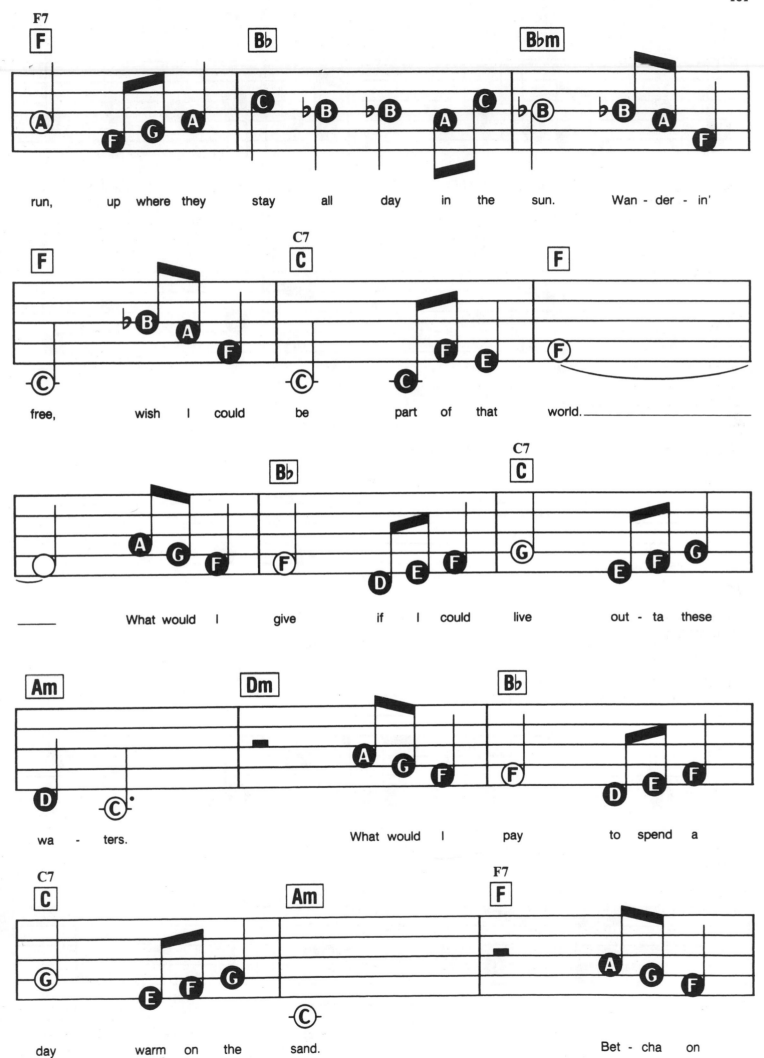

Once Upon a Dream
from Walt Disney's SLEEPING BEAUTY

Words and Music by Sammy Fain
and Jack Lawrence
Adapted from a Theme by Tchaikovsky

Registration 2
Rhythm: Waltz

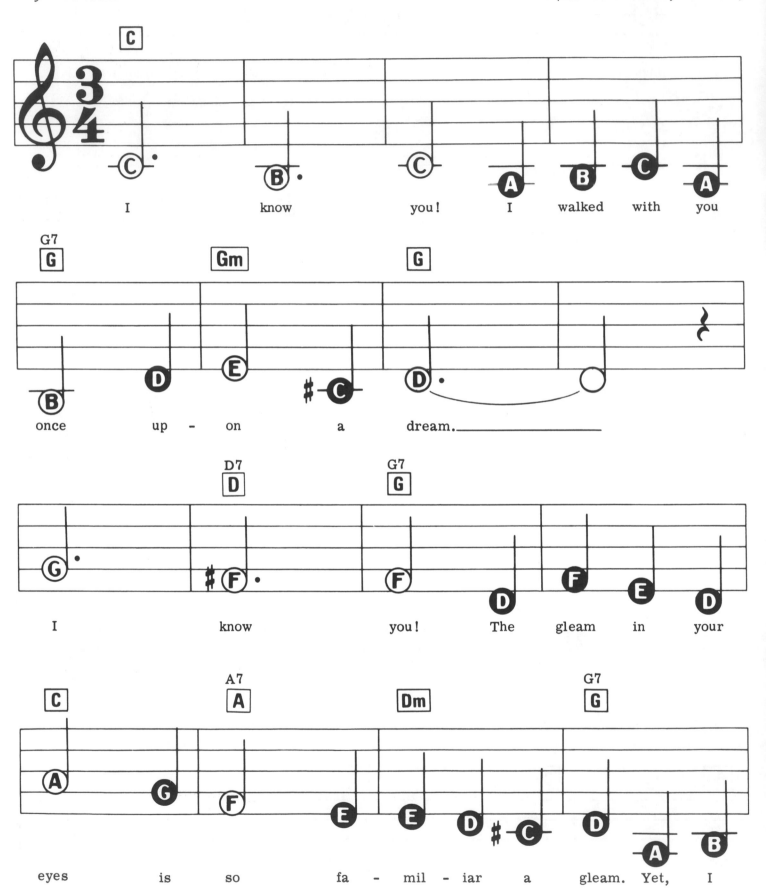

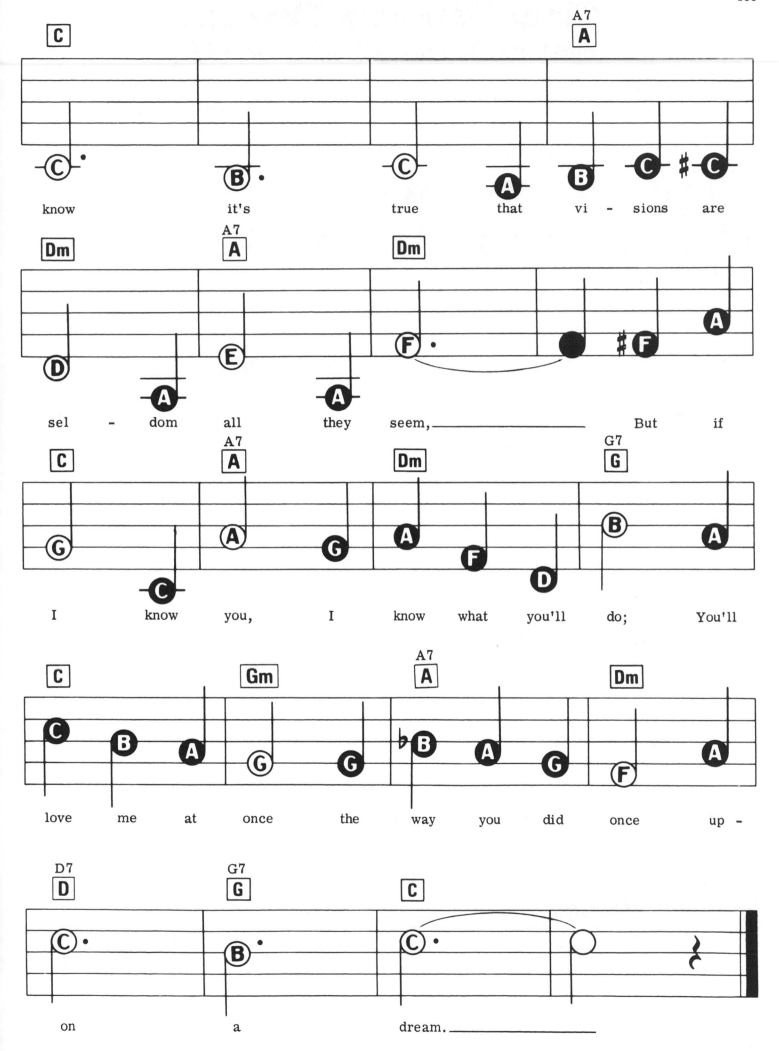

Perfect Isn't Easy
from Walt Disney's OLIVER & COMPANY

Registration 1
Rhythm: Fox Trot

Words by Jack Feldman and Bruce Sussman
Music by Barry Manilow

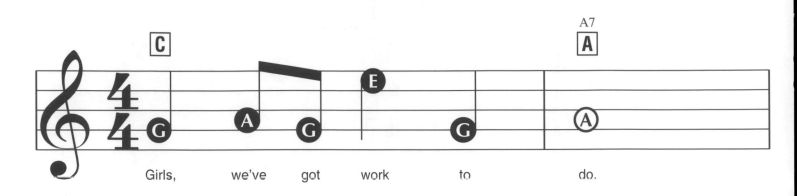

Girls, we've got work to do.

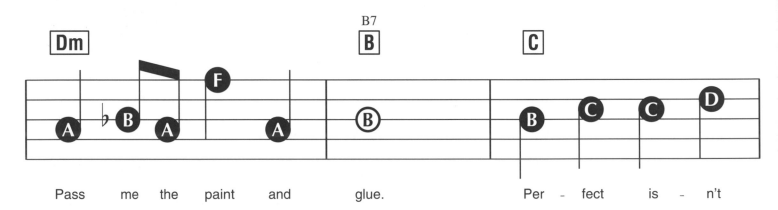

Pass me the paint and glue. Per - fect is - n't

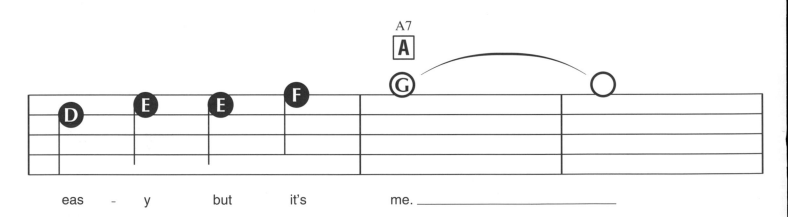

eas - y but it's me.

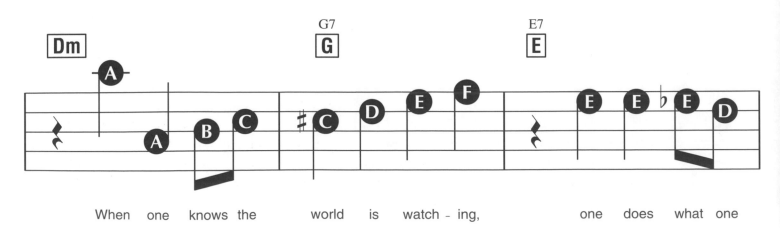

When one knows the world is watch - ing, one does what one

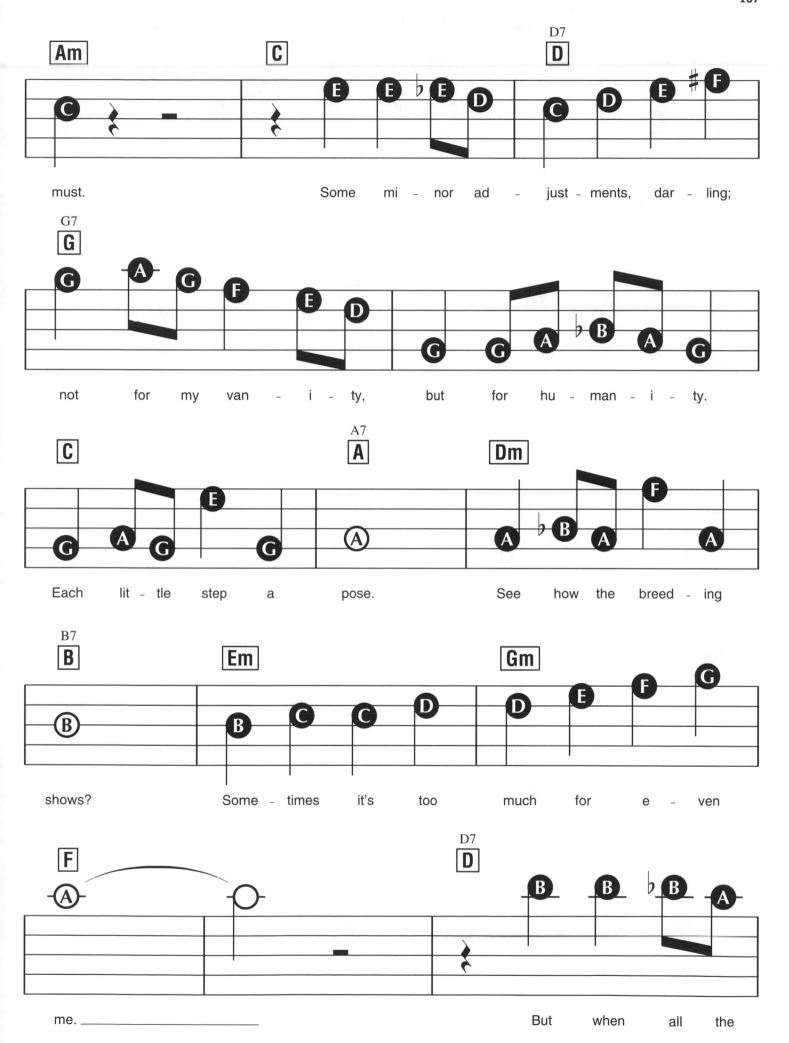

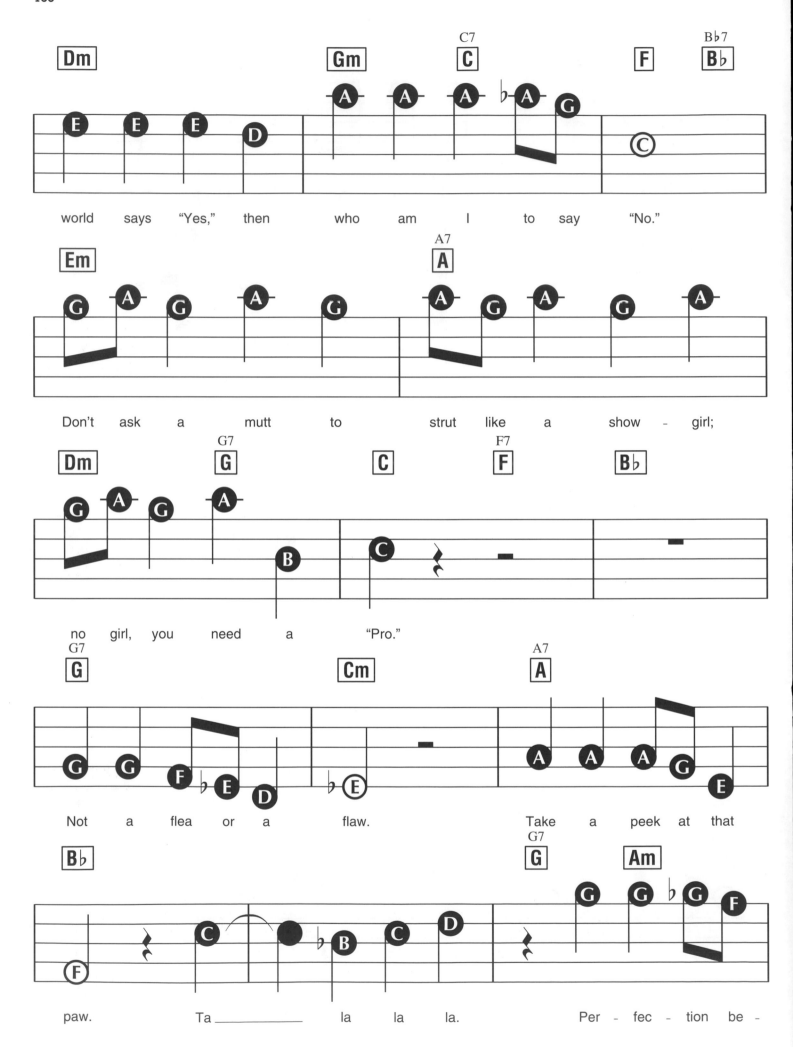

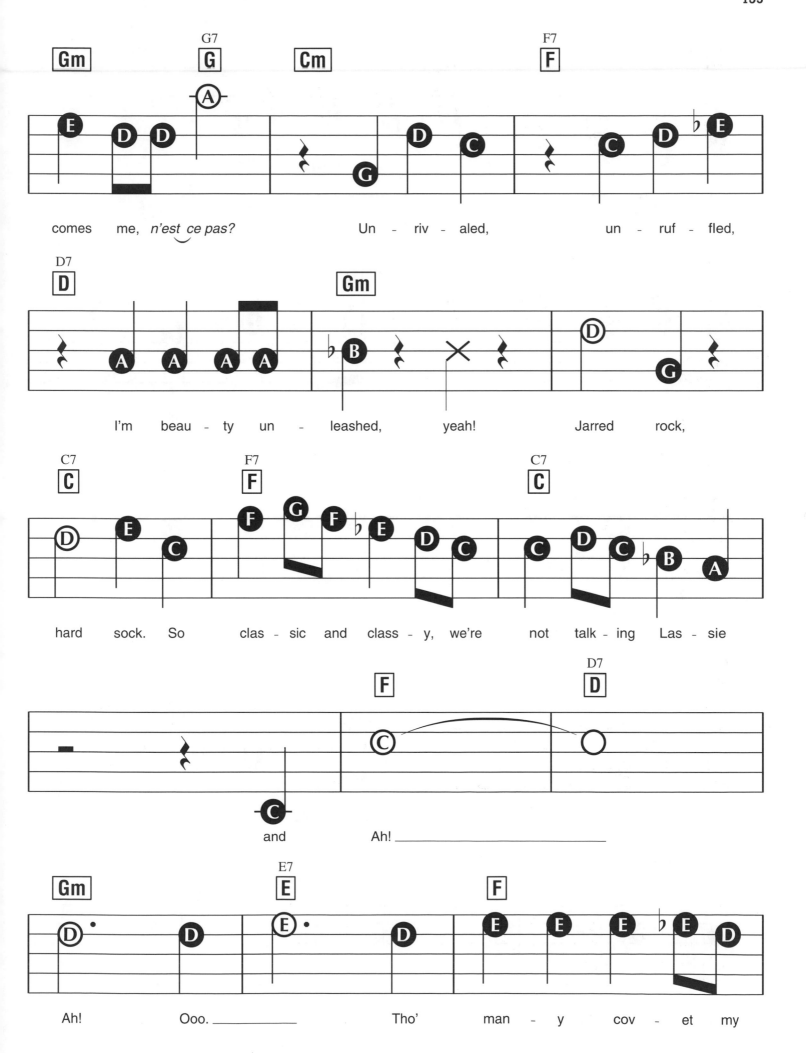

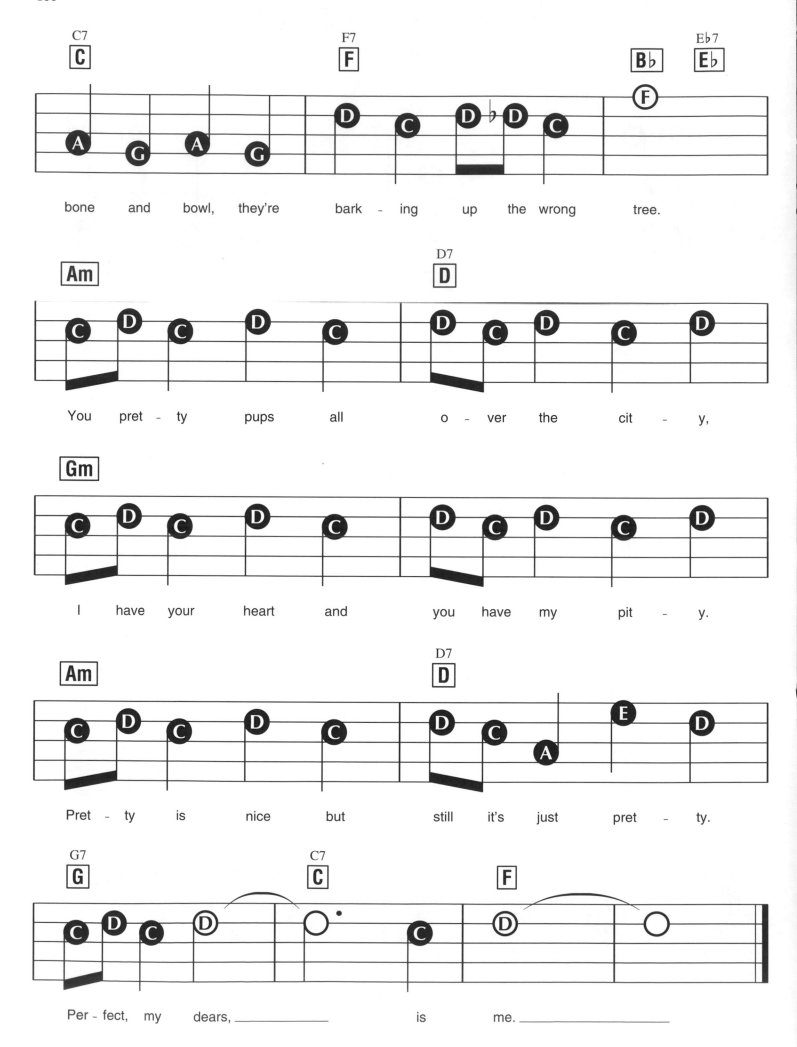

A Pirate's Life
from Walt Disney's PETER PAN

Registration 2
Rhythm: 6/8 March

Words by Ed Penner
Music by Oliver Wallace

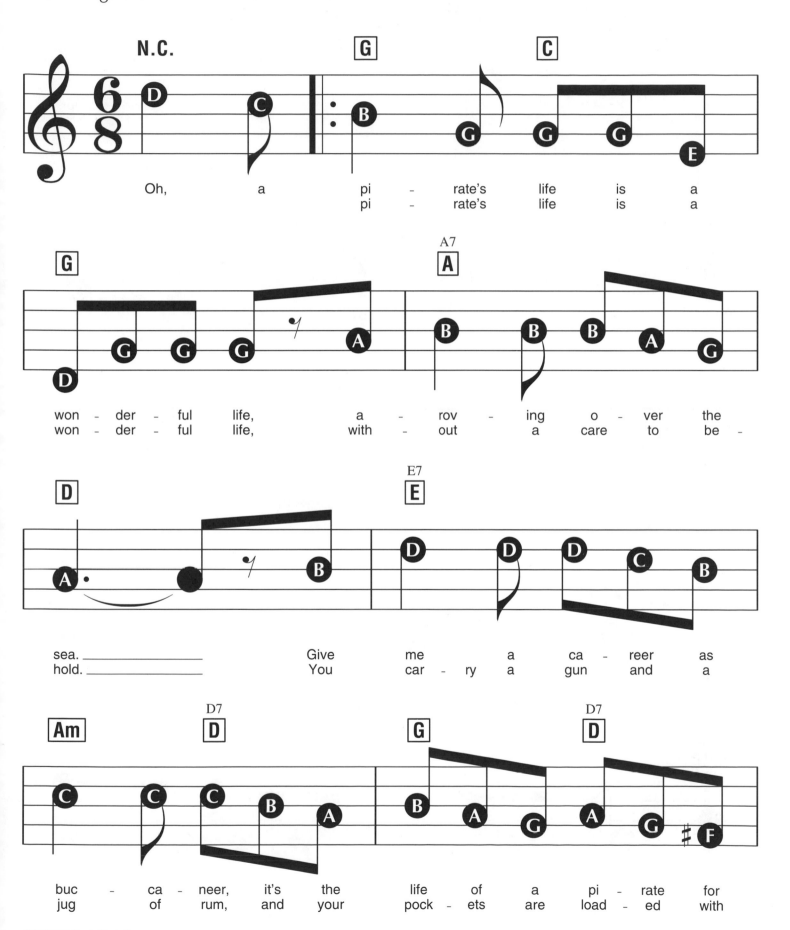

Oh, a pi - rate's life is a
pi - rate's life is a

won - der - ful life, a - rov - ing o - ver the
won - der - ful life, with - out a care to be -

sea. _____ Give me a ca - reer as
hold. _____ You car - ry a gun and a

buc - ca - neer, it's the life of a pi - rate for
jug of rum, and your pock - ets are load - ed with

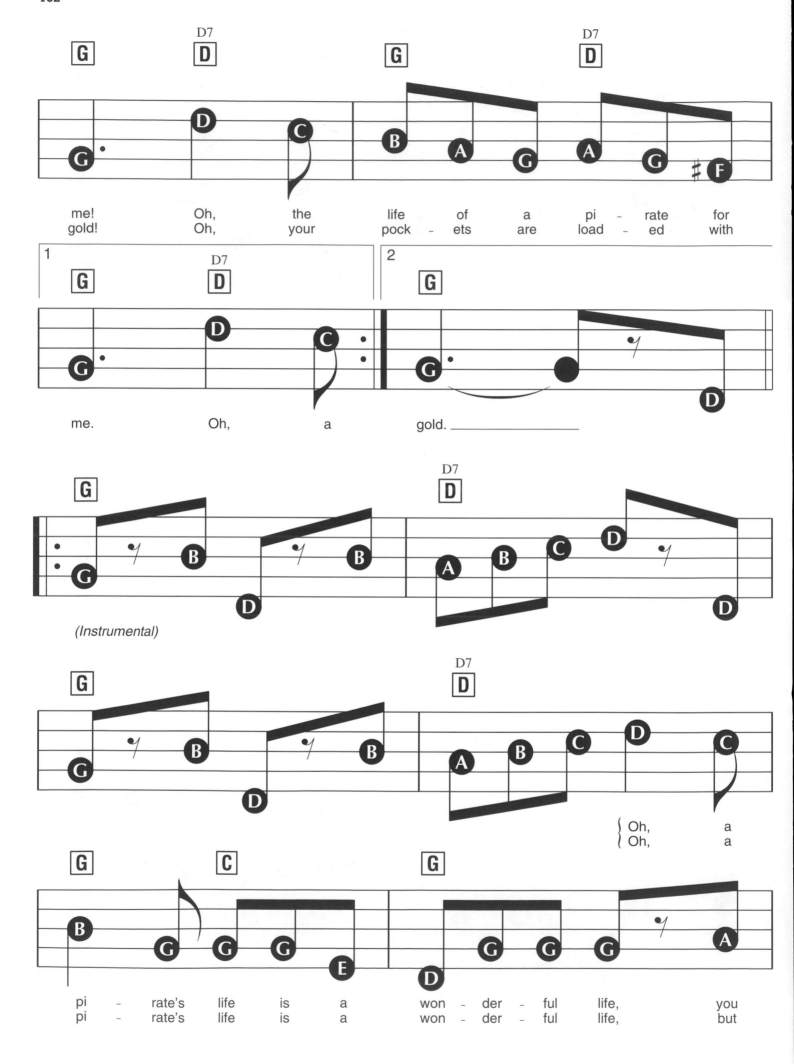

me! Oh, the life of a pi – rate for
gold! Oh, your pock – ets are load – ed with

me. Oh, a gold. _____

(Instrumental)

Oh, a
Oh, a

pi – rate's life is a won – der – ful life, you
pi – rate's life is a won – der – ful life, but

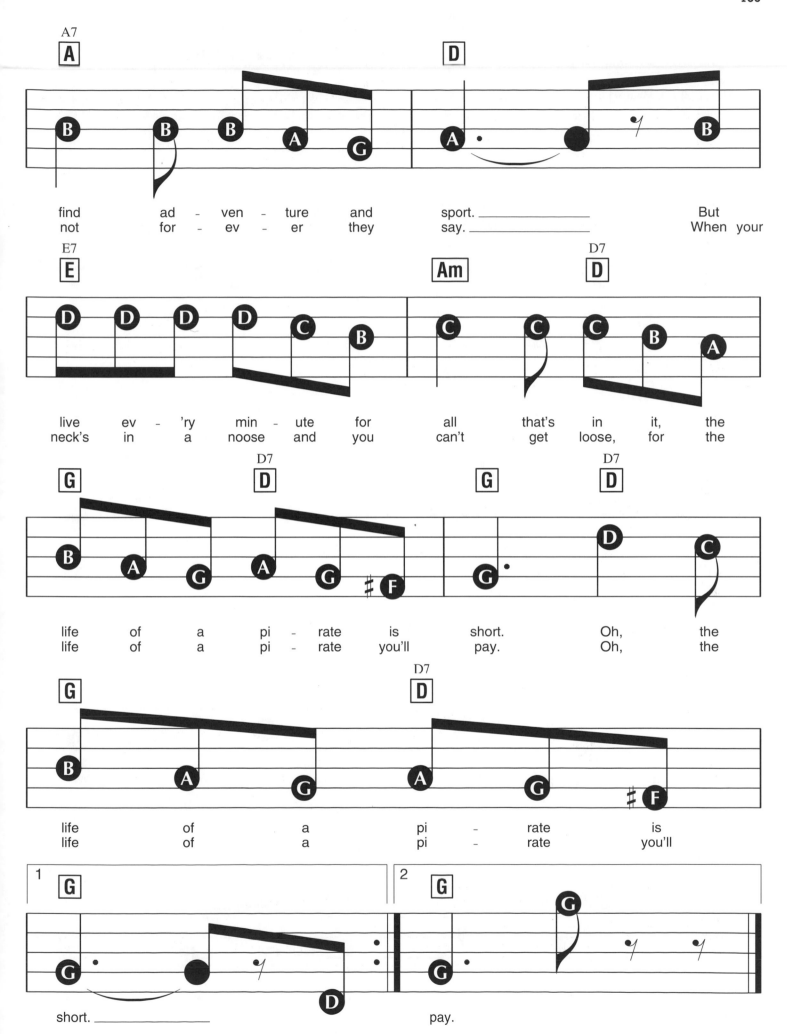

Promise
from MILLENNIUM CELEBRATION at Epcot

Registration 1
Rhythm: 4/4 Ballad or 8 Beat

Music by Gavin Greenaway
Words by Don Dorsey

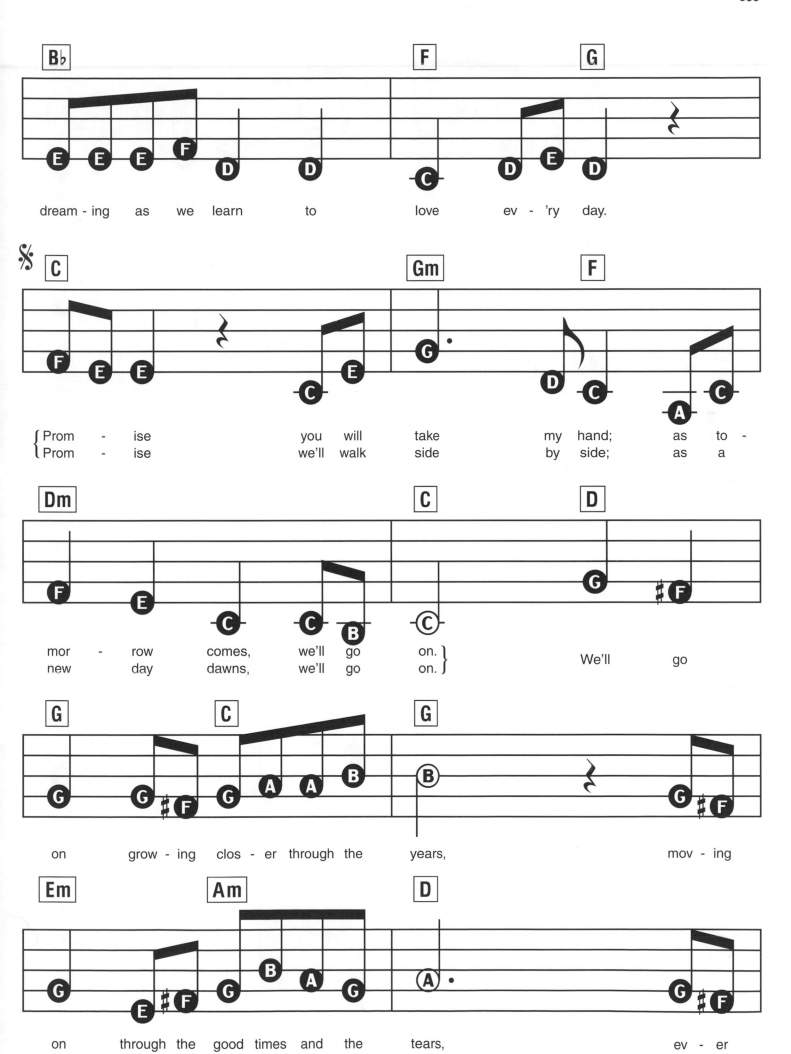

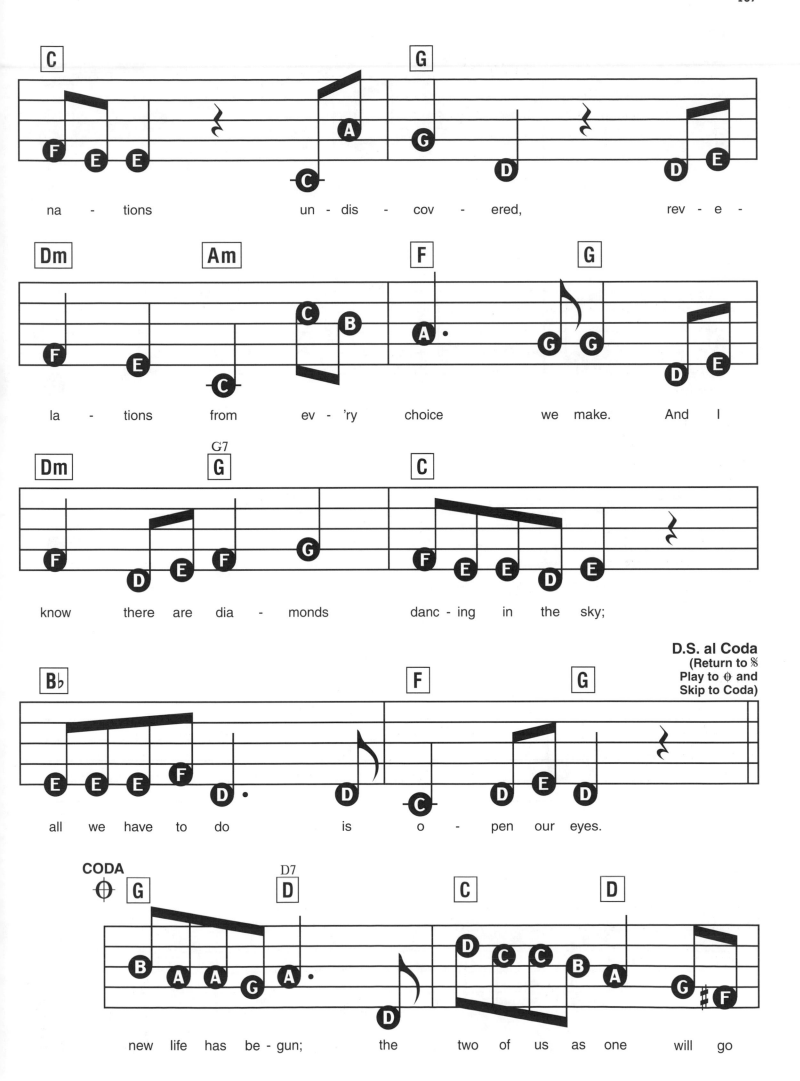

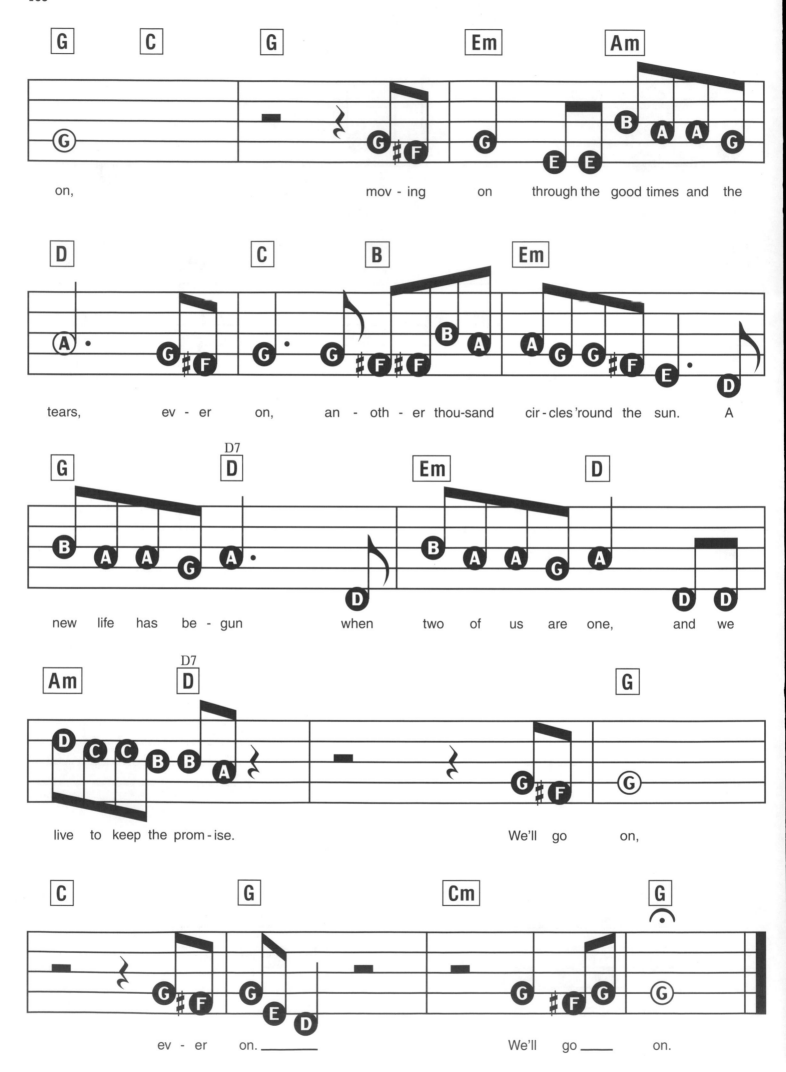

Reflection
from Walt Disney Pictures' MULAN

Registration 10
Rhythm: Ballad or 8 Beat

Music by Matthew Wilder
Lyrics by David Zippel

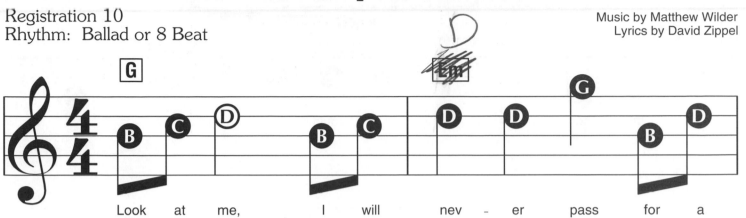

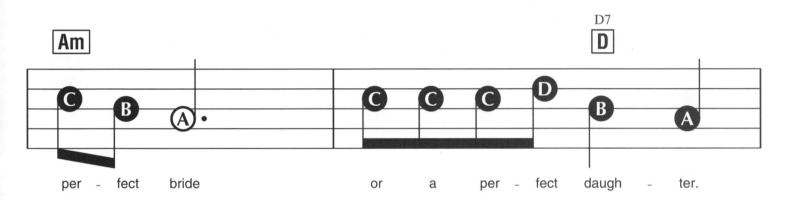

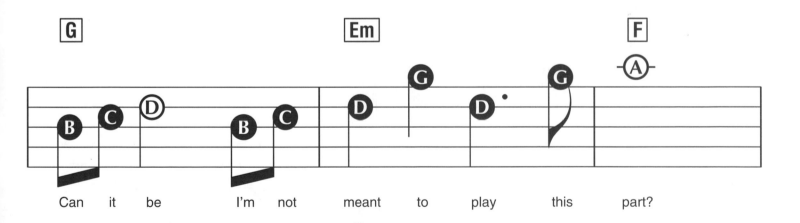

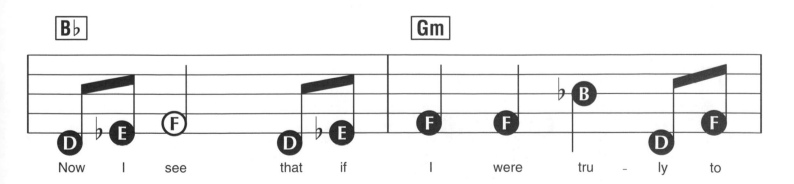

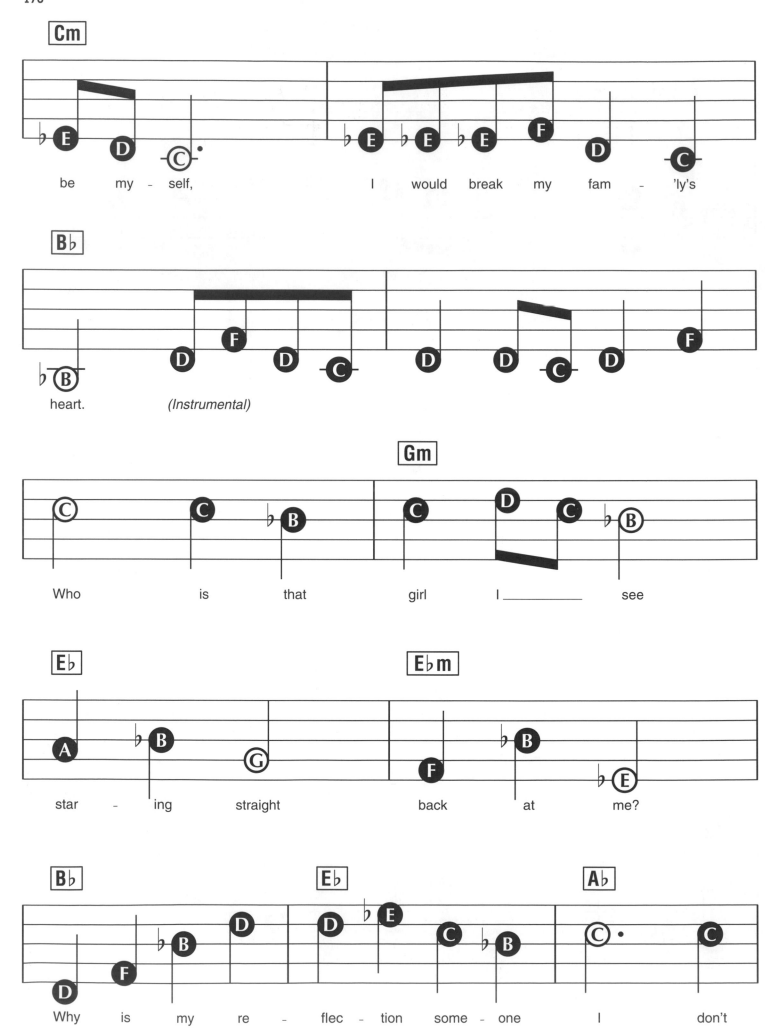

170

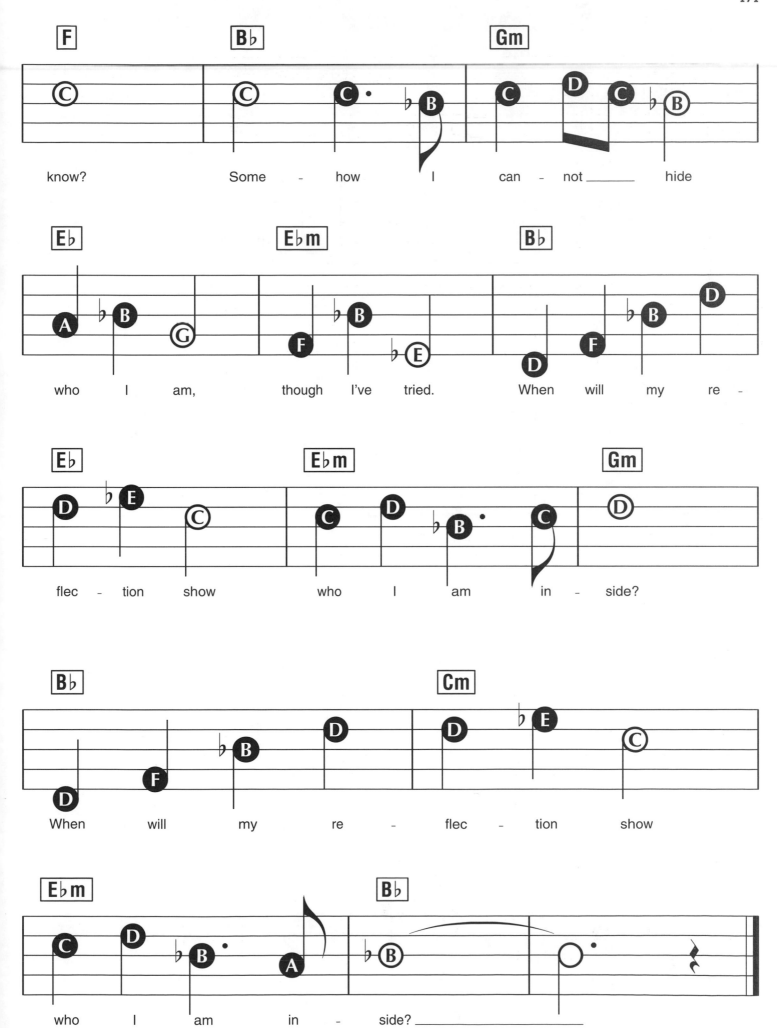

The Second Star to the Right
from Walt Disney's PETER PAN

Registration 3
Rhythm: Ballad or Fox Trot

Words by Sammy Cahn
Music by Sammy Fain

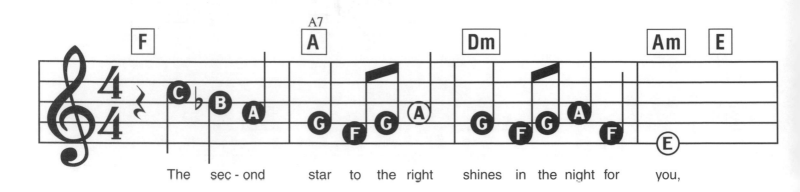

The sec-ond star to the right shines in the night for you,

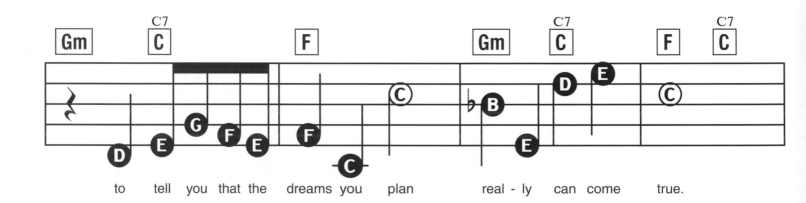

to tell you that the dreams you plan real-ly can come true.

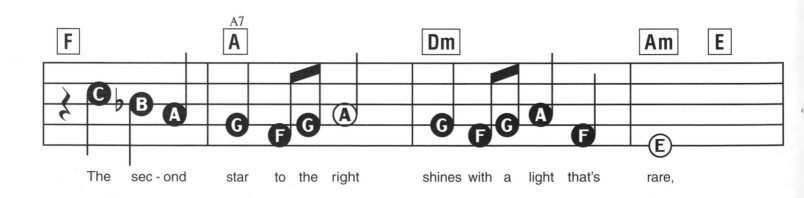

The sec-ond star to the right shines with a light that's rare,

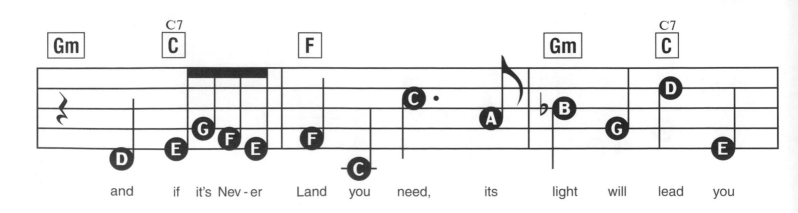

and if it's Nev-er Land you need, its light will lead you

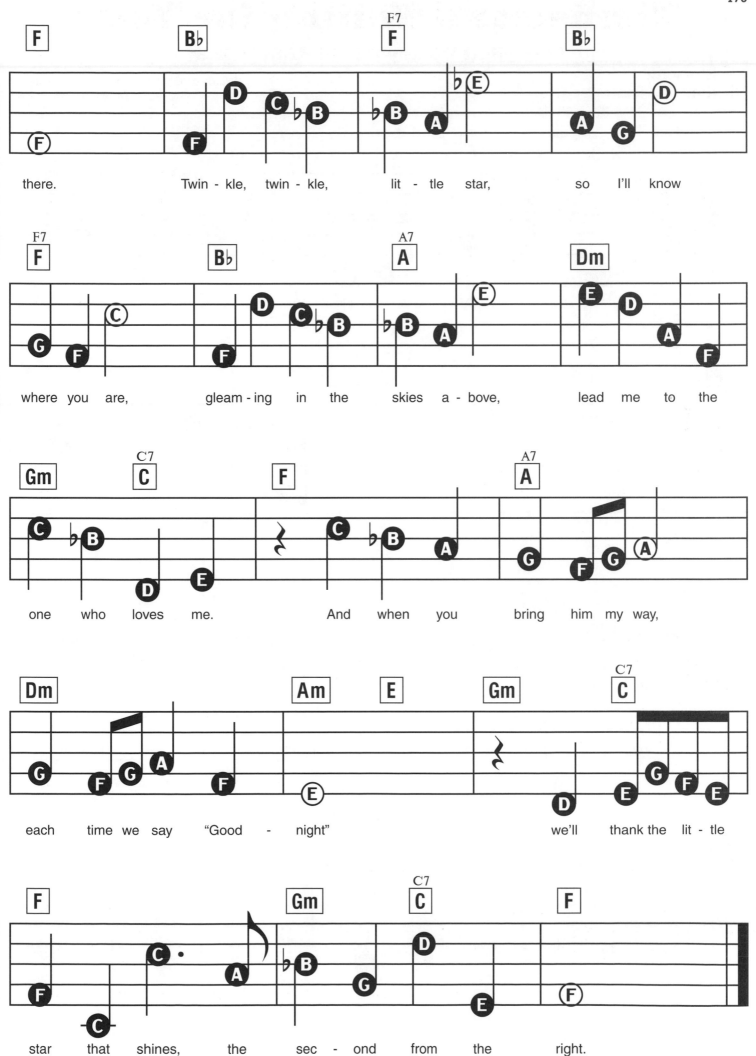

Someone's Waiting for You

from Walt Disney's THE RESCUERS

Registration 8
Rhythm: Fox Trot

Words by Carol Connors and Ayn Robbins
Music by Sammy Fain

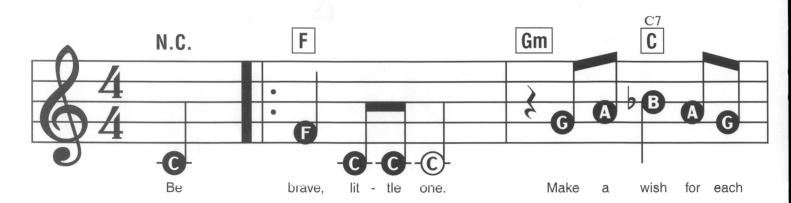

Be brave, lit - tle one. Make a wish for each

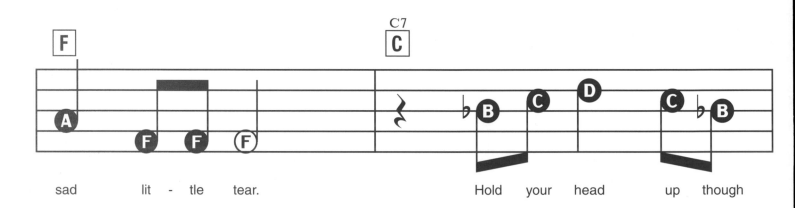

sad lit - tle tear. Hold your head up though

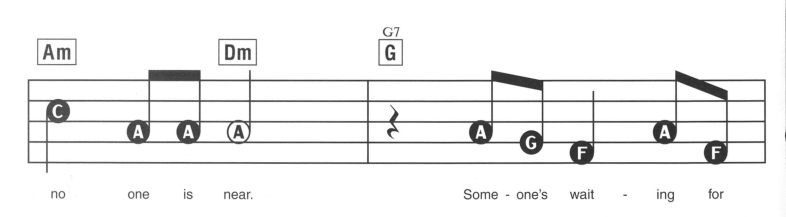

no one is near. Some - one's wait - ing for

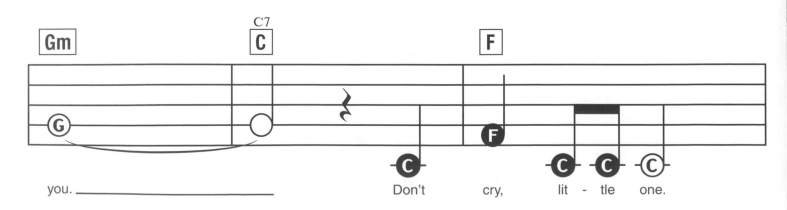

you. Don't cry, lit - tle one.

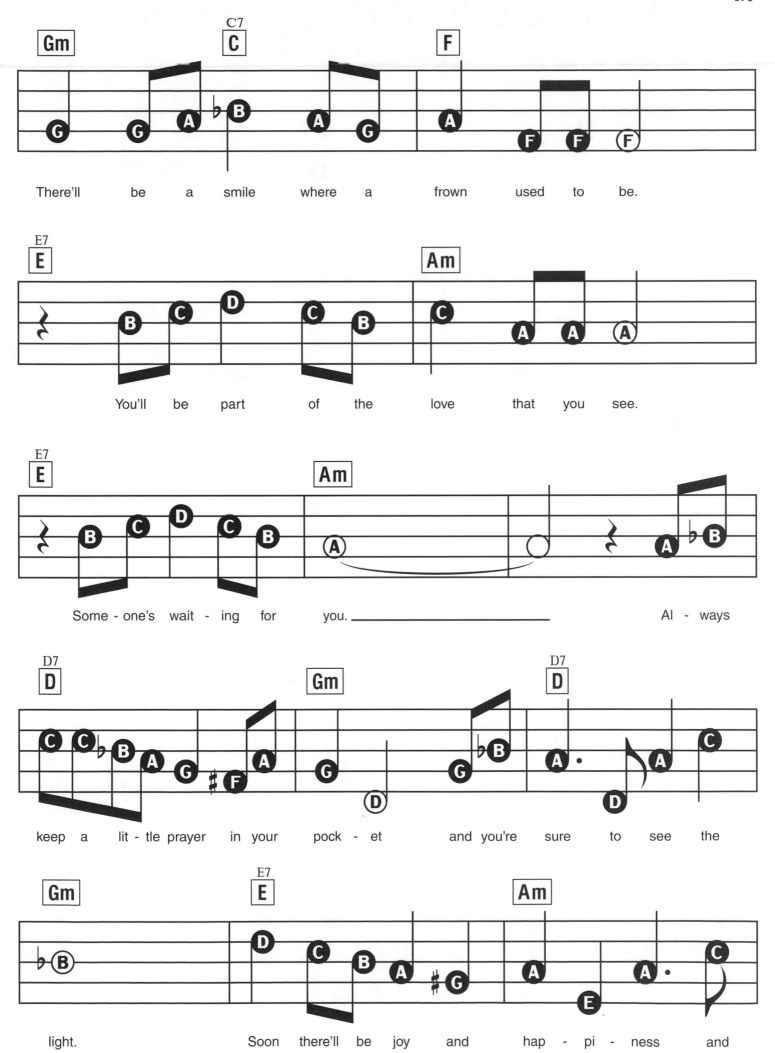

Seize the Day
from Walt Disney's NEWSIES

Registration 2
Rhythm: None

Lyrics by Jack Feldman
Music by Alan Menken

C

David: O - pen the gates and seize the day.

Dm **C**

Bb **F**

Don't be a - fraid and don't de - lay.

C **Am** **Fm**

Noth - ing can break us. No one can make us

C **G** (G7) **Am** **D** (D7)

give our rights a - way. _____ A -

Rhythm: Broadway or Fox Trot

C **G** (G7) **C**

rise and seize the day.

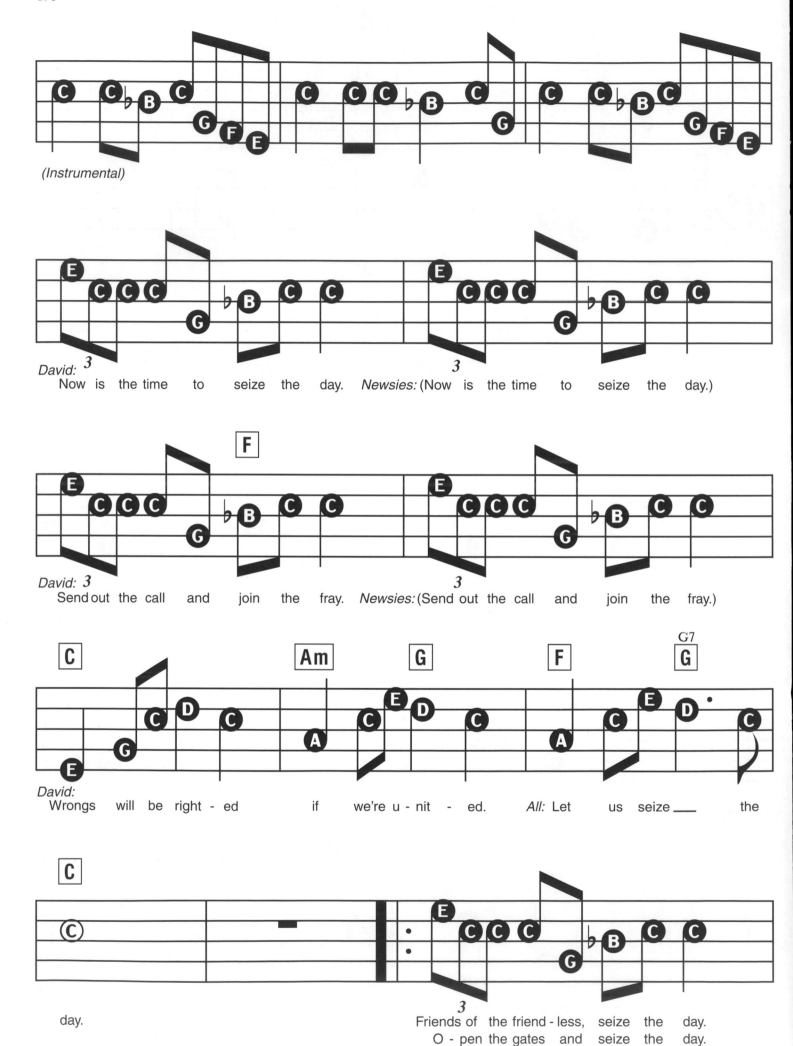

(Instrumental)

David:
Now is the time to seize the day. *Newsies:* (Now is the time to seize the day.)

David:
Send out the call and join the fray. *Newsies:* (Send out the call and join the fray.)

David:
Wrongs will be right-ed if we're u-nit-ed. *All:* Let us seize ___ the

day.

Friends of the friend-less, seize the day.
O - pen the gates and seize the day.

The Siamese Cat Song
from Walt Disney's LADY AND THE TRAMP

Registration 1
Rhythm: Rock

Words and Music by Peggy Lee
and Sonny Burke

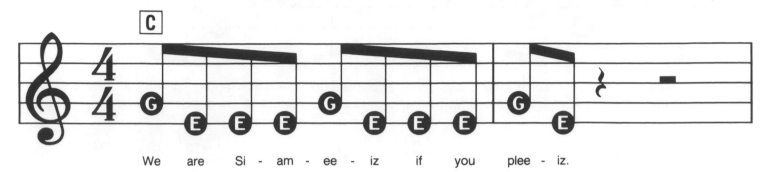

We are Si - am - ee - iz if you plee - iz.

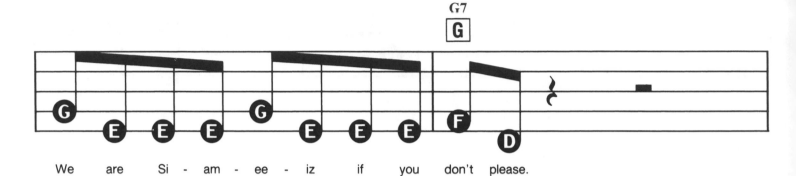

We are Si - am - ee - iz if you don't please.

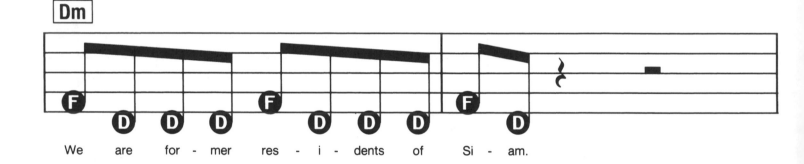

We are for - mer res - i - dents of Si - am.

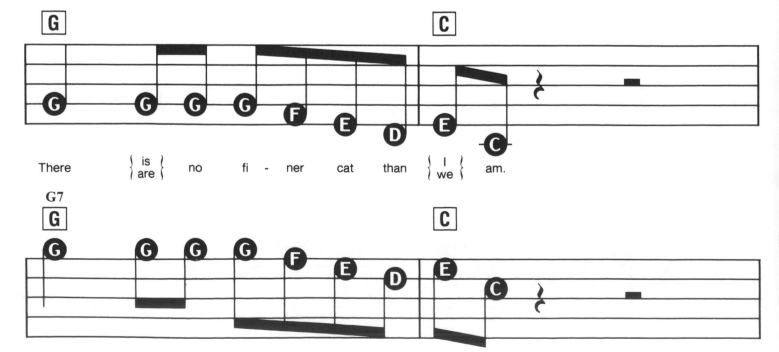

There {is / are} no fi - ner cat than {I / we} am.

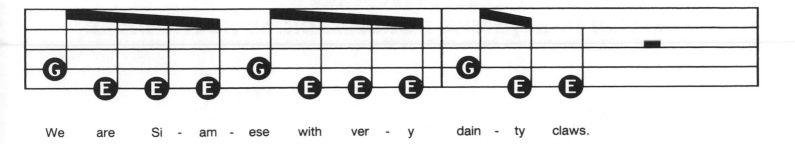

We are Si - am - ese with ver - y dain - ty claws.

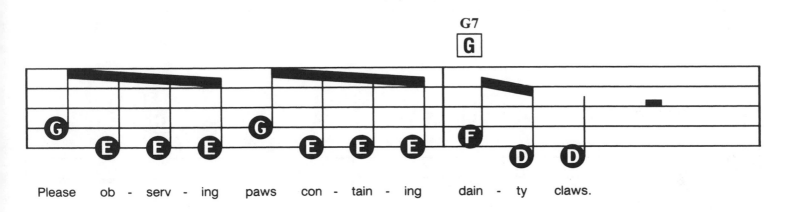

Please ob - serv - ing paws con - tain - ing dain - ty claws.

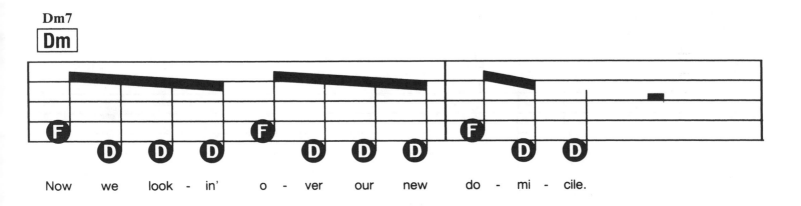

Now we look - in' o - ver our new do - mi - cile.

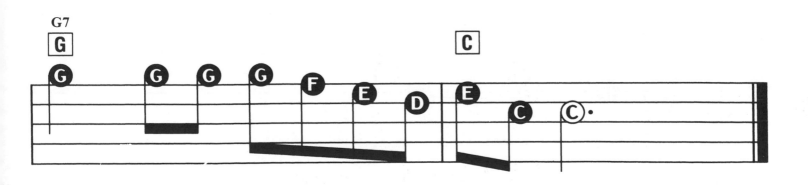

Someday
from Walt Disney's THE HUNCHBACK OF NOTRE DAME

Registration 1
Rhythm: Waltz

Music by Alan Menken
Lyrics by Stephen Schwartz

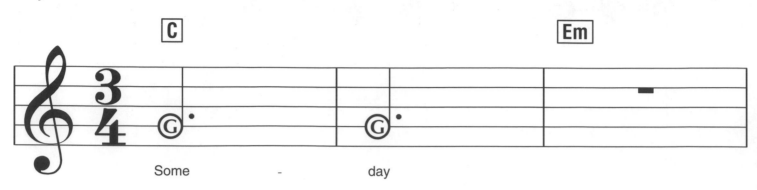

Some - day

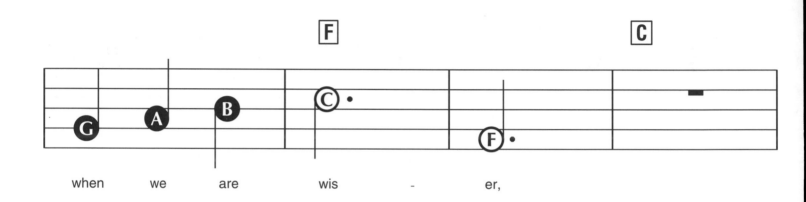

when we are wis - er,

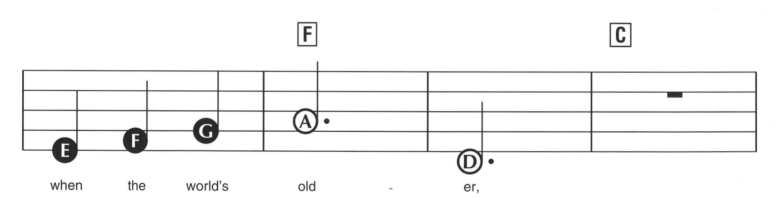

when the world's old - er,

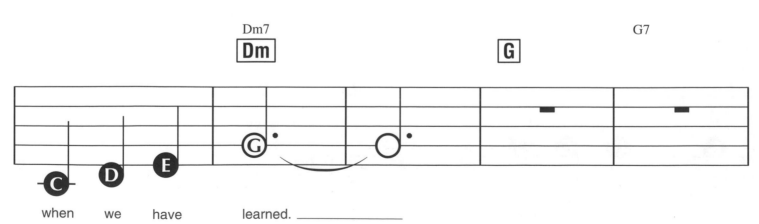

when we have learned. _____

183

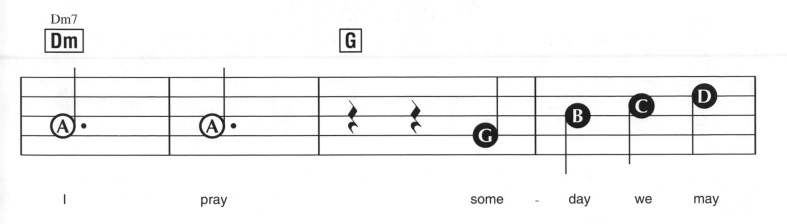

I   pray   some - day   we   may

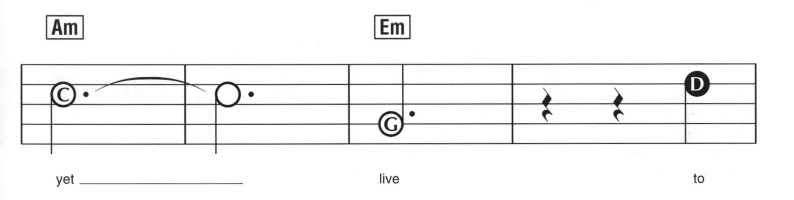

yet _____   live   to

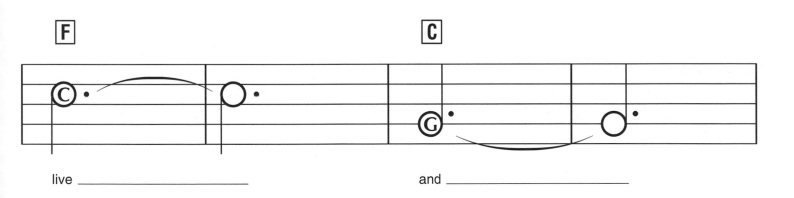

live _____   and _____

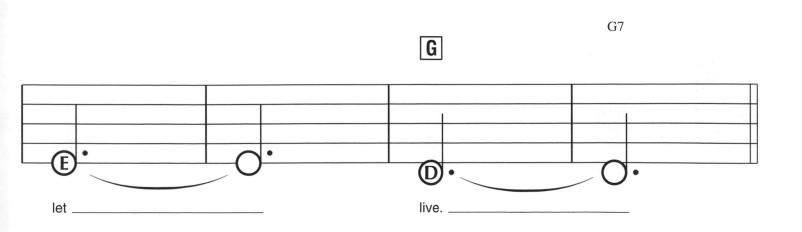

let _____   live. _____

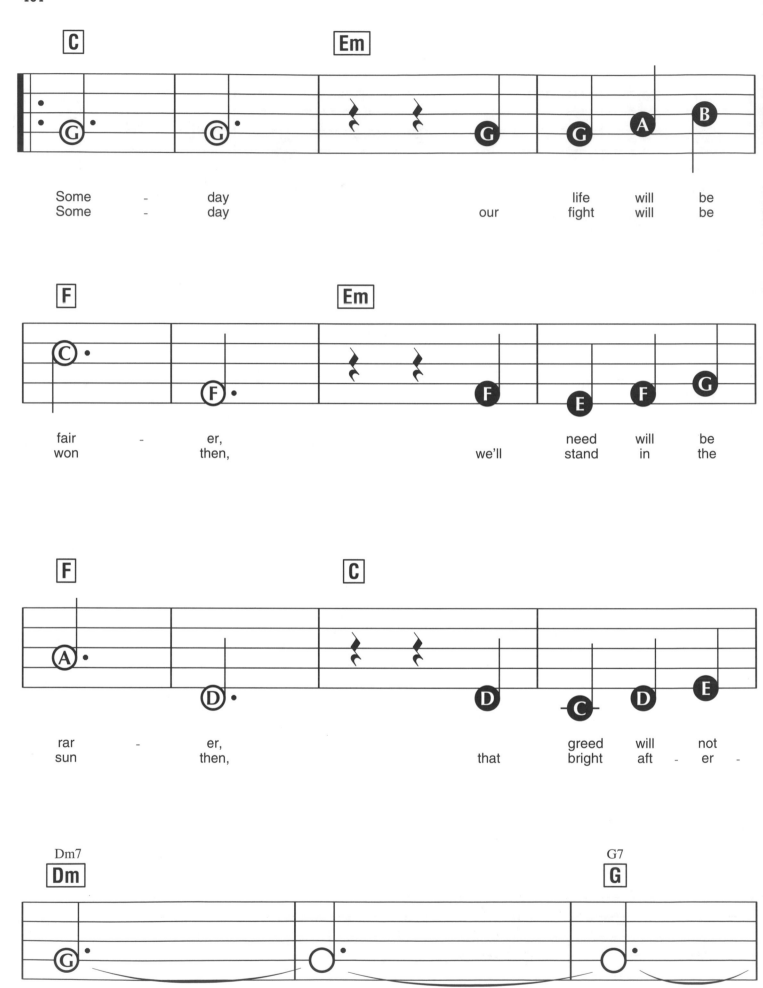

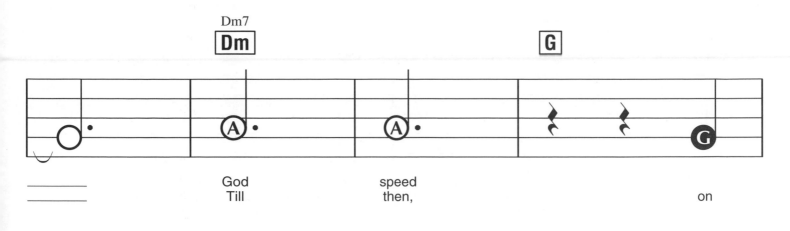

God speed
Till then, on

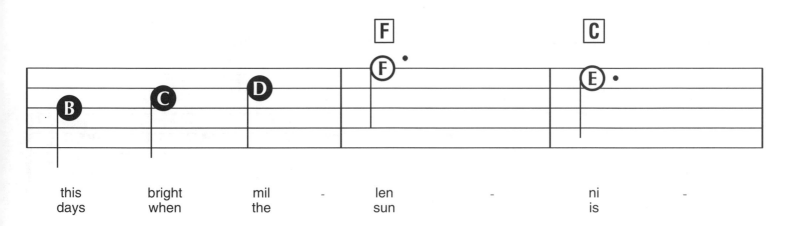

this bright mil - len - ni -
days when the sun is

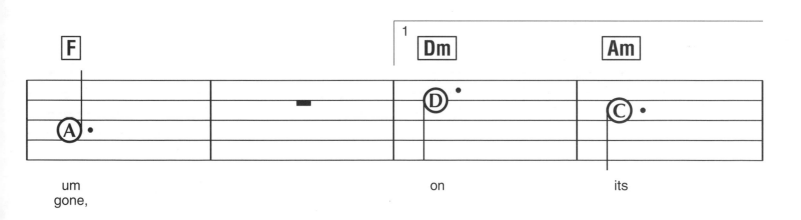

um on its
gone,

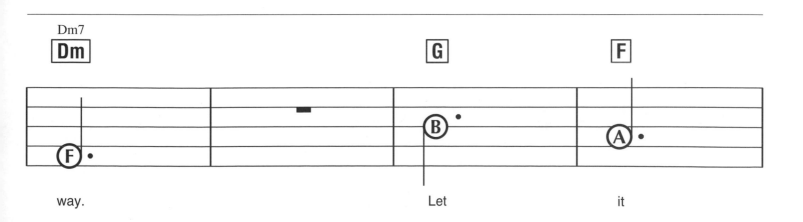

way. Let it

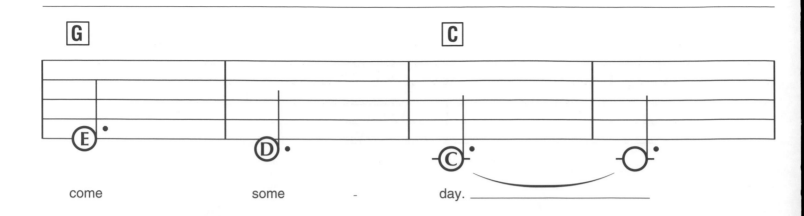

come   some -   day.

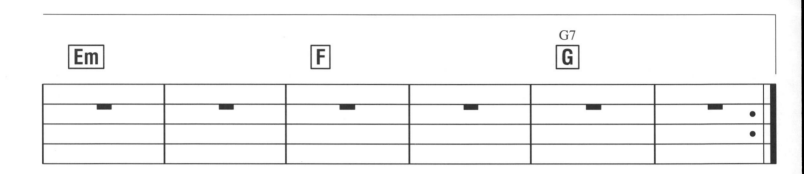

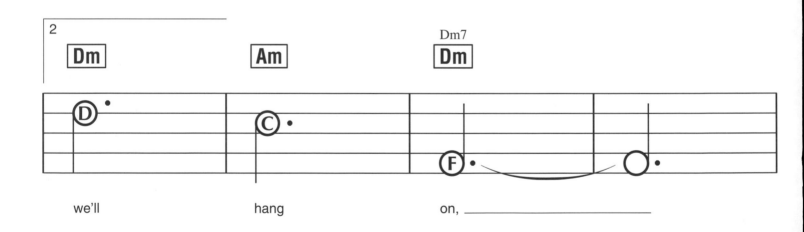

we'll   hang   on,

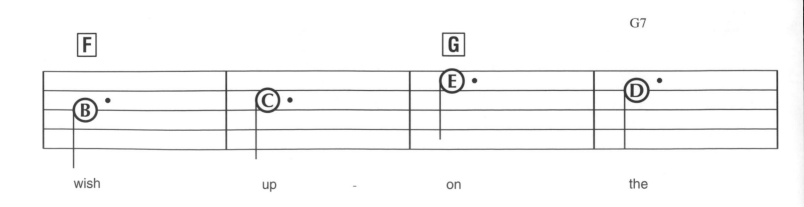

wish   up -   on   the

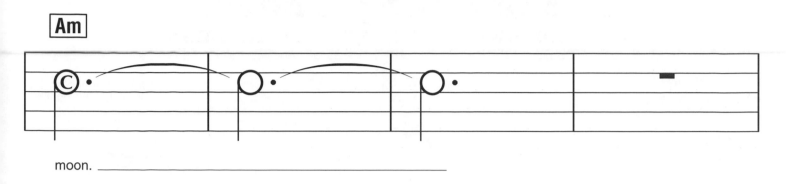

moon.

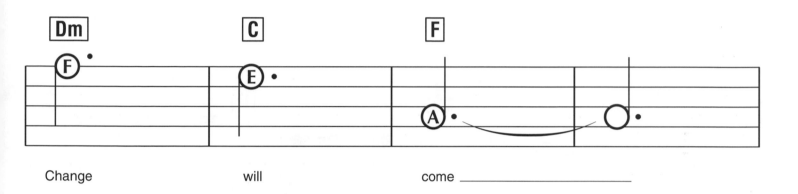

Change will come

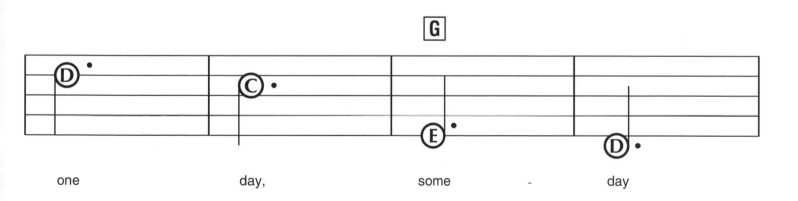

one day, some - day

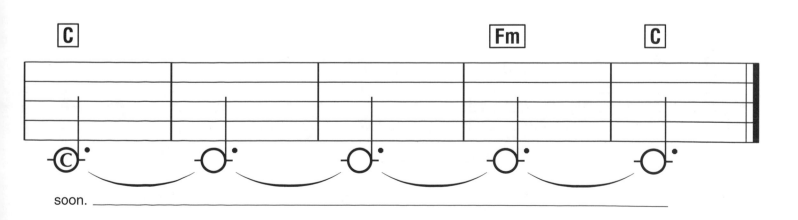

soon.

Something There
from Walt Disney's BEAUTY AND THE BEAST

Registration 7
Rhythm: 8 Beat or Pops

Lyrics by Howard Ashman
Music by Alan Menken

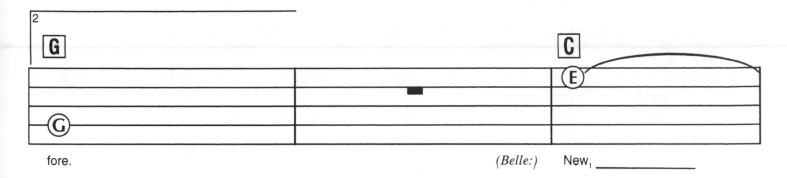

fore.   *(Belle:)*   New, _____

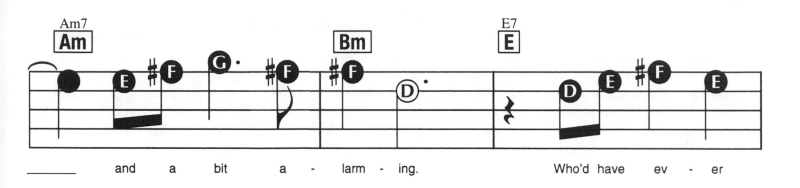

_____ and a bit a - larm - ing.   Who'd have ev - er

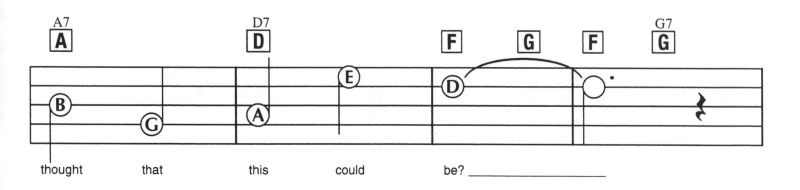

thought that this could be? _____

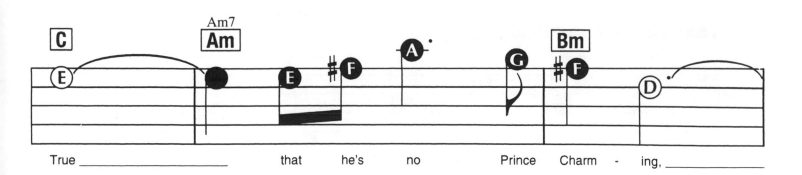

True _____ that he's no Prince Charm - ing, _____

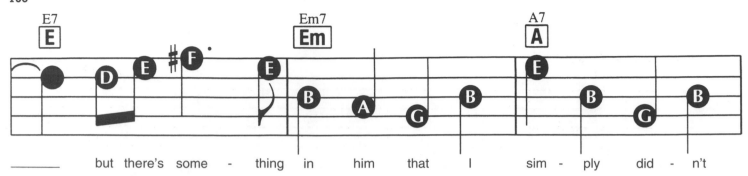

but there's some - thing in him that I sim - ply did - n't

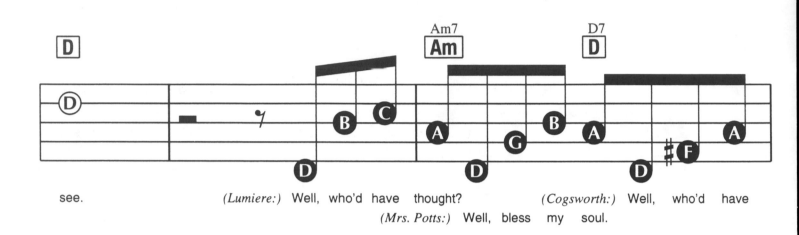

see.   (Lumiere:) Well, who'd have thought?   (Cogsworth:) Well, who'd have

(Mrs. Potts:) Well, bless my soul.

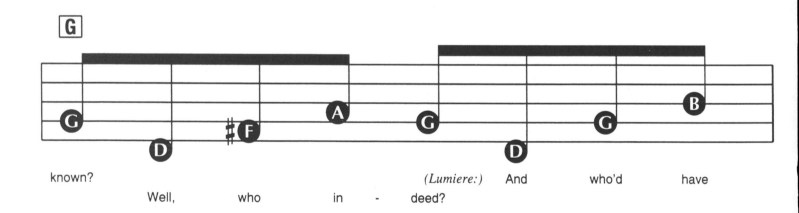

known?   (Lumiere:) And who'd have

Well, who in - deed?

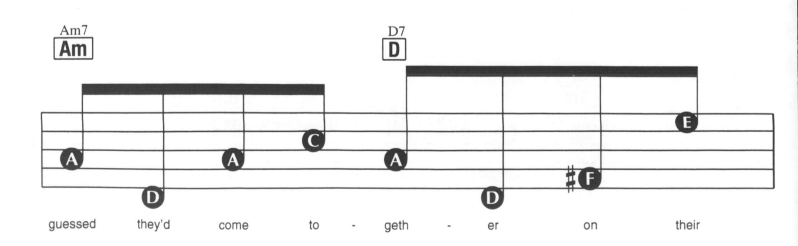

guessed they'd come to - geth - er on their

own?
It's so pe - cul - iar! *(Both:)* We'll wait and see *(All Three:)* a few days

more. There may be some - thing there that was - n't there be -

fore. *(Cogsworth:)* You know, per - haps there's

some - thing there that was - n't there be - fore.

(Mrs. Potts:) There may be some - thing there that was - n't there be - fore.

A Spoonful of Sugar
from Walt Disney's MARY POPPINS

Registration 3
Rhythm: Fox Trot or Swing

Words and Music by Richard M. Sherman
and Robert B. Sherman

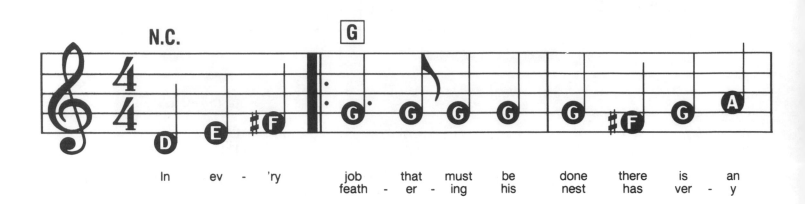

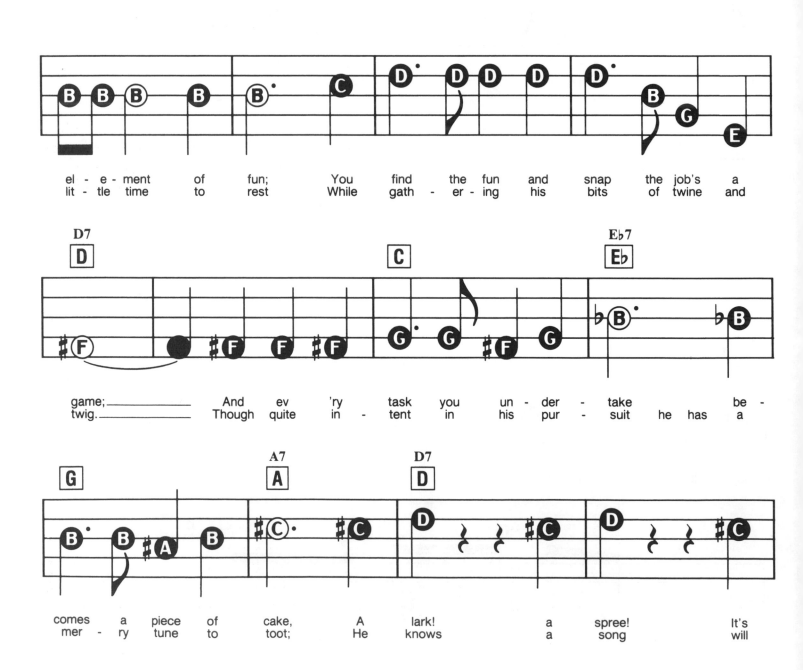

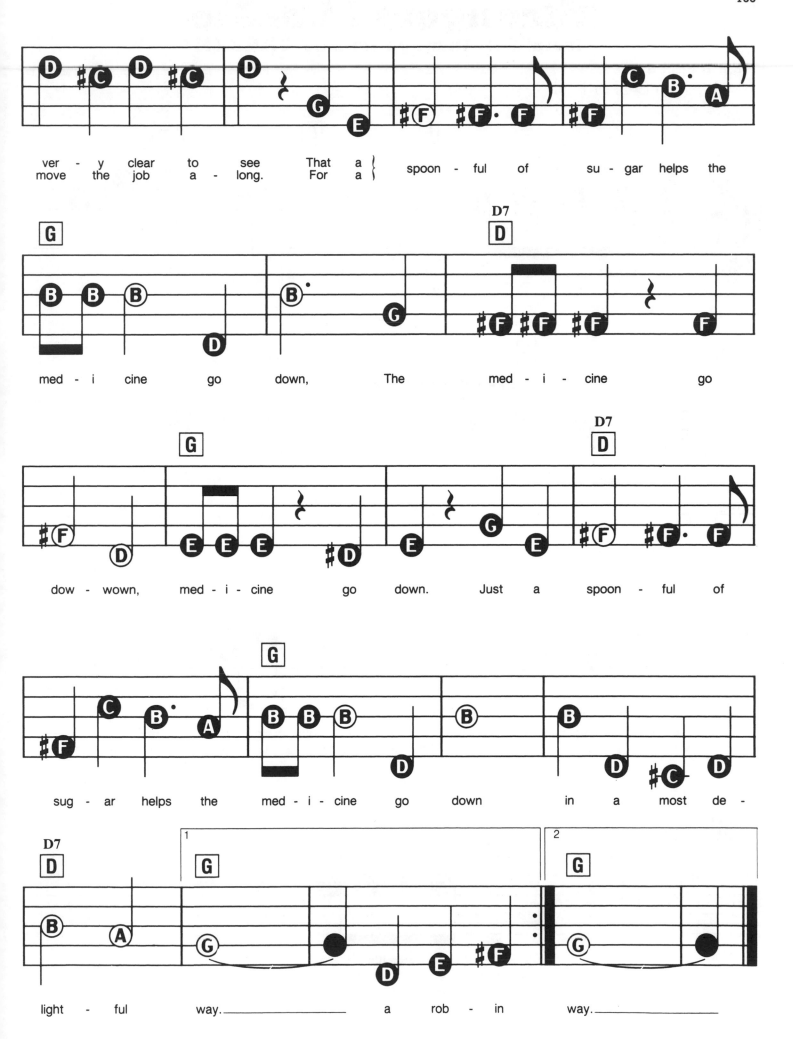

Strangers Like Me
from Walt Disney Pictures' TARZAN™

Registration 4
Rhythm: 16 Beat or Funk

Words and Music by
Phil Collins

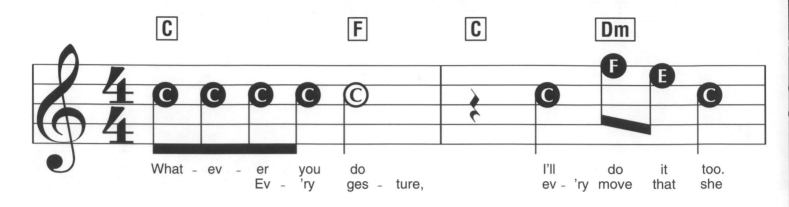

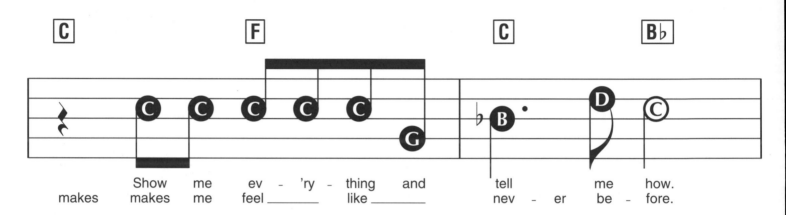

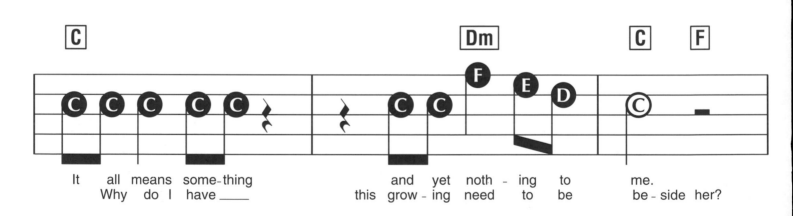

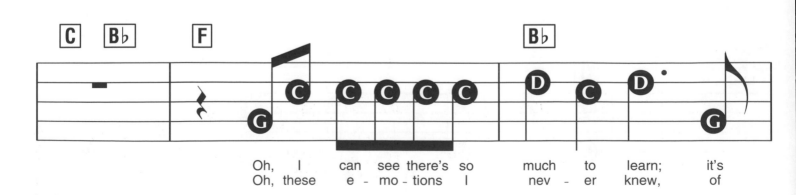

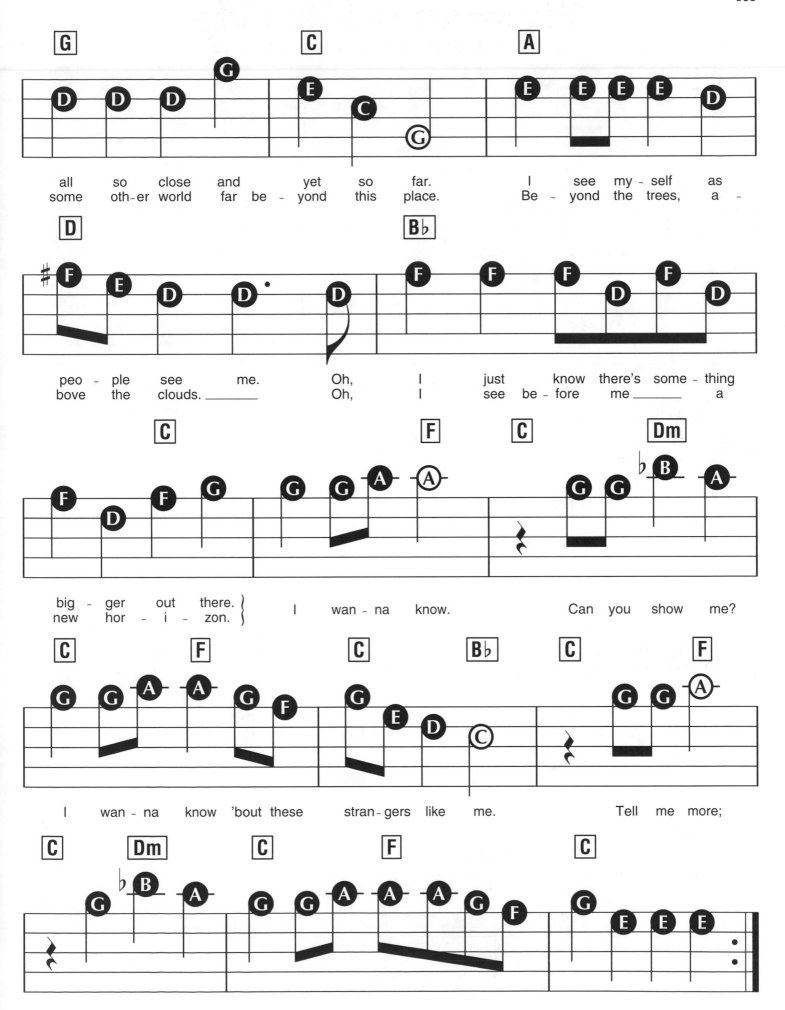

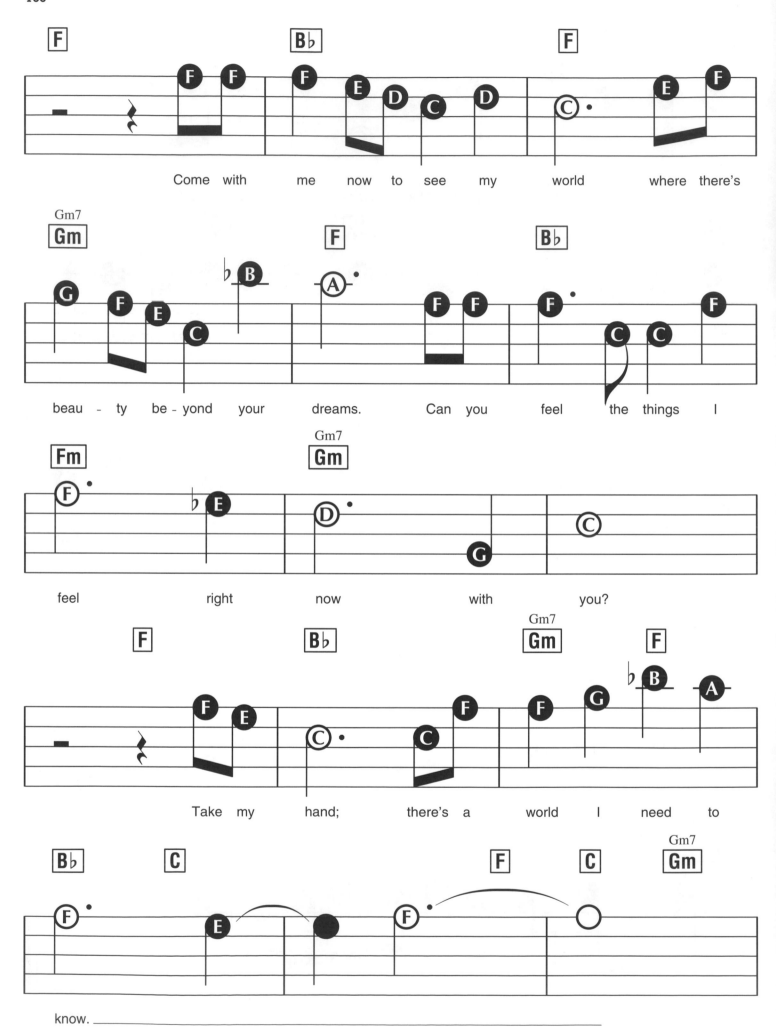

Come with me now to see my world where there's

beau - ty be - yond your dreams. Can you feel the things I

feel right now with you?

Take my hand; there's a world I need to

know.

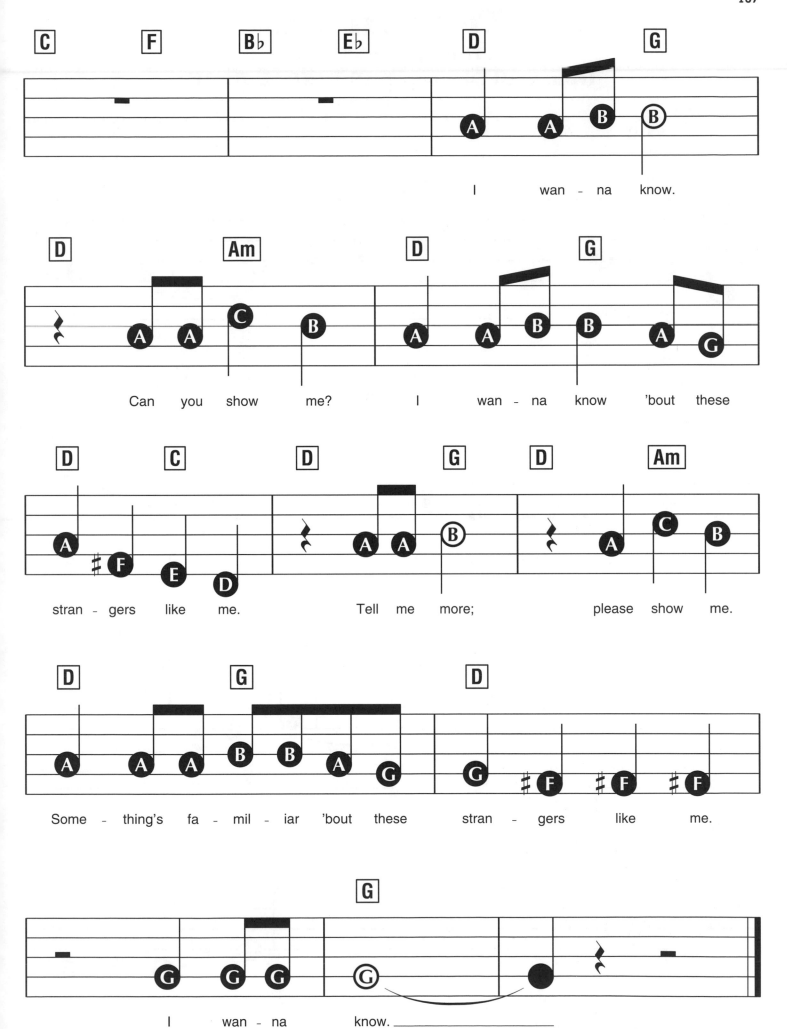

Trust in Me
(The Python's Song)
from Walt Disney's THE JUNGLE BOOK

Registration 7
Rhythm: Fox Trot

Words and Music by Richard M. Sherman
and Robert B. Sherman

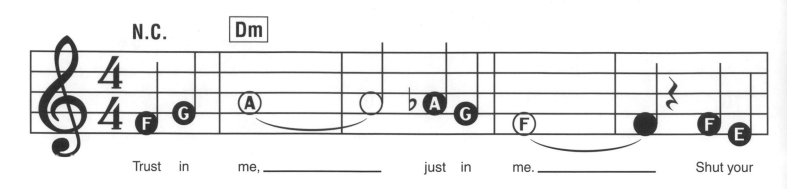

Trust in me, _____ just in me. _____ Shut your

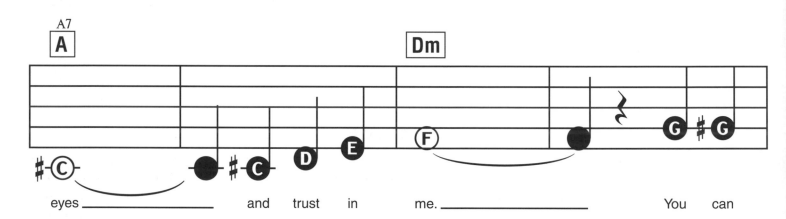

eyes _____ and trust in me. _____ You can

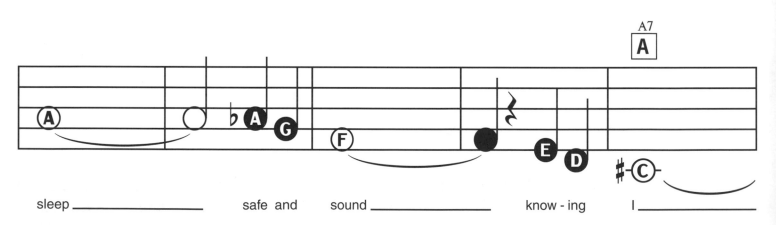

sleep _____ safe and sound _____ know - ing I _____

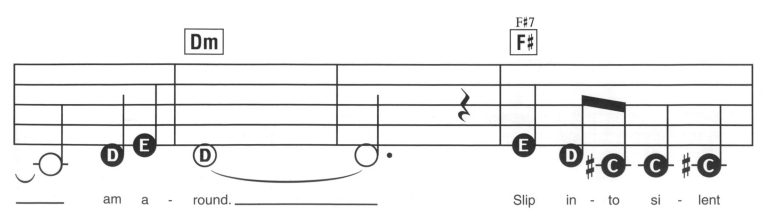

_____ am a - round. _____ Slip in - to si - lent

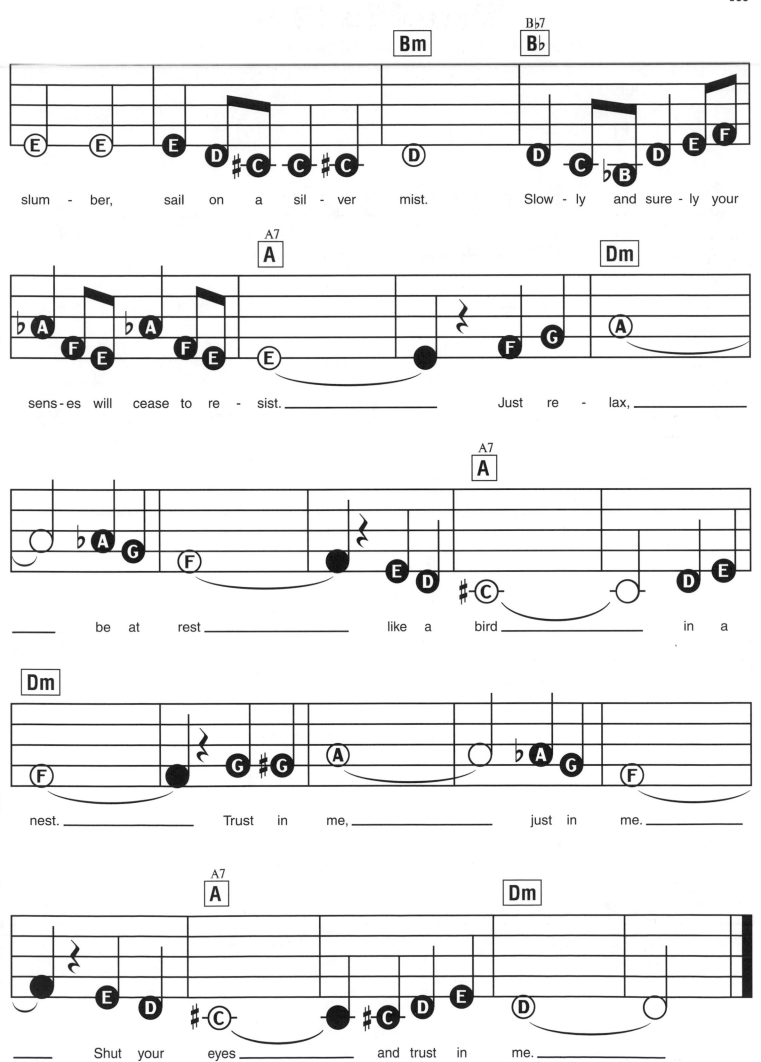

Two Worlds
from Walt Disney Pictures' TARZAN™

Registration 5
Rhythm: Rock or Pops

Words and Music by
Phil Collins

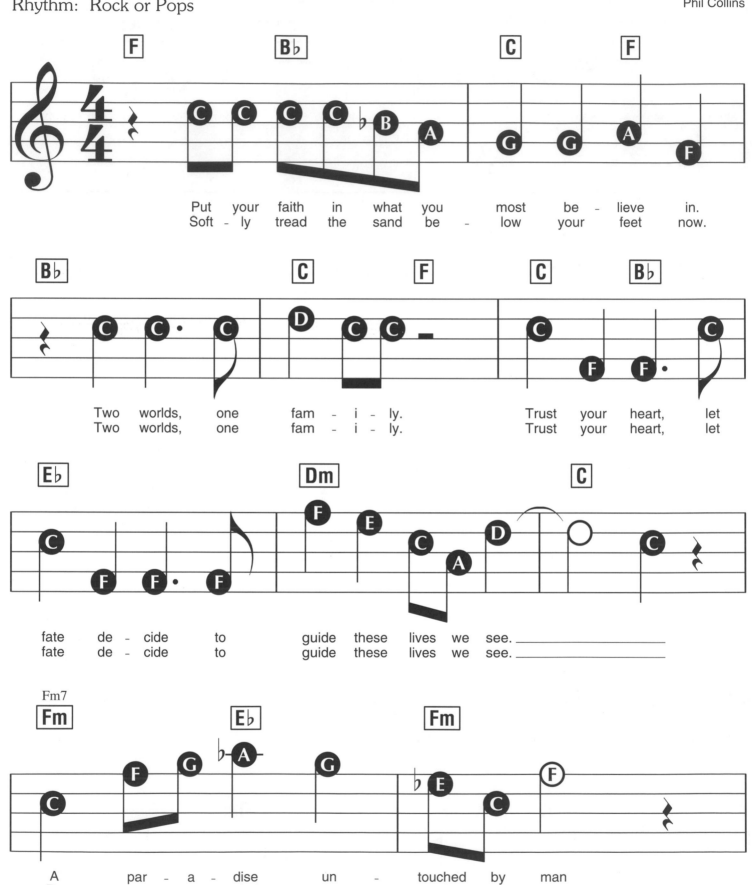

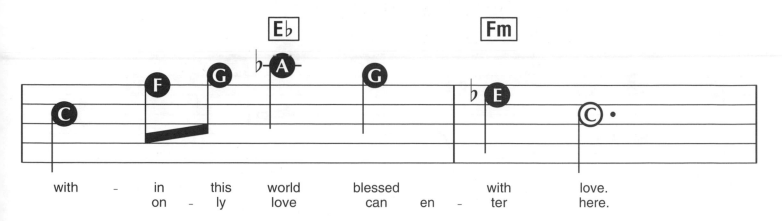

with - in this world blessed with love.
on - ly love can en - ter here.

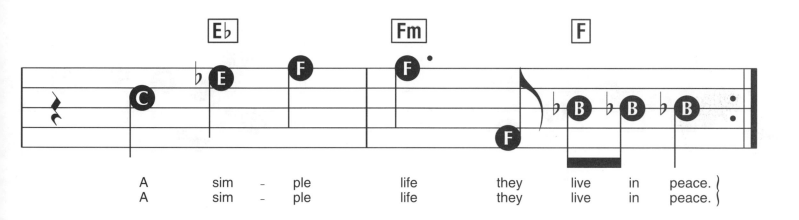

A sim - ple life they live in peace.
A sim - ple life they live in peace.

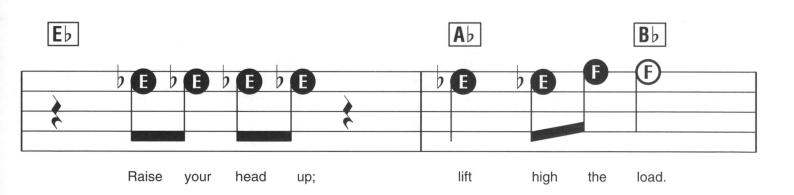

Raise your head up; lift high the load.

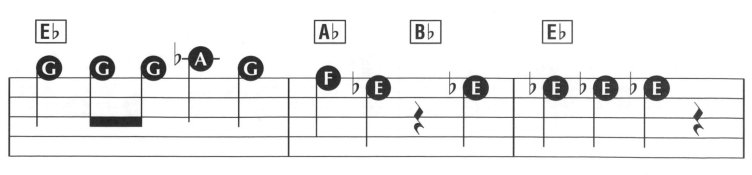

Take strength from those that need you. Build high the walls,

202

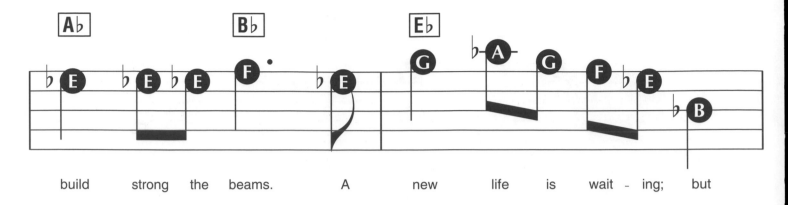

build strong the beams. A new life is wait - ing; but

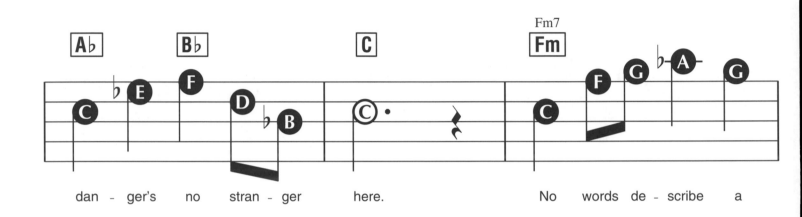

dan - ger's no stran - ger here. No words de - scribe a

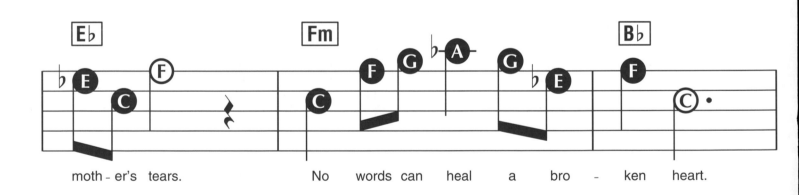

moth - er's tears. No words can heal a bro - ken heart.

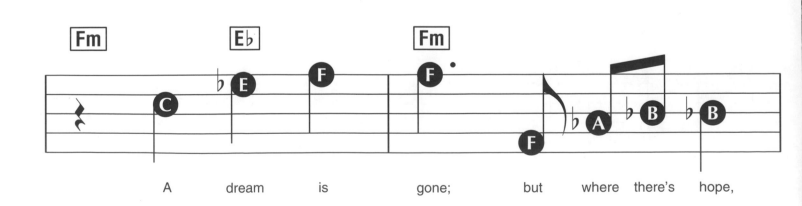

A dream is gone; but where there's hope,

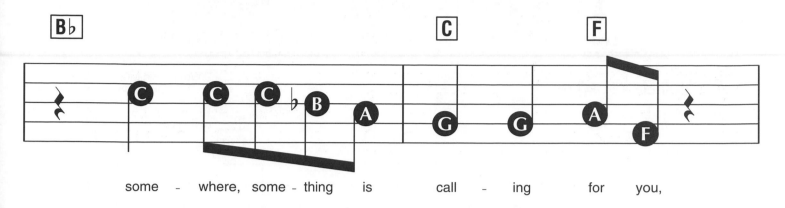

some - where, some - thing is call - ing for you,

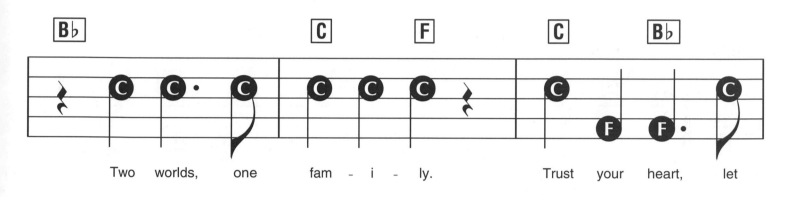

Two worlds, one fam - i - ly. Trust your heart, let

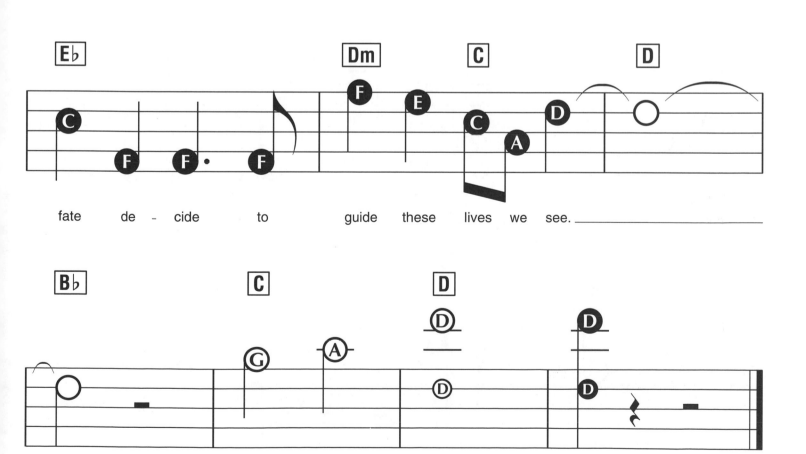

fate de - cide to guide these lives we see. _____

The Unbirthday Song
from Walt Disney's ALICE IN WONDERLAND

Registration 2
Rhythm: Ballad or Fox Trot

Words and Music by Mack David,
Al Hoffman and Jerry Livingston

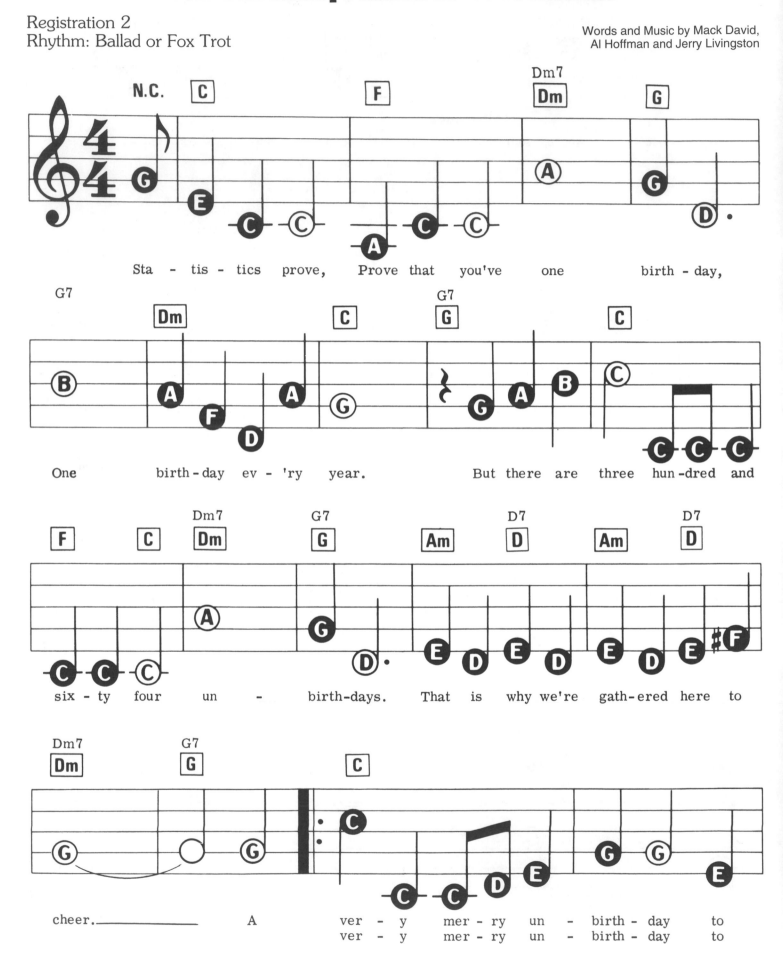

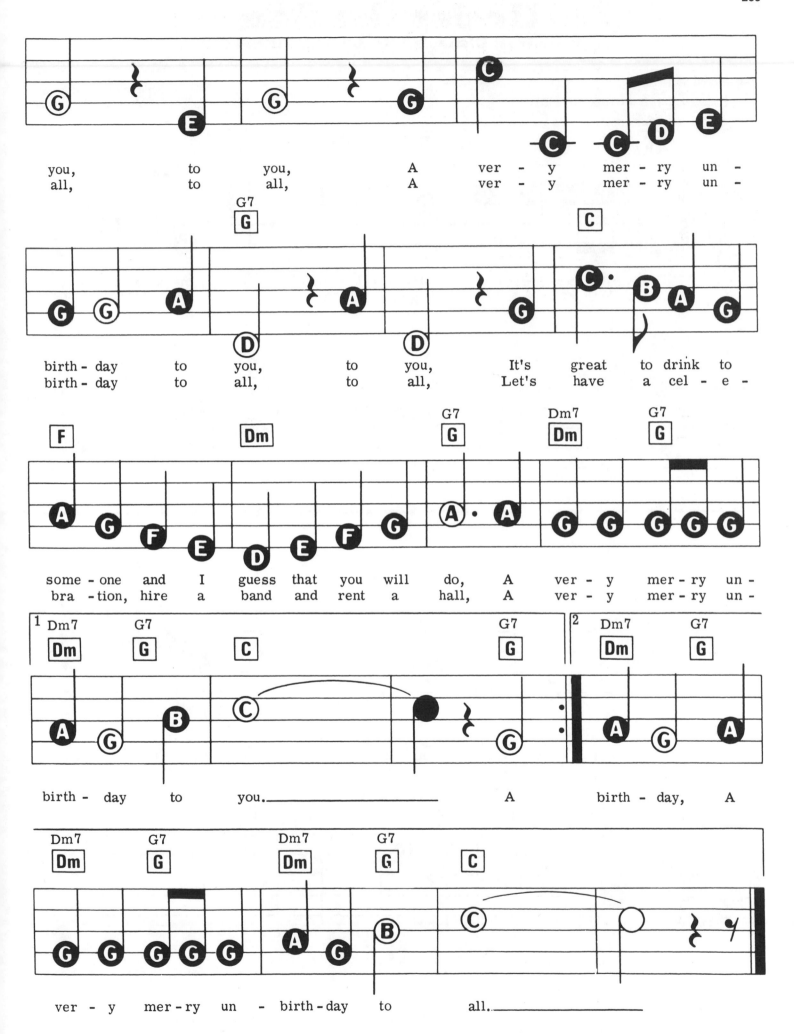

Under the Sea
from Walt Disney's THE LITTLE MERMAID

Registration 7
Rhythm: Bossa Nova or Latin

Lyrics by Howard Ashman
Music by Alan Menken

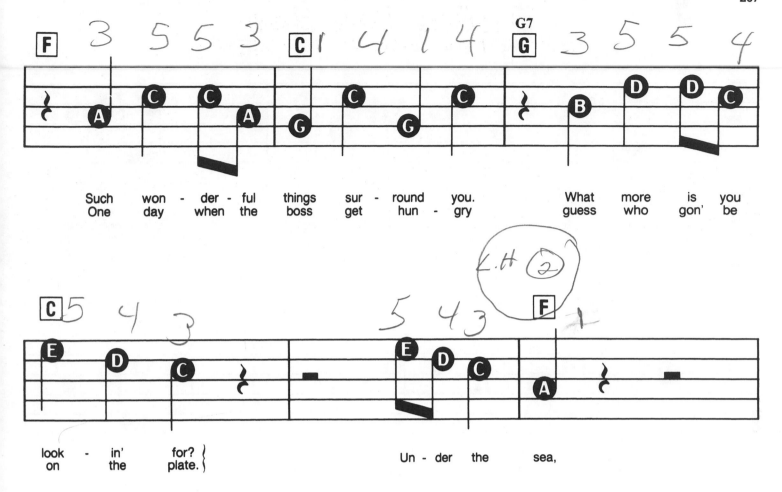

Such won-der-ful things sur-round you. What more is you
One day when the boss get hun-gry guess who gon' be

look-in' for?
on the plate.

Un-der the sea,

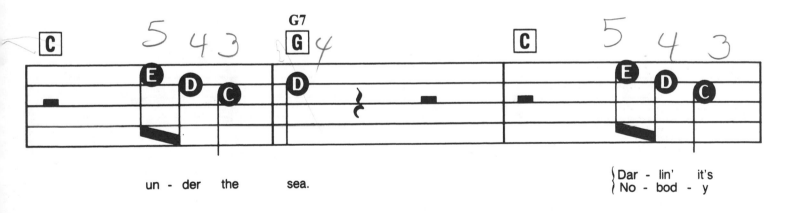

un-der the sea.

Dar-lin' it's
No-bod-y

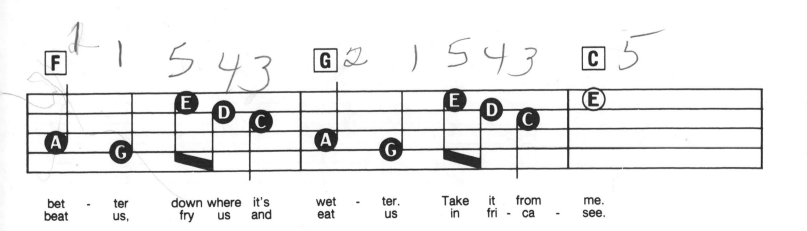

bet-ter down where it's wet-ter. Take it from me.
beat us, fry us and eat us in fri-ca-see.

208

Up on the shore they work all day.
We what the land folks loves to cook.

Out in the
Un - der the

sun they slave a - way.
sea we off the hook.

While we de - vo - tin' full - time to
We got no trou - bles, life is the

float - in' un - der the sea.
bub - bles un - der the

sea.

Un - der the sea.

209

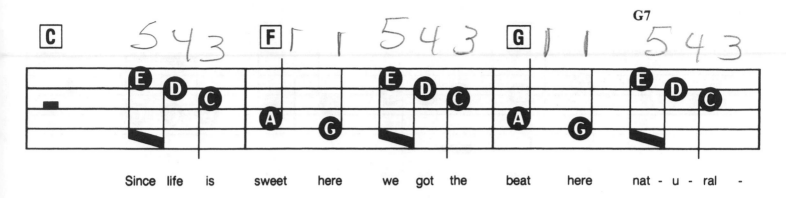

Since life is sweet here we got the beat here nat - u - ral -

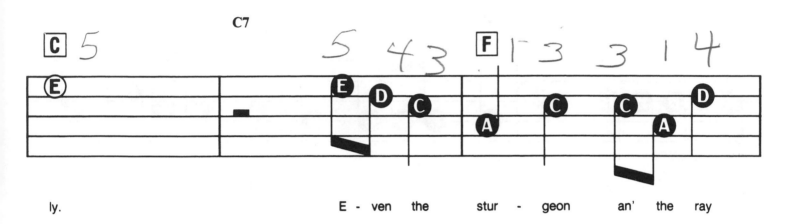

ly. E - ven the stur - geon an' the ray

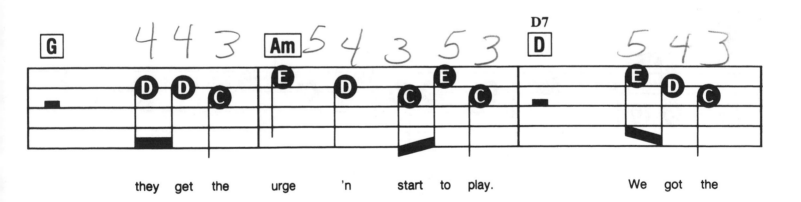

they get the urge 'n start to play. We got the

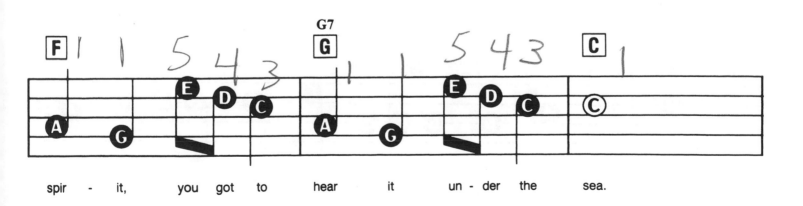

spir - it, you got to hear it un - der the sea.

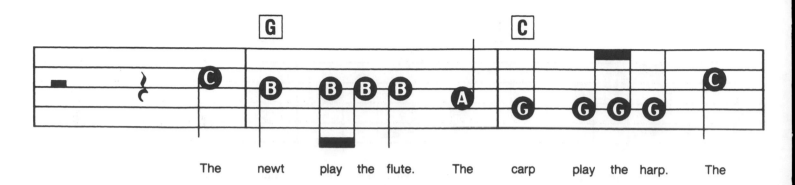

The newt play the flute. The carp play the harp. The

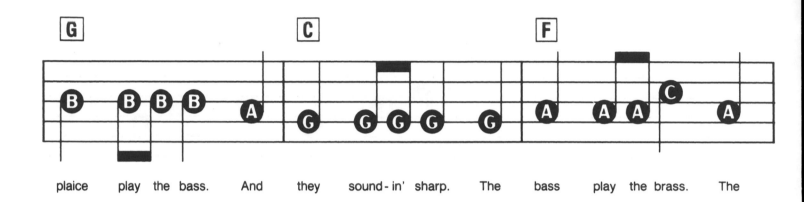

plaice play the bass. And they sound-in' sharp. The bass play the brass. The

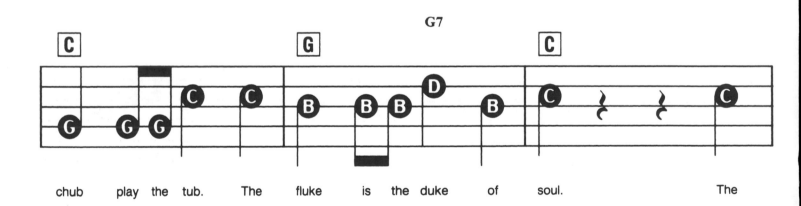

chub play the tub. The fluke is the duke of soul. The

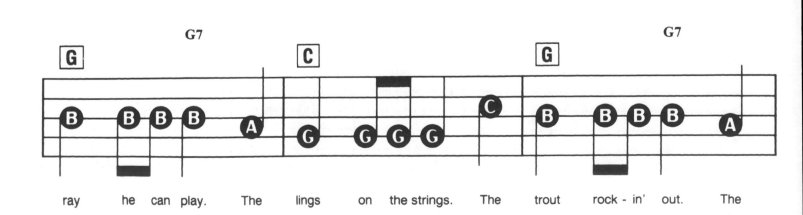

ray he can play. The lings on the strings. The trout rock-in' out. The

211

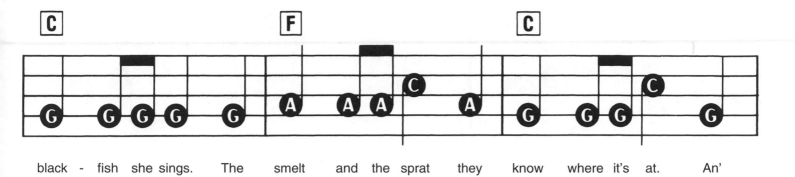

black - fish she sings. The smelt and the sprat they know where it's at. An'

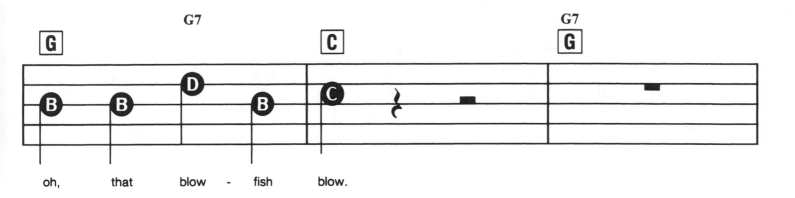

oh, that blow - fish blow.

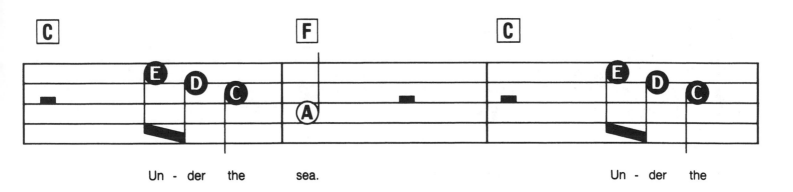

Un - der the sea. Un - der the

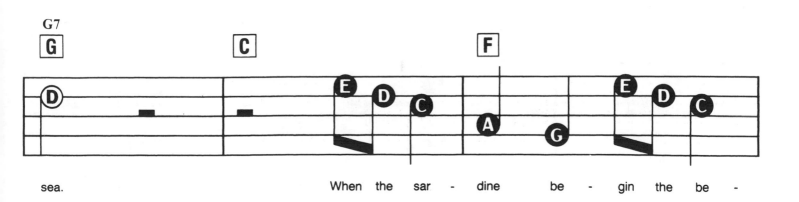

sea. When the sar - dine be - gin the be -

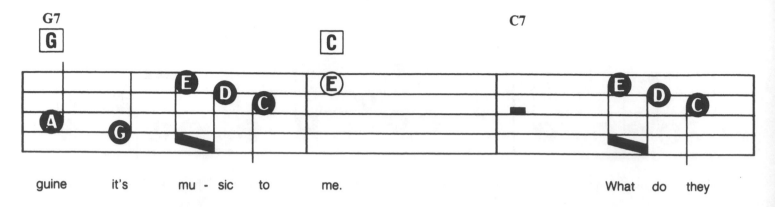

guine it's mu - sic to me. What do they

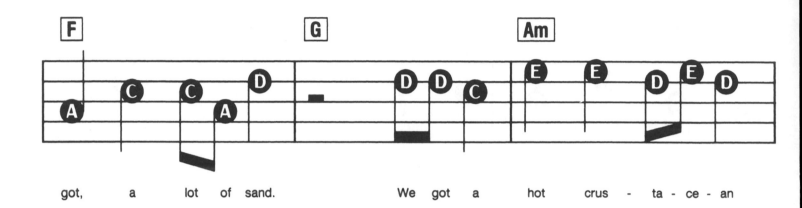

got, a lot of sand. We got a hot crus - ta - ce - an

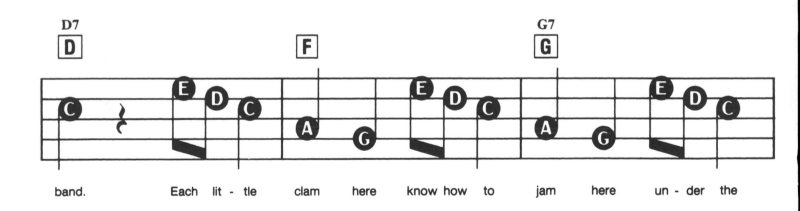

band. Each lit - tle clam here know how to jam here un - der the

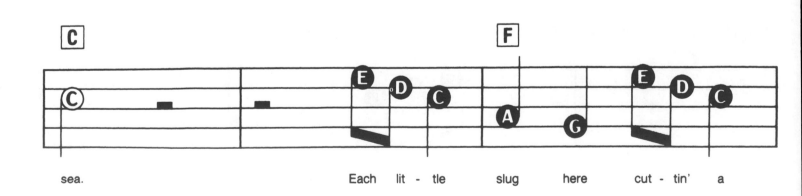

sea. Each lit - tle slug here cut - tin' a

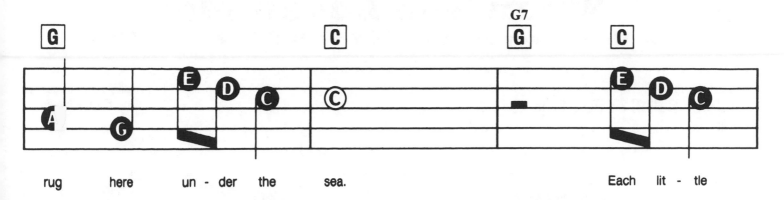

rug   here   un - der   the   sea.   Each   lit - tle

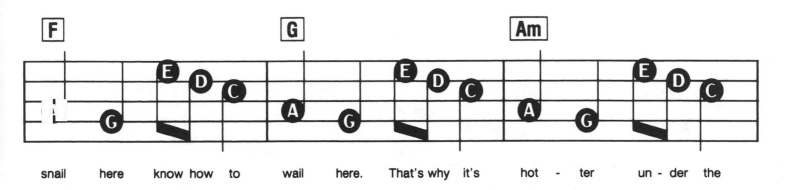

snail   here   know how to   wail   here.   That's why it's   hot - ter   un - der the

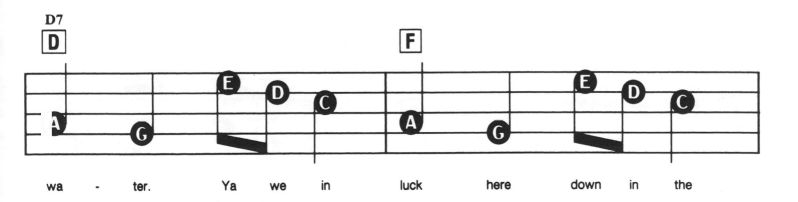

wa - ter.   Ya   we   in   luck   here   down   in   the

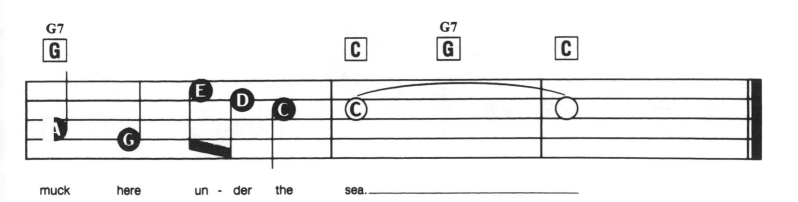

muck   here   un - der   the   sea._____

When She Loved Me
from Walt Disney Pictures' TOY STORY 2 - A Pixar Film

Registration 8
Rhythm: Ballad or Fox Trot

Music and Lyrics by
Randy Newman

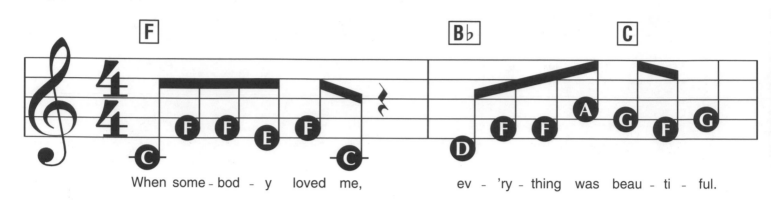

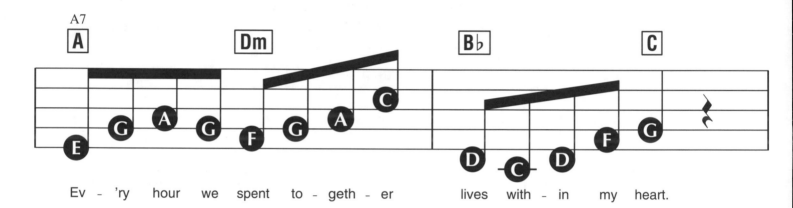

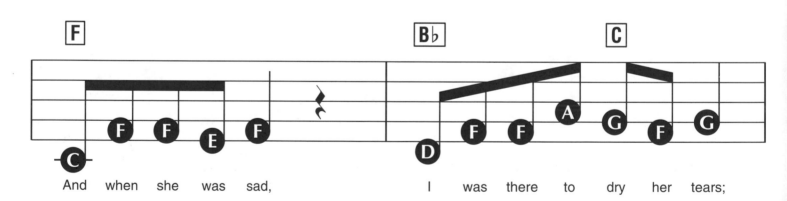

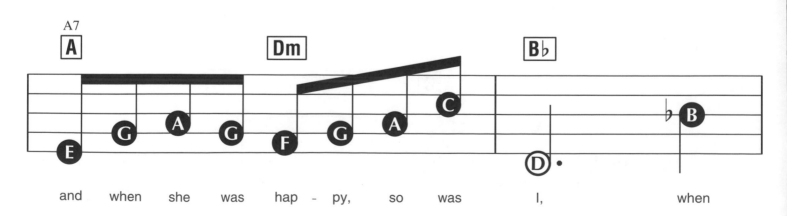

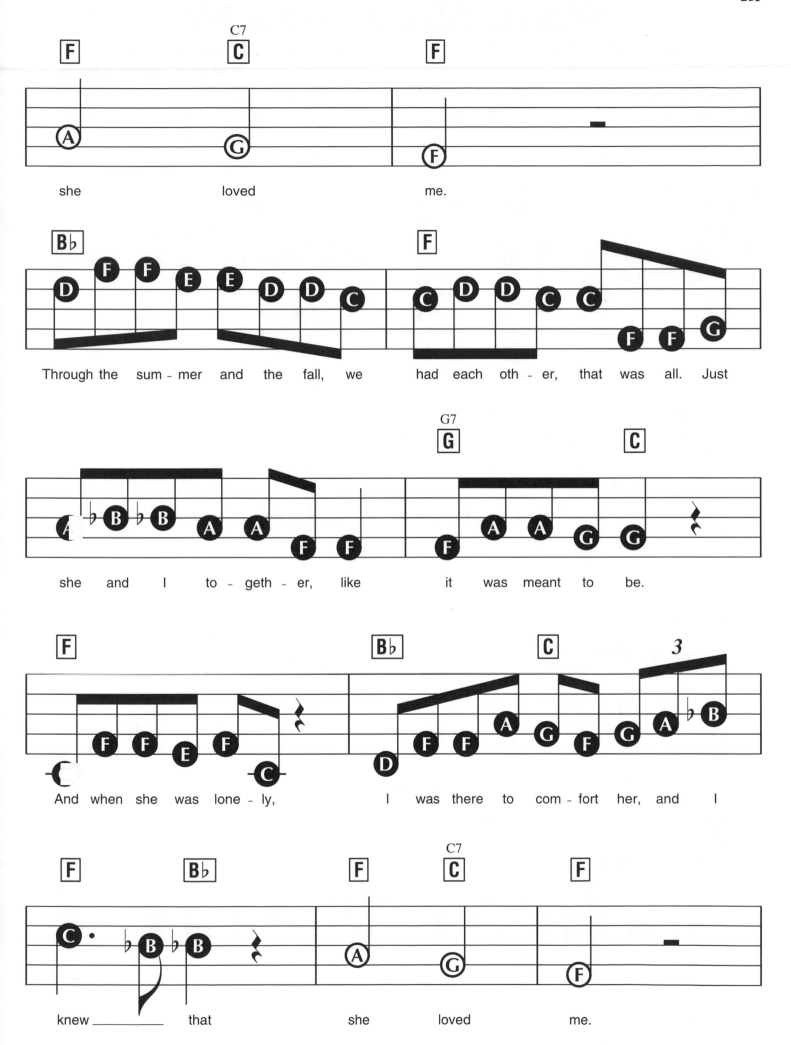

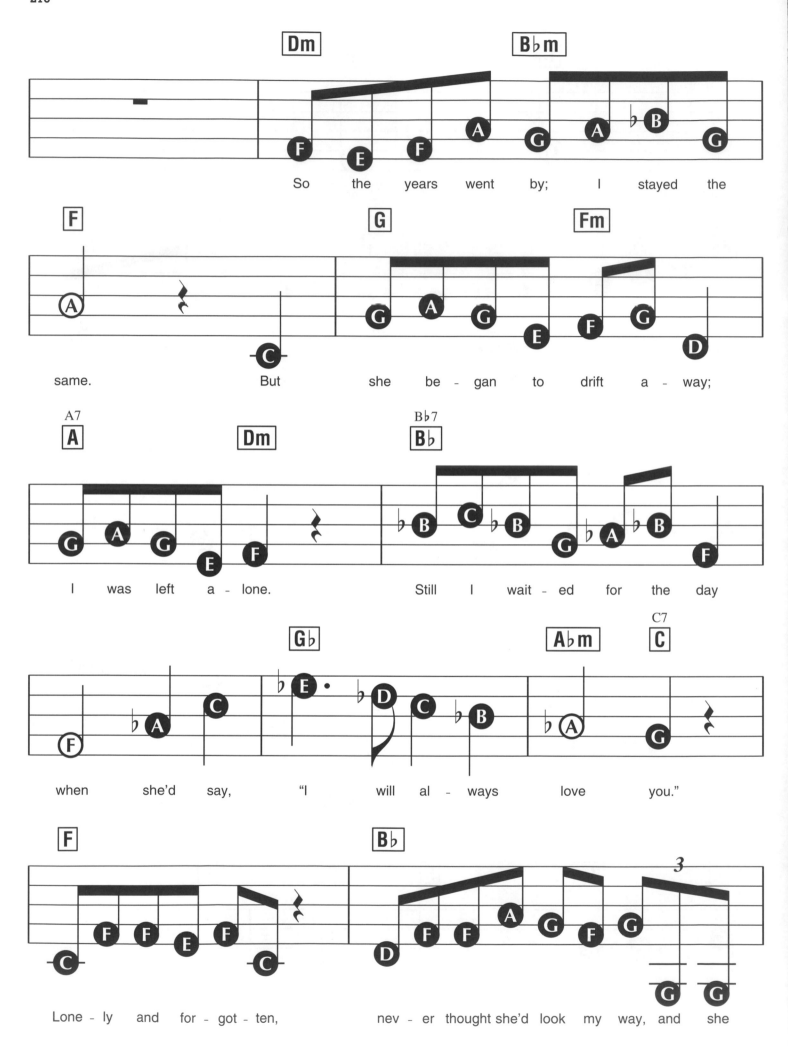

Where the Dream Takes You

from Walt Disney Pictures' ATLANTIS: THE LOST EMPIRE

Registration 1
Rhythm: Ballad

Lyrics by Diane Warren
Music by Diane Warren and James Newton Howard

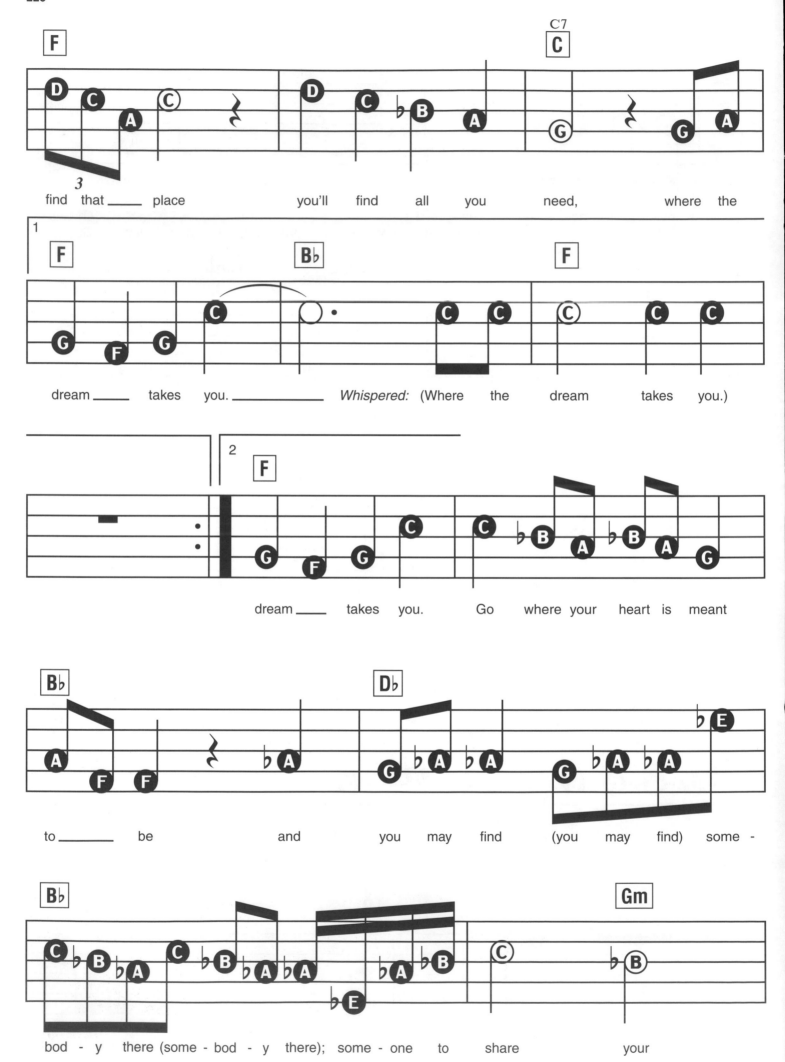

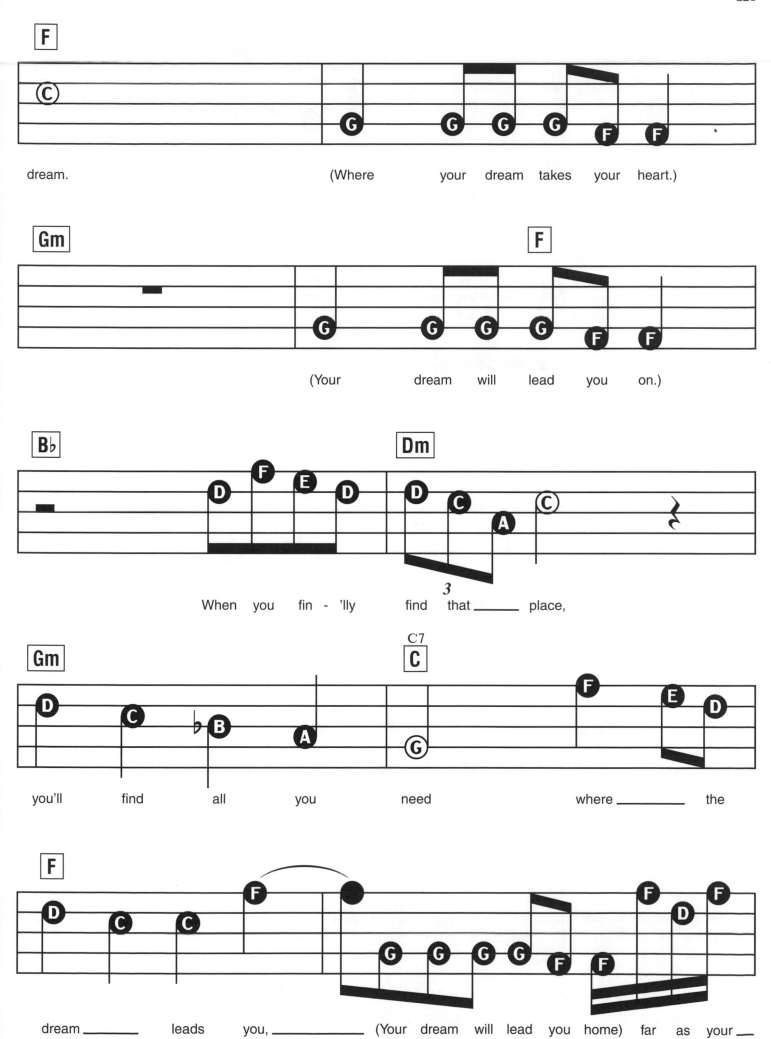

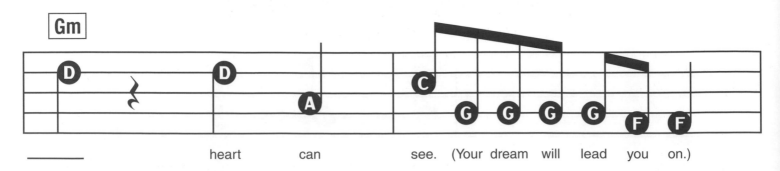

Gm

_____ heart can see. (Your dream will lead you on.)

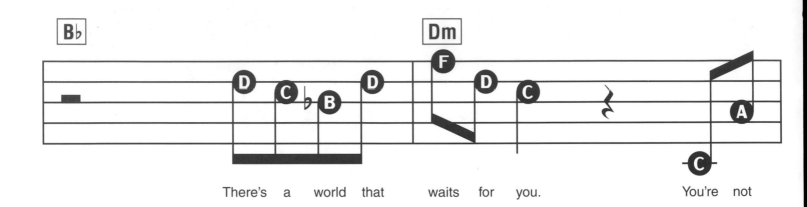

Bb **Dm**

There's a world that waits for you. You're not

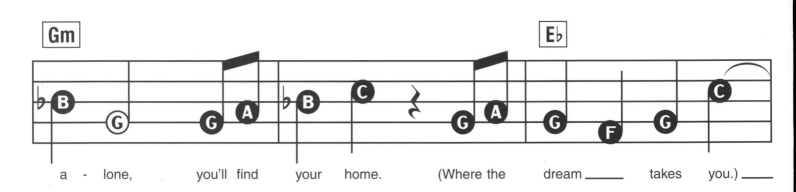

Gm **Eb**

a - lone, you'll find your home. (Where the dream _____ takes you.) _____

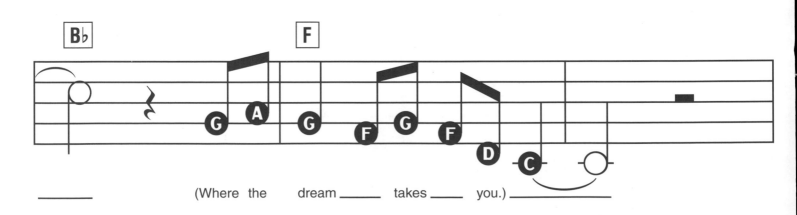

Bb **F**

_____ (Where the dream _____ takes _____ you.) _____

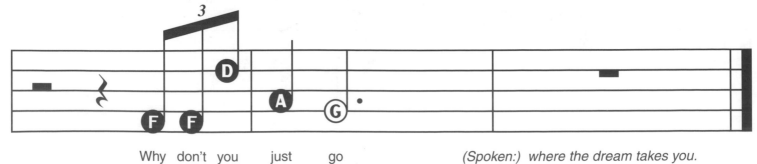

3

Why don't you just go (Spoken:) where the dream takes you.

A Whole New World

from Walt Disney's ALADDIN

Registration 1
Rhythm: 8 Beat or Pops

Music by Alan Menken
Lyrics by Tim Rice

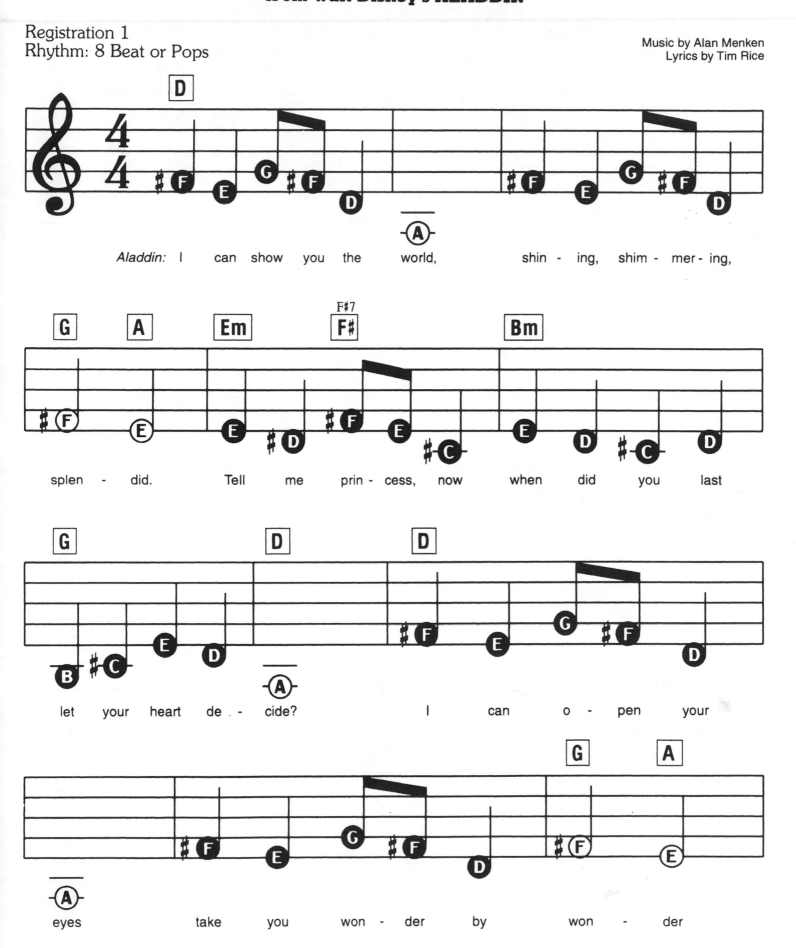

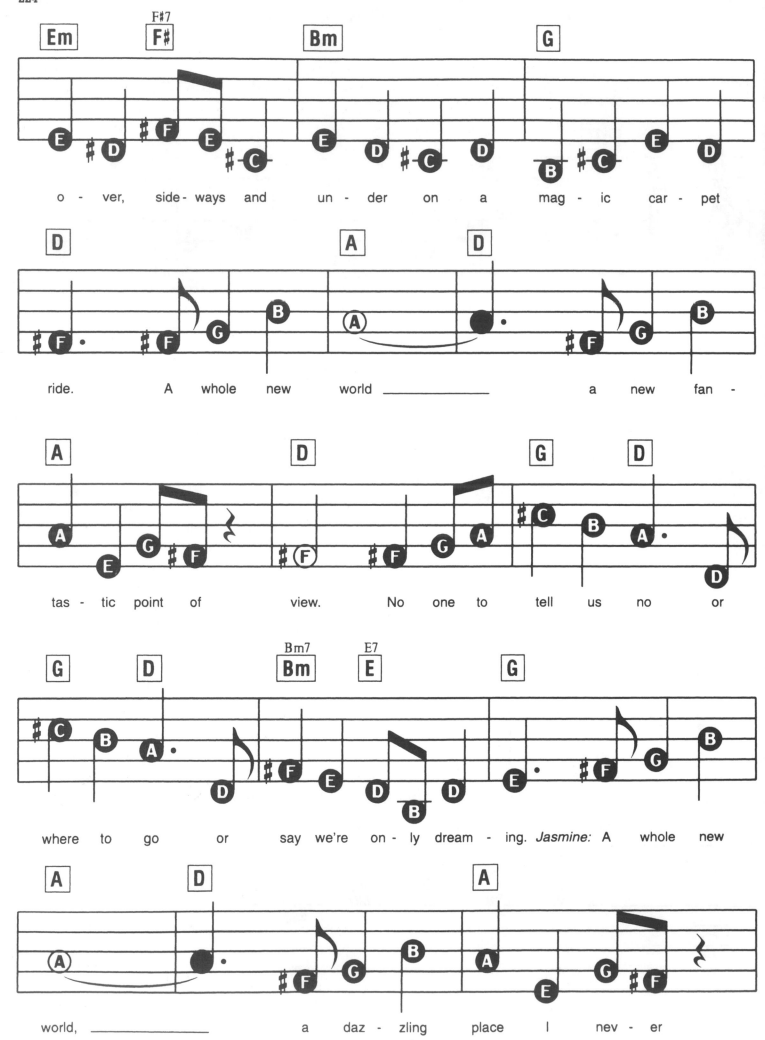

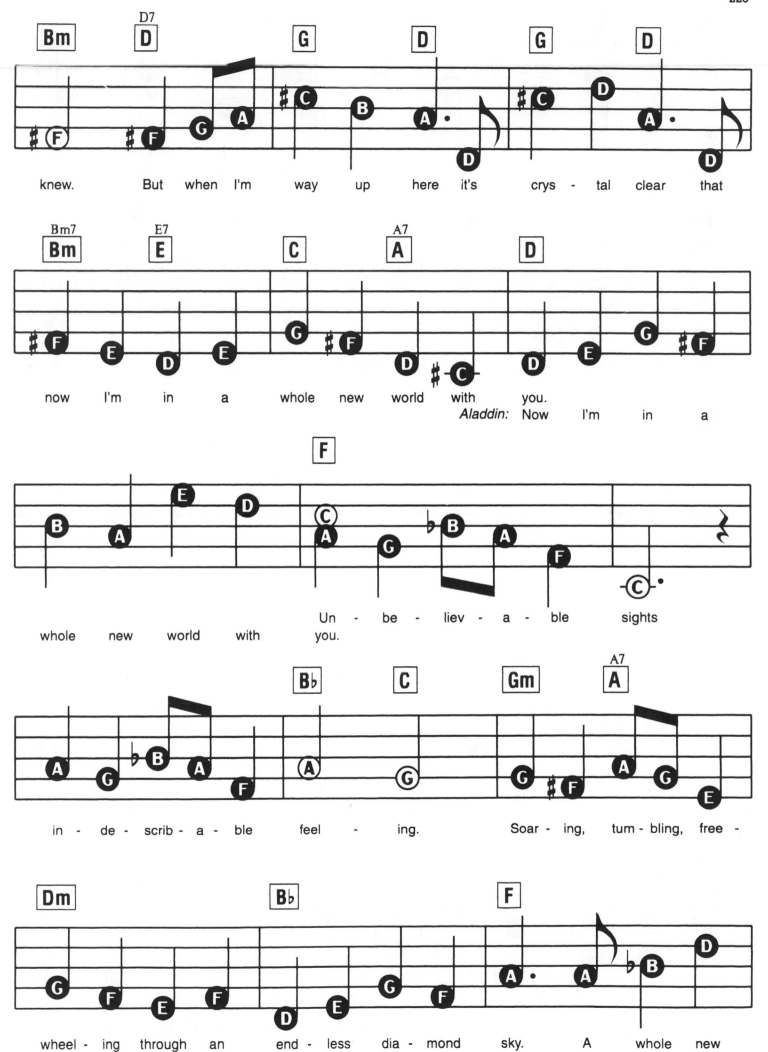

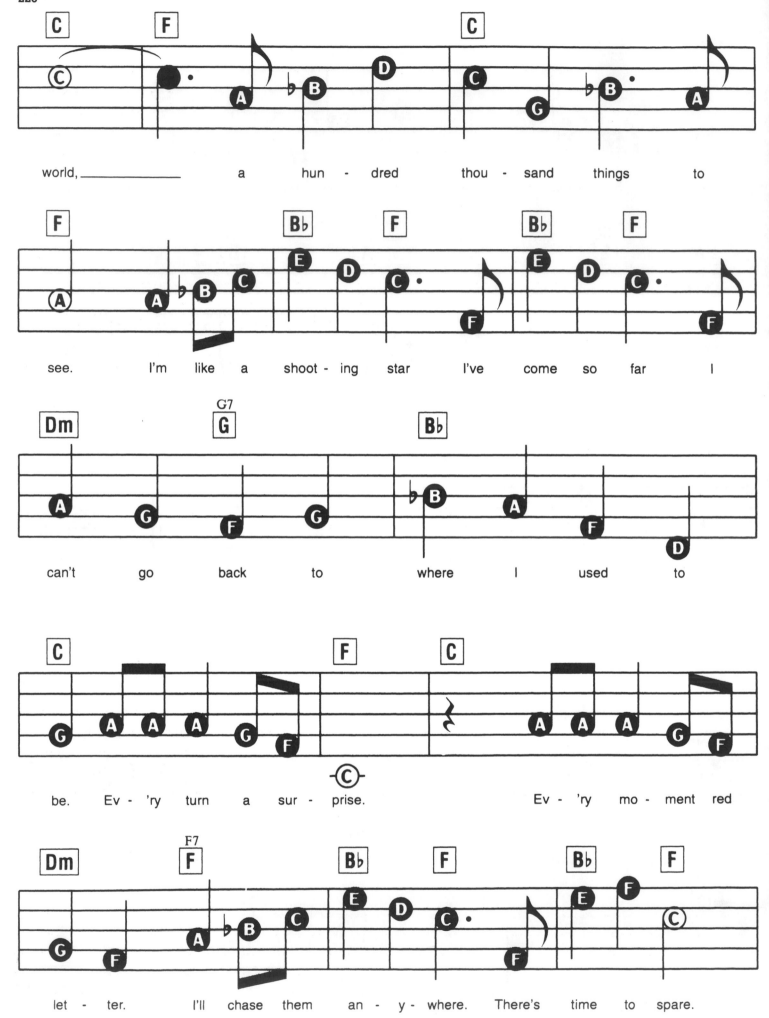

world, _____ a hun - dred thou - sand things to

see. I'm like a shoot - ing star I've come so far I

can't go back to where I used to

be. Ev - 'ry turn a sur - prise. Ev - 'ry mo - ment red

let - ter. I'll chase them an - y - where. There's time to spare.

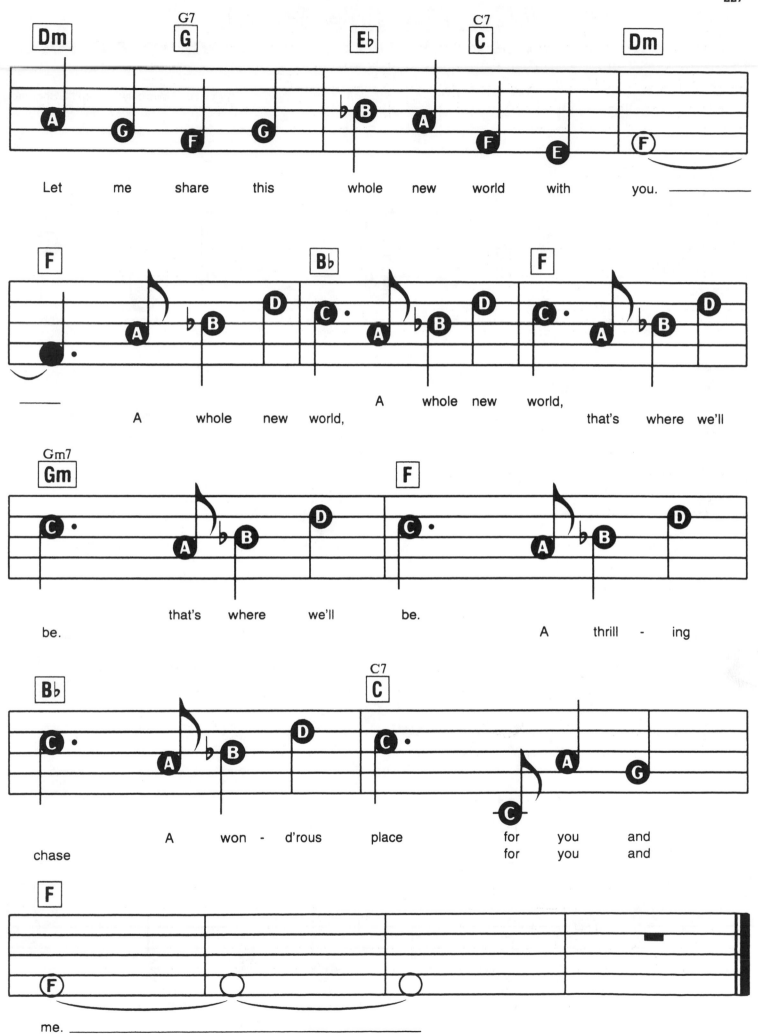

Winnie the Pooh
from Walt Disney's THE MANY ADVENTURES OF WINNIE THE POOH

Registration 2
Rhythm: Fox Trot or Ballad

Words and Music by Richard M. Sherman
and Robert B. Sherman

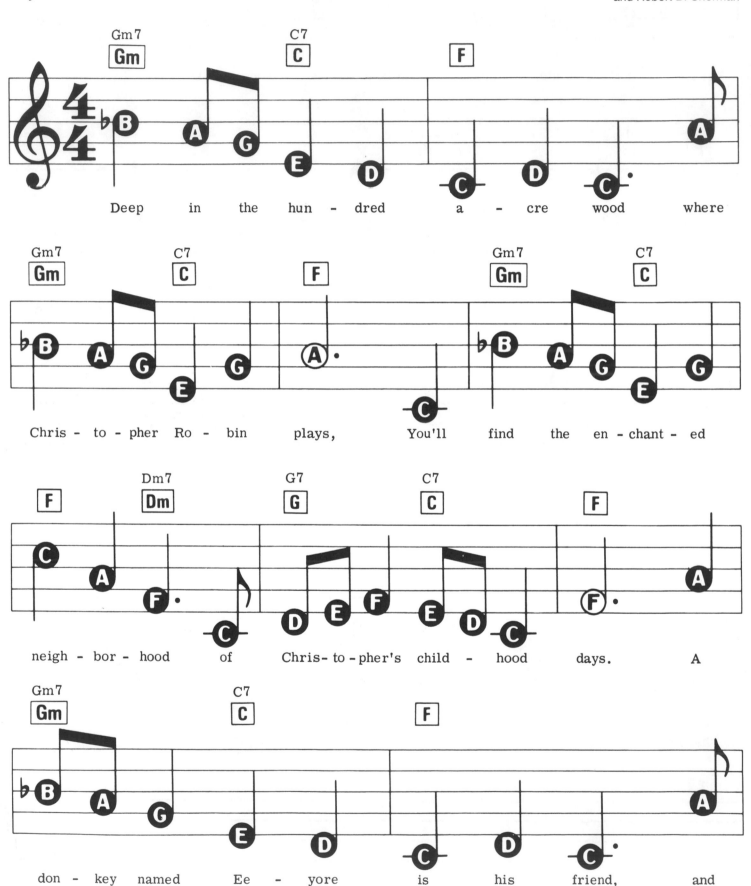

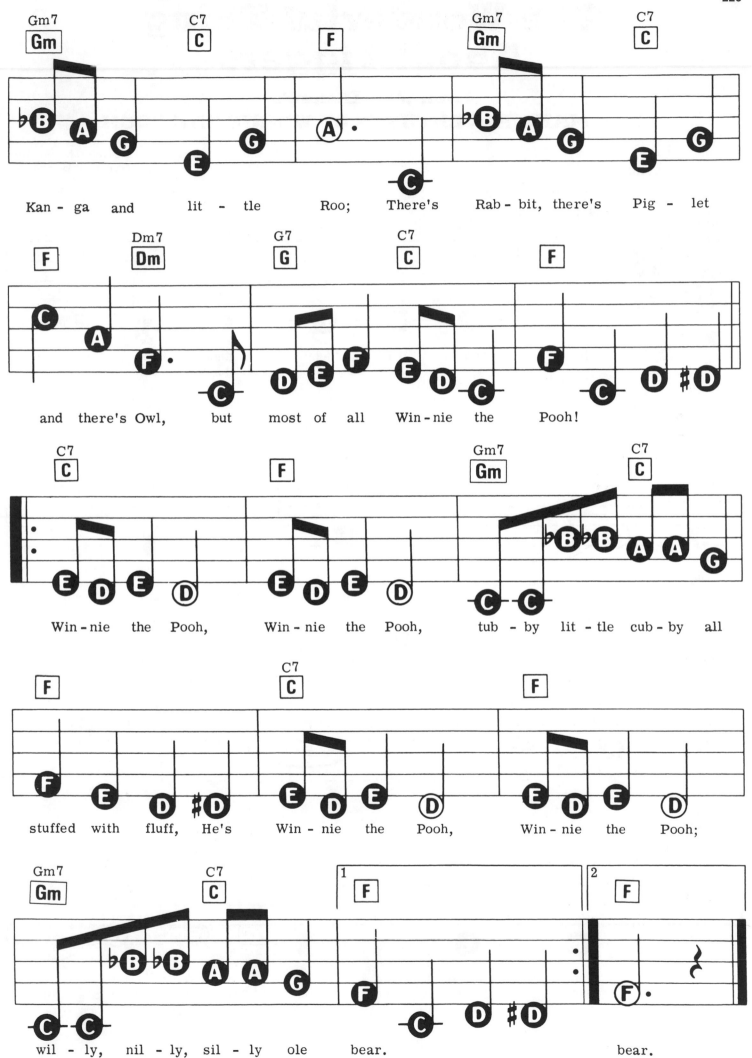

The Wonderful Thing About Tiggers

from Walt Disney's
THE MANY ADVENTURES OF WINNIE THE POOH

Registration 1
Rhythm: Waltz

Words and Music by Richard M. Sherman
and Robert B. Sherman

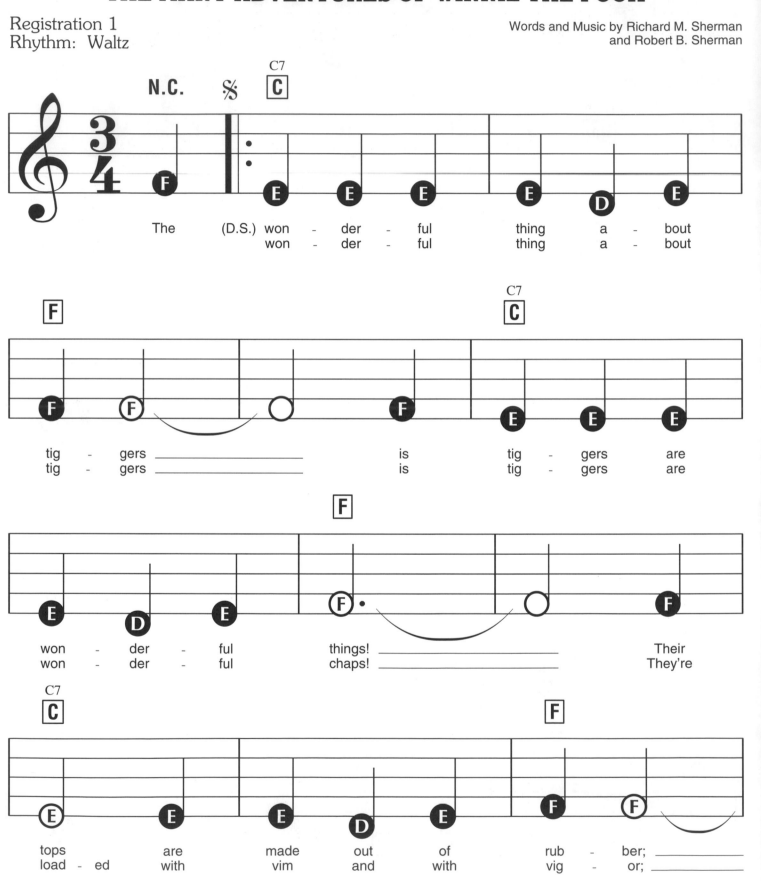

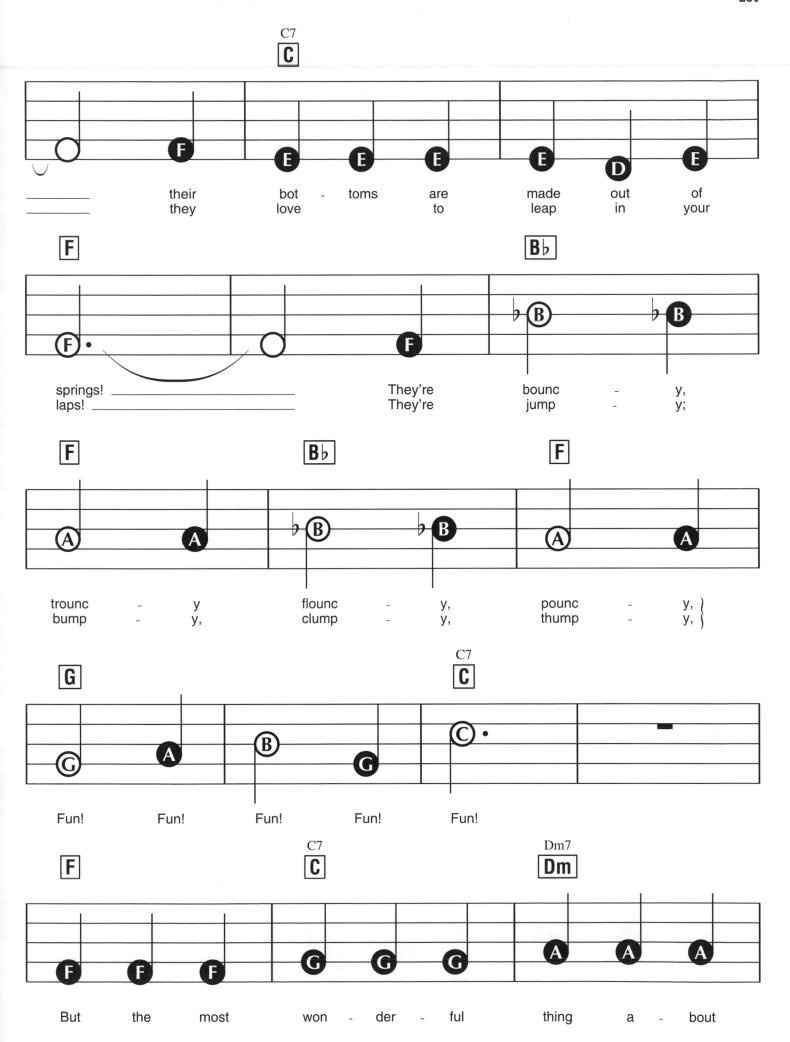

their bot - toms are made out of
they love to leap in your

springs! _____
laps! _____

They're bounc - y,
They're jump - y;

trounc - y
bump - y,

flounc - y,
clump - y,

pounc - y,
thump - y,

Fun! Fun! Fun! Fun! Fun!

But the most won - der - ful thing a - bout

232

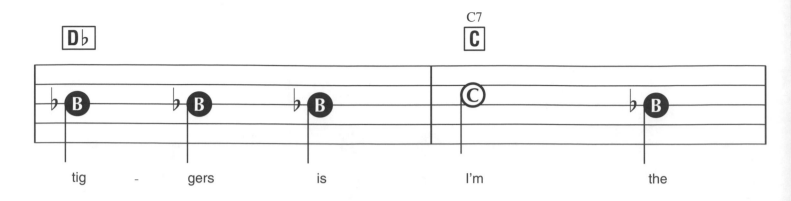

tig - gers is I'm the

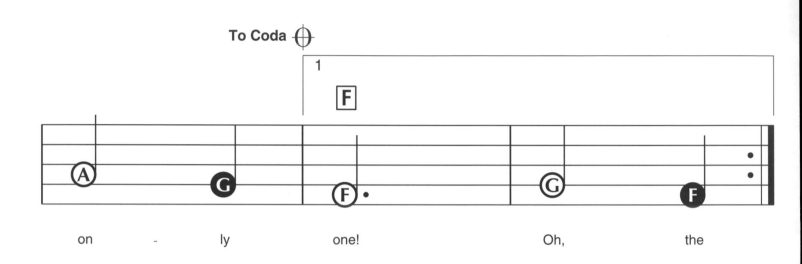

on - ly one! Oh, the

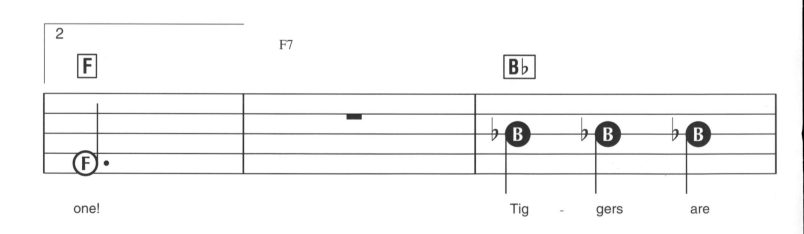

one! Tig - gers are

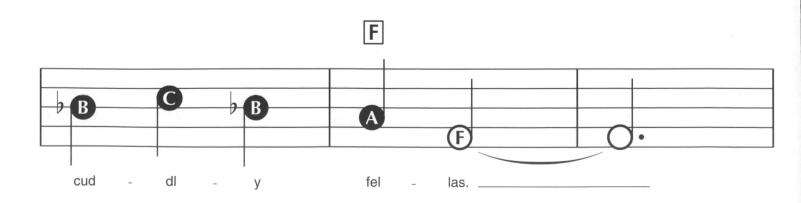

cud - dl - y fel - las.

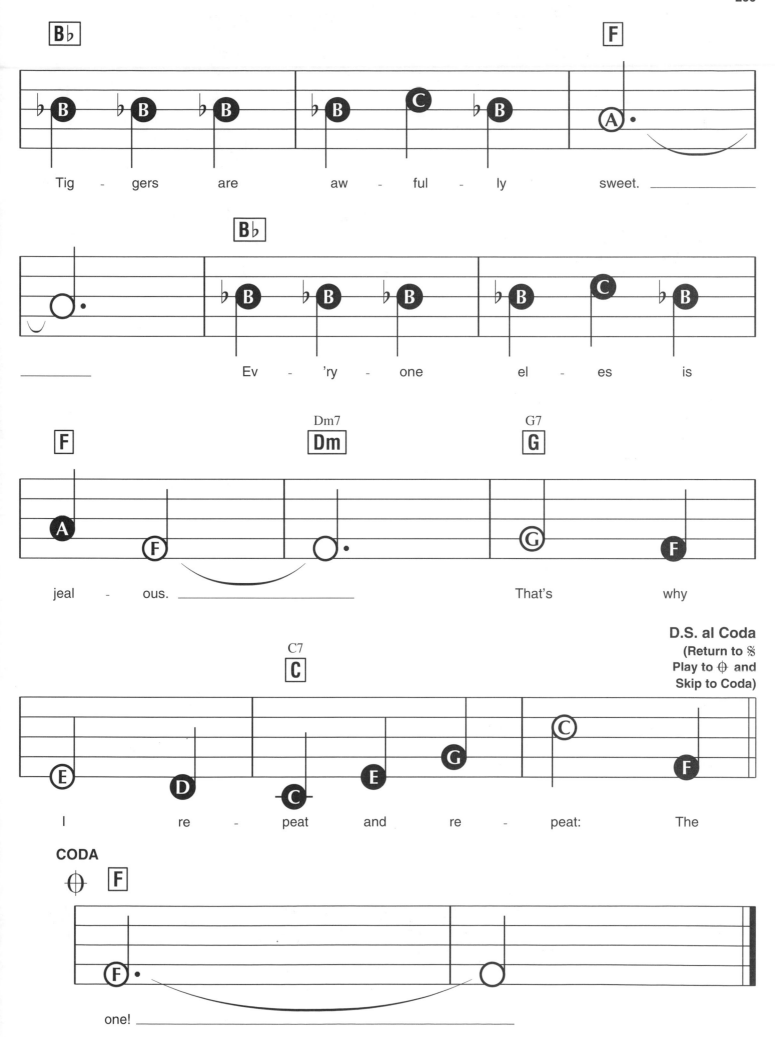

Woody's Roundup

from Walt Disney Pictures' TOY STORY 2 - A Pixar Film

Registration 2
Rhythm: Fox Trot

Music and Lyrics by
Randy Newman

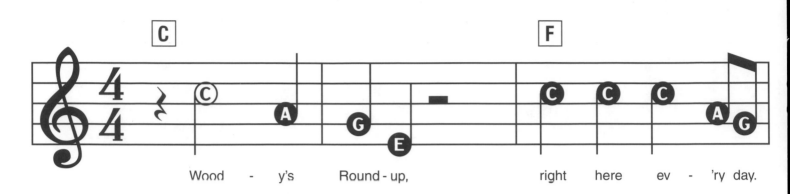

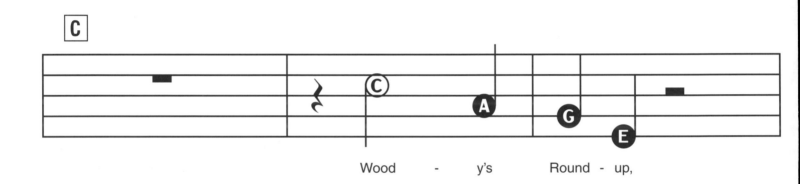

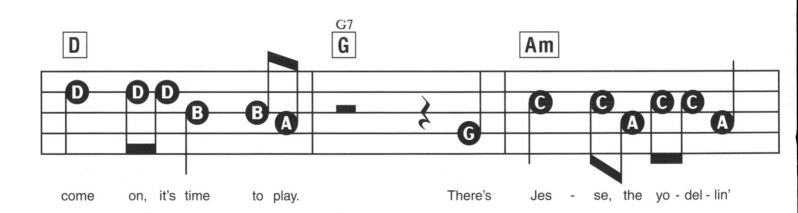

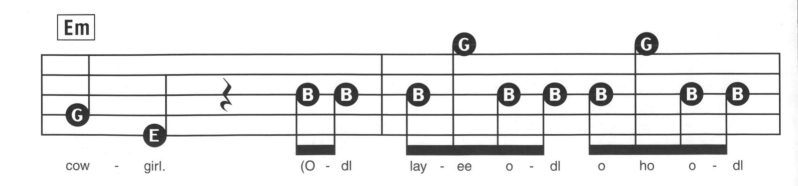

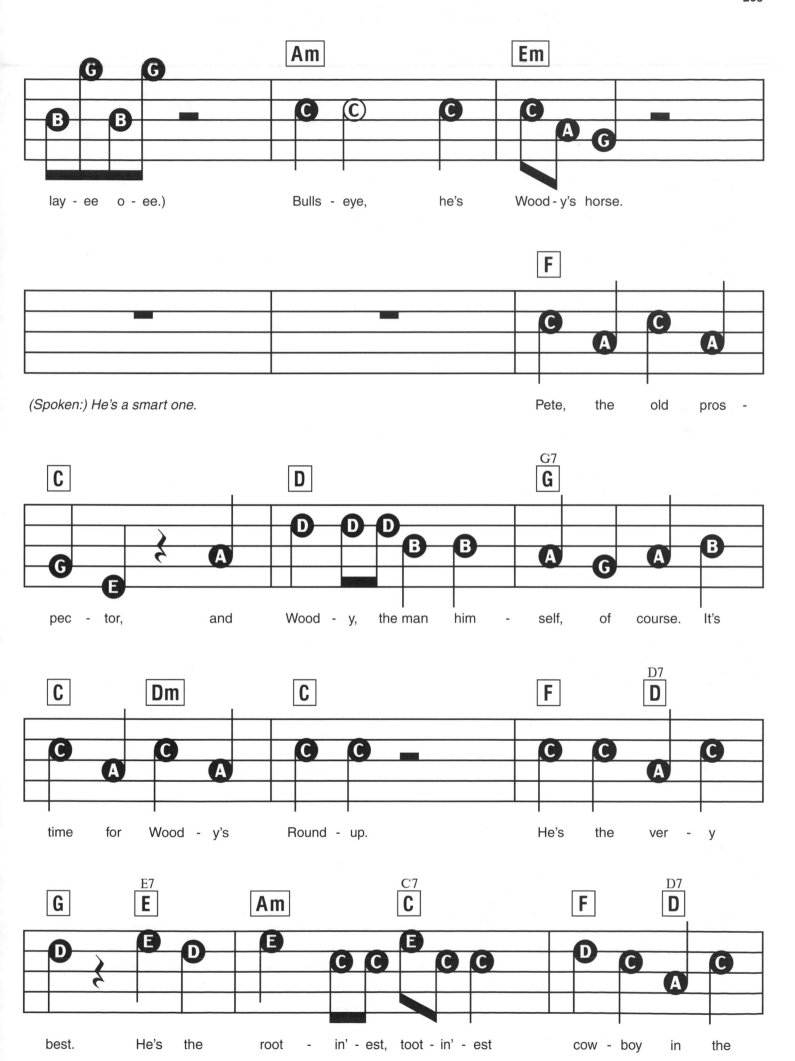

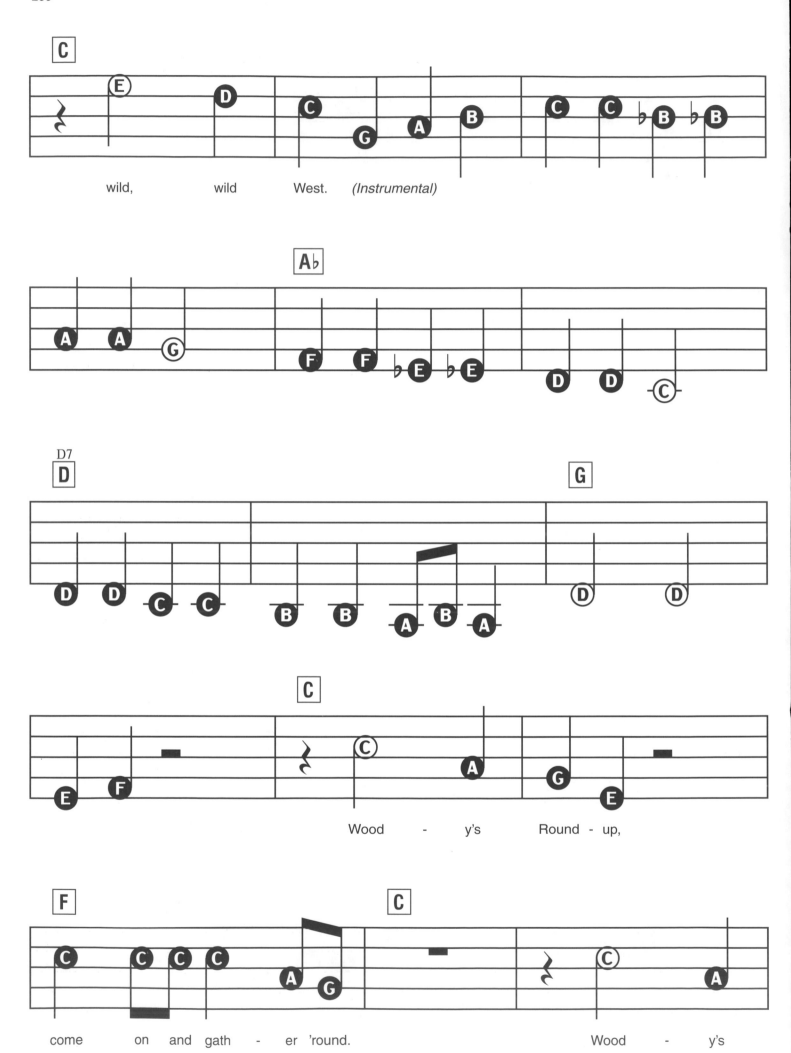

wild,   wild   West.   *(Instrumental)*

Wood - y's   Round - up,

come   on and gath - er 'round.   Wood - y's

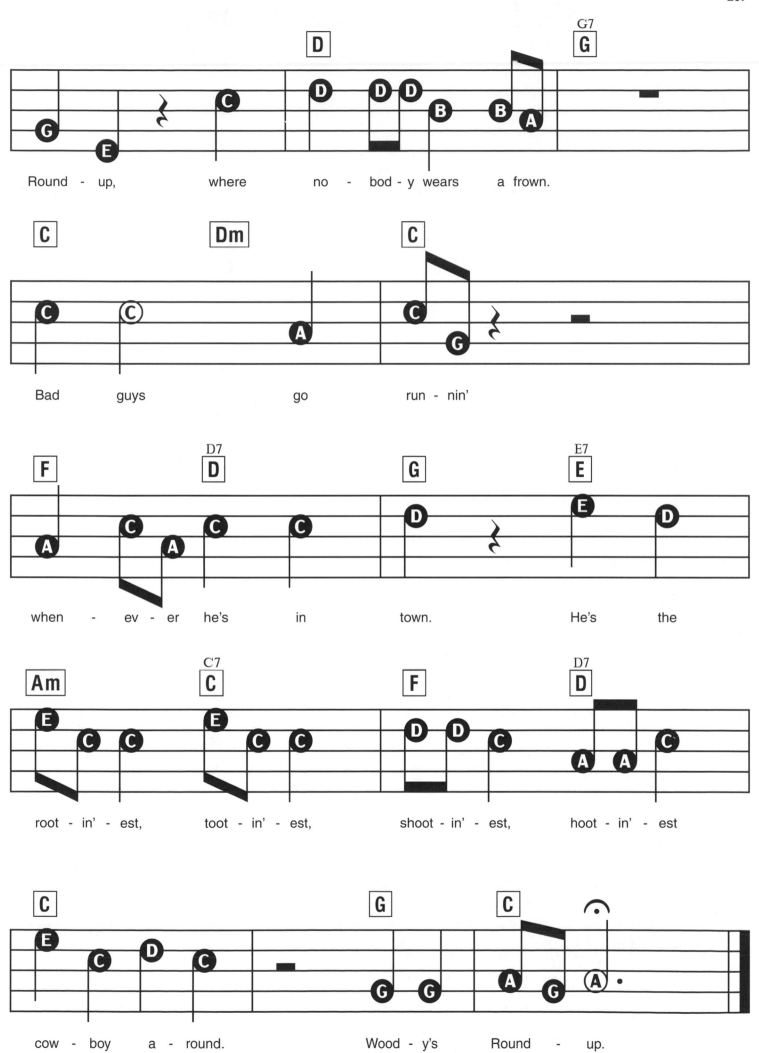

Written in the Stars
from Elton John and Tim Rice's AIDA

Registration 5
Rhythm: 8 Beat

Music by Elton John
Lyrics by Tim Rice

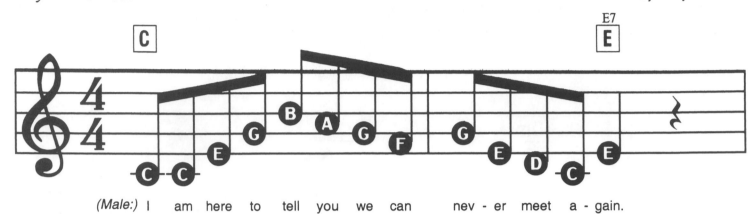

(Male:) I am here to tell you we can nev - er meet a - gain.

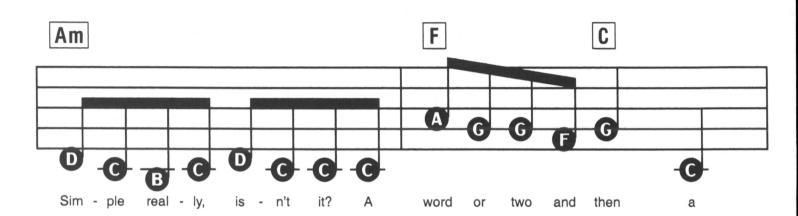

Sim - ple real - ly, is - n't it? A word or two and then a

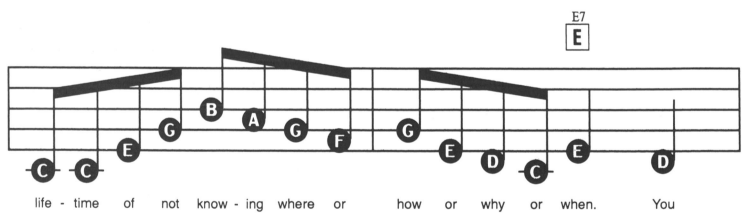

life - time of not know - ing where or how or why or when. You

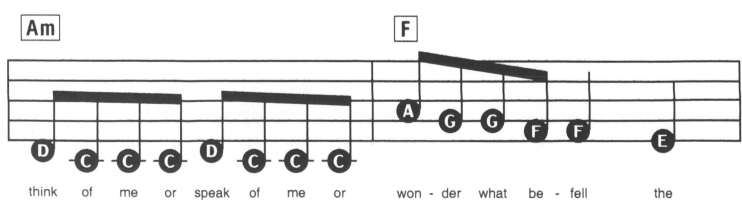

think of me or speak of me or won - der what be - fell the

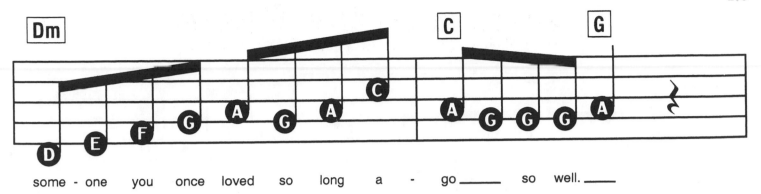

some - one you once loved so long a - go _____ so well. _____

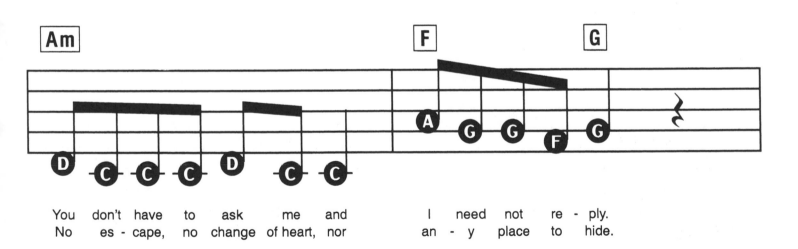

(Female:) Nev - er won - der what I'll feel _____ as liv - ing shuf - fles by.
(Male:) Noth - ing can be al - tered. Oh, there is noth - ing to de - cide.

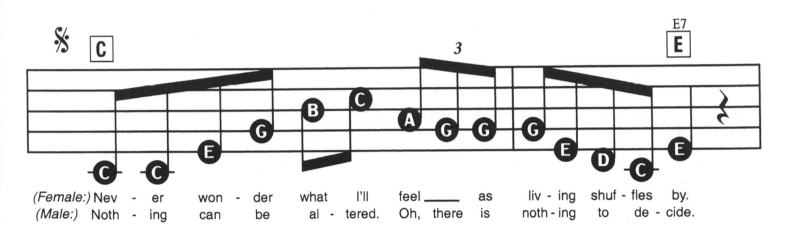

You don't have to ask me and I need not re - ply.
No es - cape, no change of heart, nor an - y place to hide.

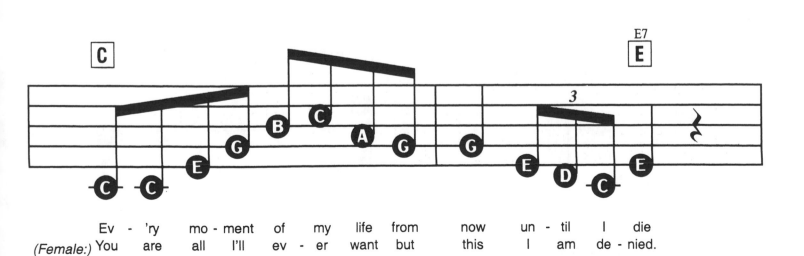

Ev - 'ry mo - ment of my life from now un - til I die
(Female:) You are all I'll ev - er want but this I am de - nied.

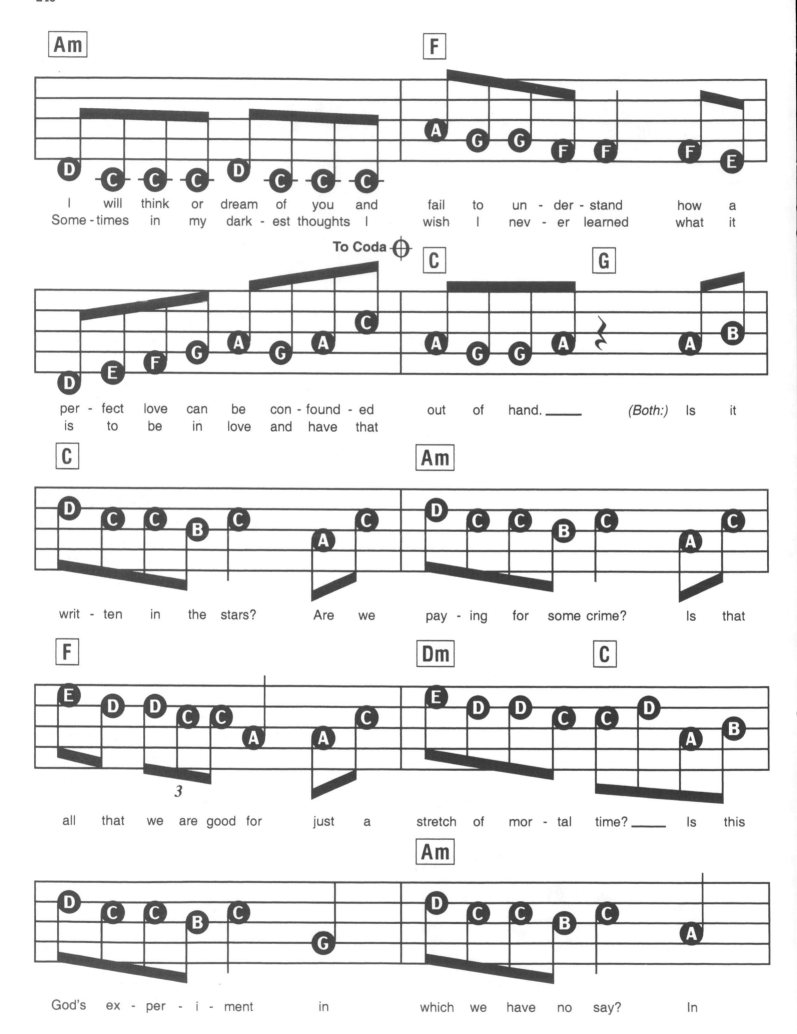

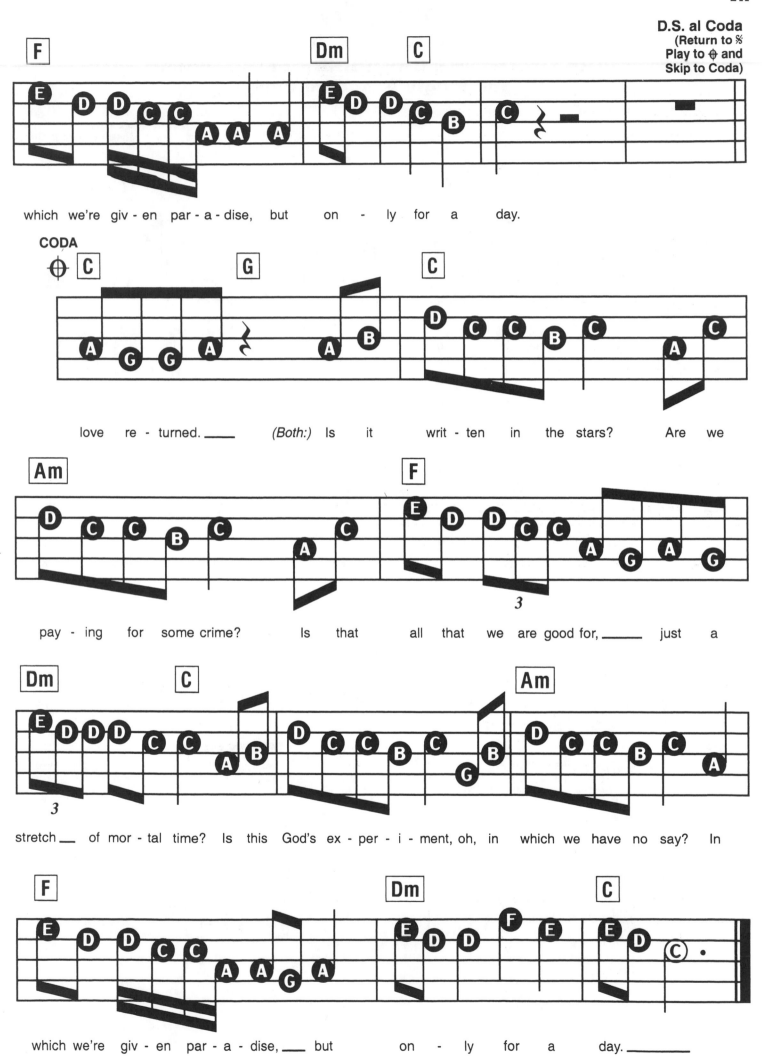

D.S. al Coda
(Return to %
Play to ⊕ and
Skip to Coda)

which we're giv-en par-a-dise, but on - ly for a day.

CODA

love re - turned. ___ *(Both:)* Is it writ - ten in the stars? Are we

pay - ing for some crime? Is that all that we are good for, ___ just a

stretch ___ of mor - tal time? Is this God's ex - per - i - ment, oh, in which we have no say? In

which we're giv - en par - a - dise, ___ but on - ly for a day. ___

Yo Ho
(A Pirate's Life for Me)
from PIRATES OF THE CARIBBEAN at Disneyland Park
and Magic Kingdom Park

Registration 8
Rhythm: 6/8 March

Words by Xavier Atencio
Music by George Bruns

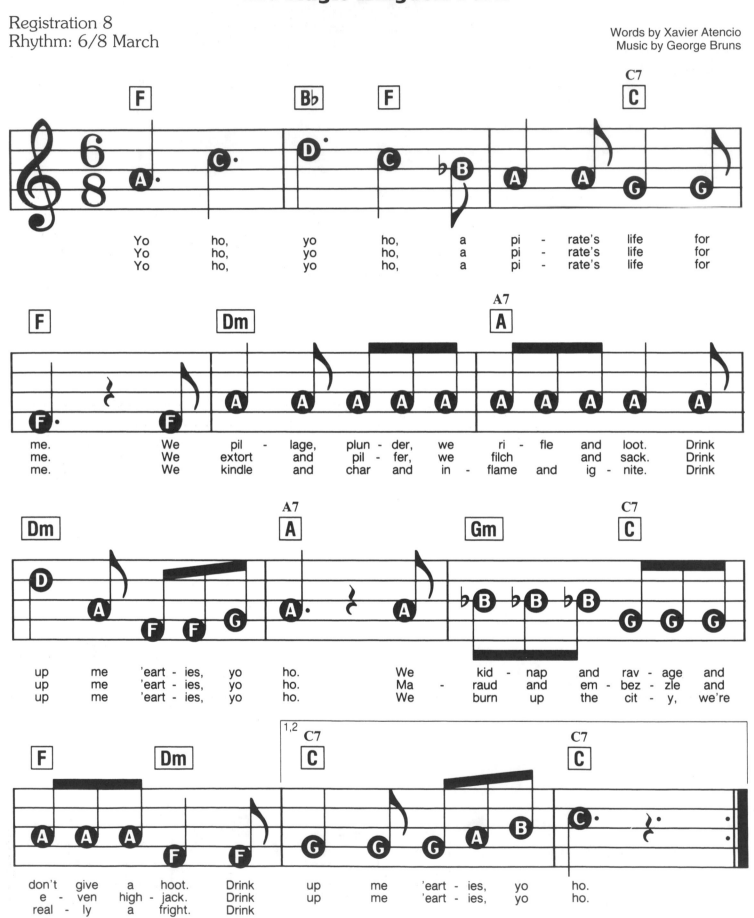

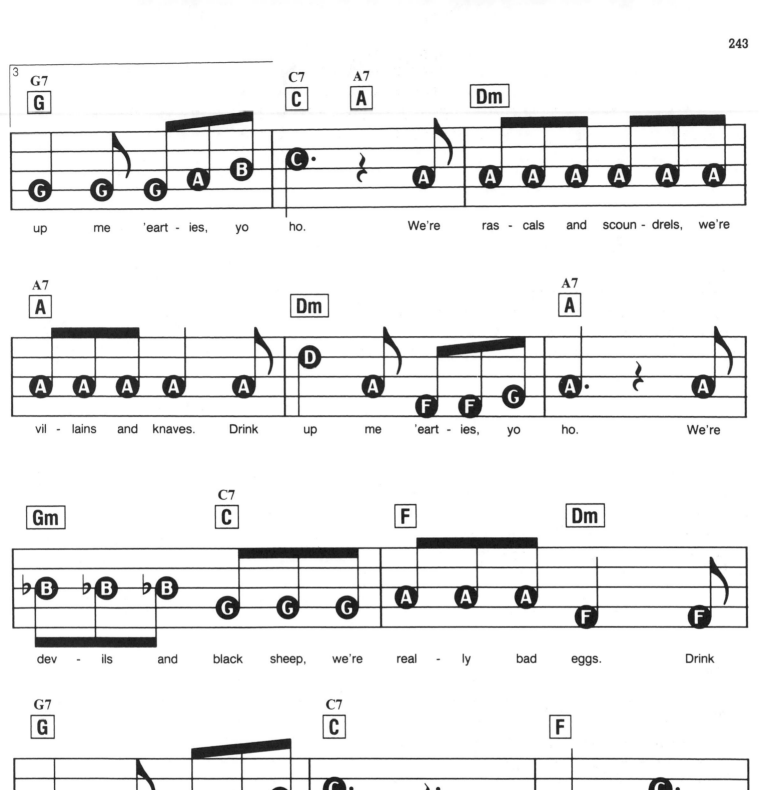

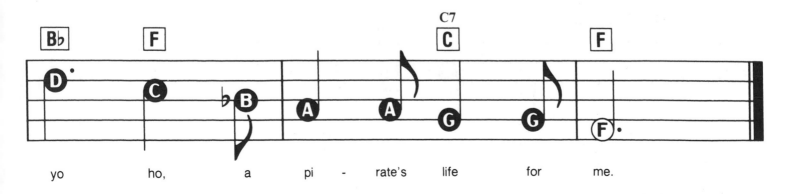

You Can Fly! You Can Fly! You Can Fly!
from Walt Disney's PETER PAN

Registration 8
Rhythm: Fox Trot or Swing

Words by Sammy Cahn
Music by Sammy Fain

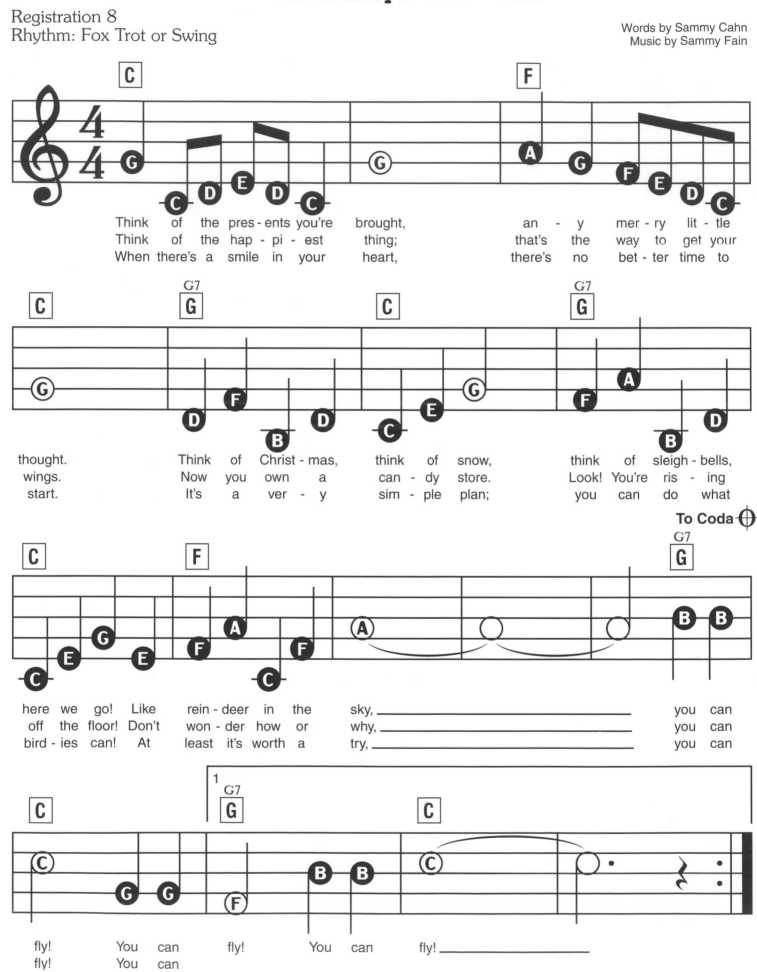

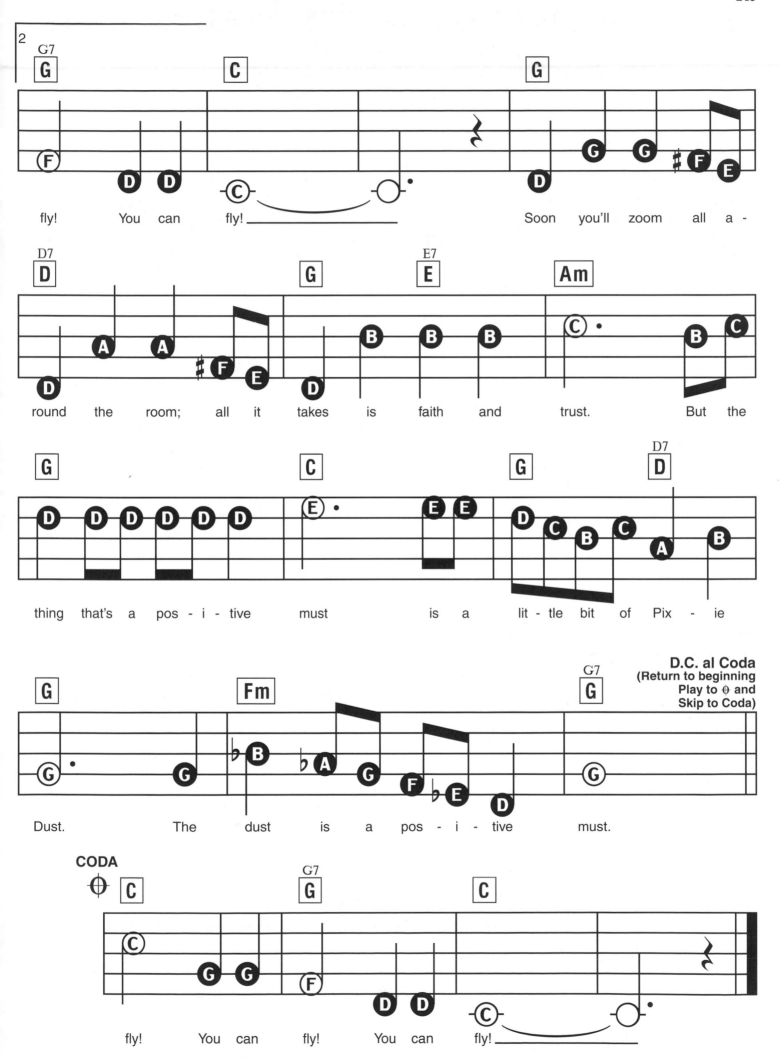

You'll Be in My Heart

(Pop Version)
from Walt Disney Pictures' TARZAN™
As Performed by Phil Collins

Registration 1
Rhythm: Rock or Pops

Words and Music by
Phil Collins

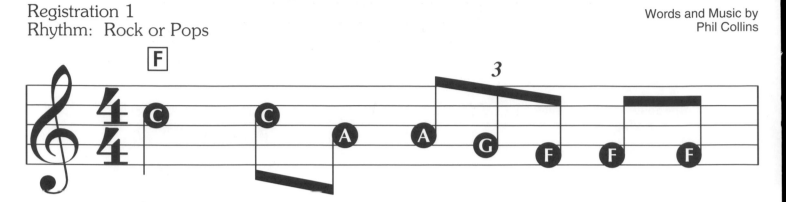

Come stop your cry - ing; _____ it will

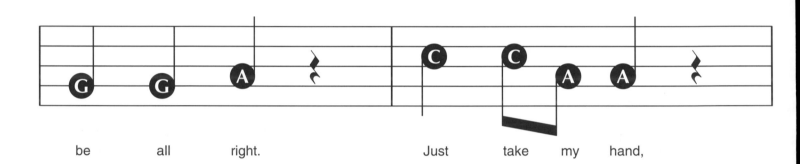

be all right. Just take my hand,

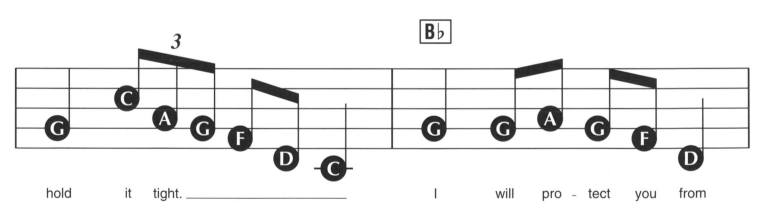

hold it tight. _____ I will pro - tect you from

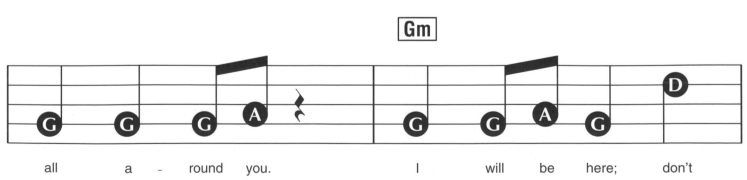

all a - round you. I will be here; don't

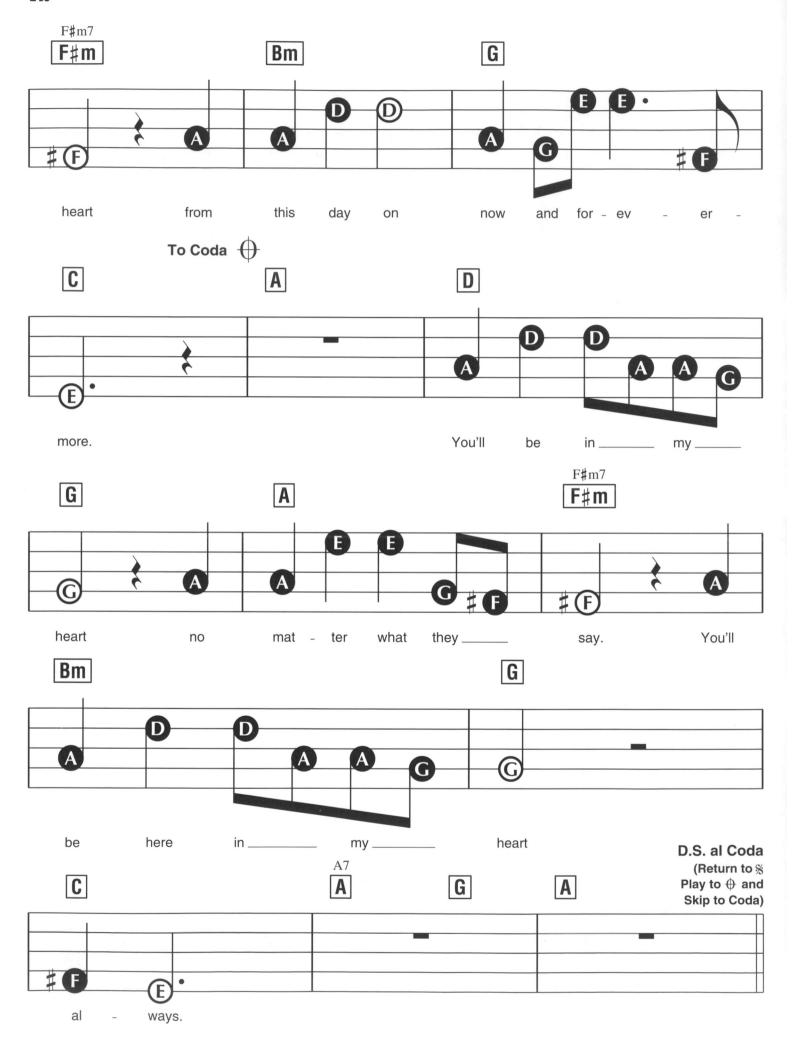

heart from this day on now and for - ev - er -

To Coda

more. You'll be in _____ my _____

heart no mat - ter what they _____ say. You'll

be here in _____ my _____ heart

D.S. al Coda
(Return to %
Play to and
Skip to Coda)

al - ways.

CODA

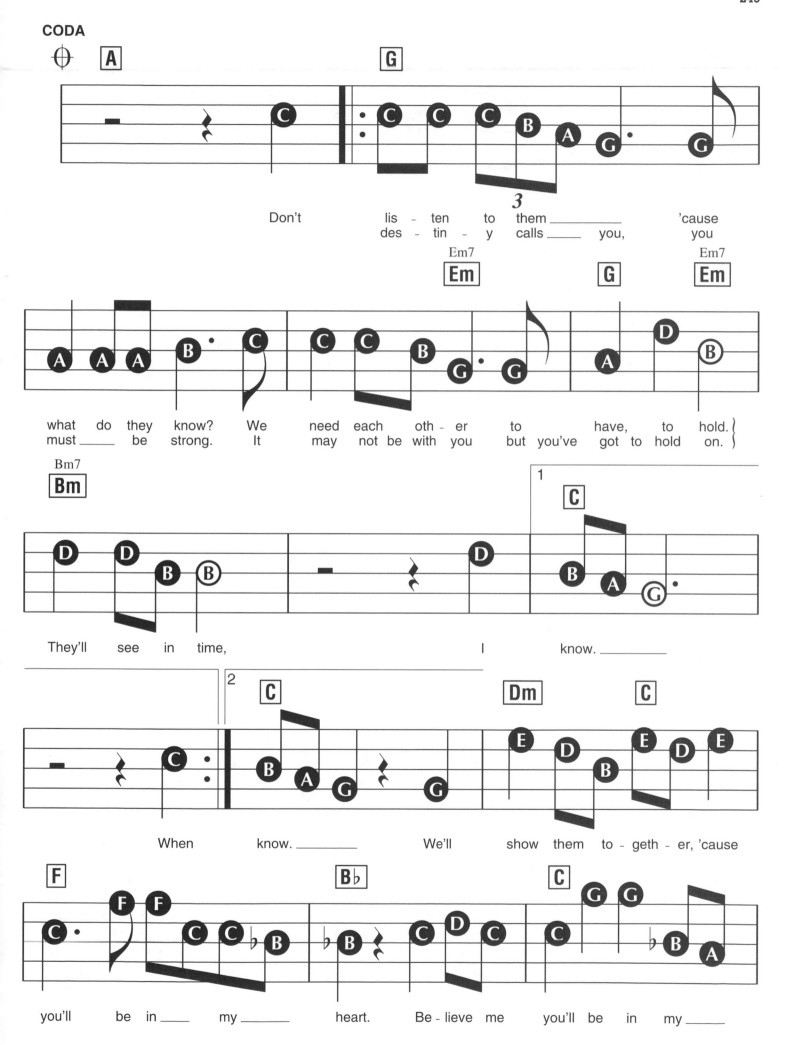

Don't listen to them _____ 'cause
des - tin - y calls _____ you, you

what do they know? We need each oth - er to have, to hold.
must _____ be strong. It may not be with you but you've got to hold on.

They'll see in time, I know. _____

When know. _____ We'll show them to - geth - er, 'cause

you'll be in _____ my _____ heart. Be - lieve me you'll be in my _____

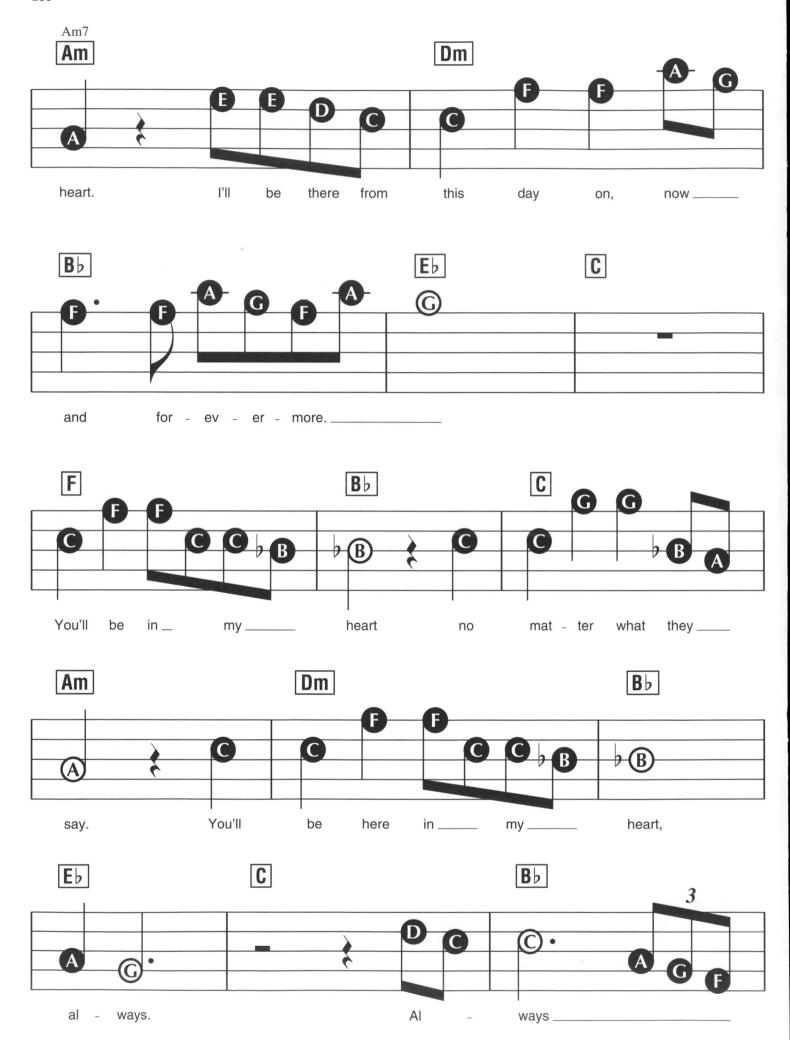

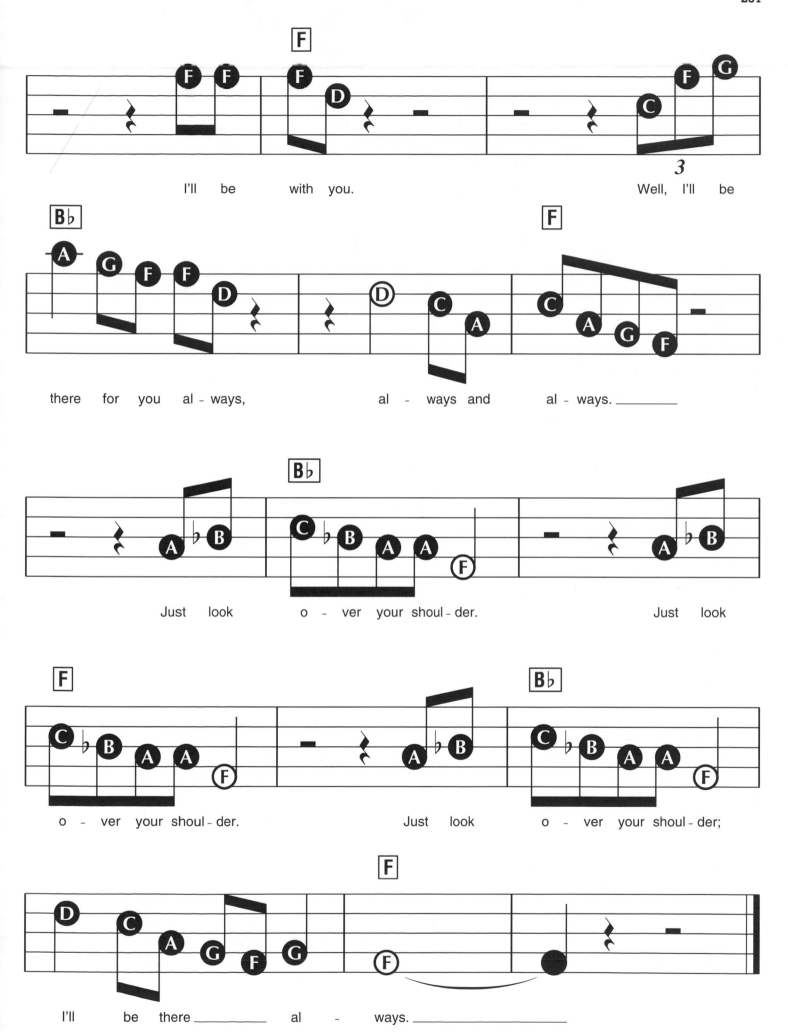

You've Got a Friend in Me
from Walt Disney's TOY STORY

Registration 7
Rhythm: Shuffle

Music and Lyrics by
Randy Newman

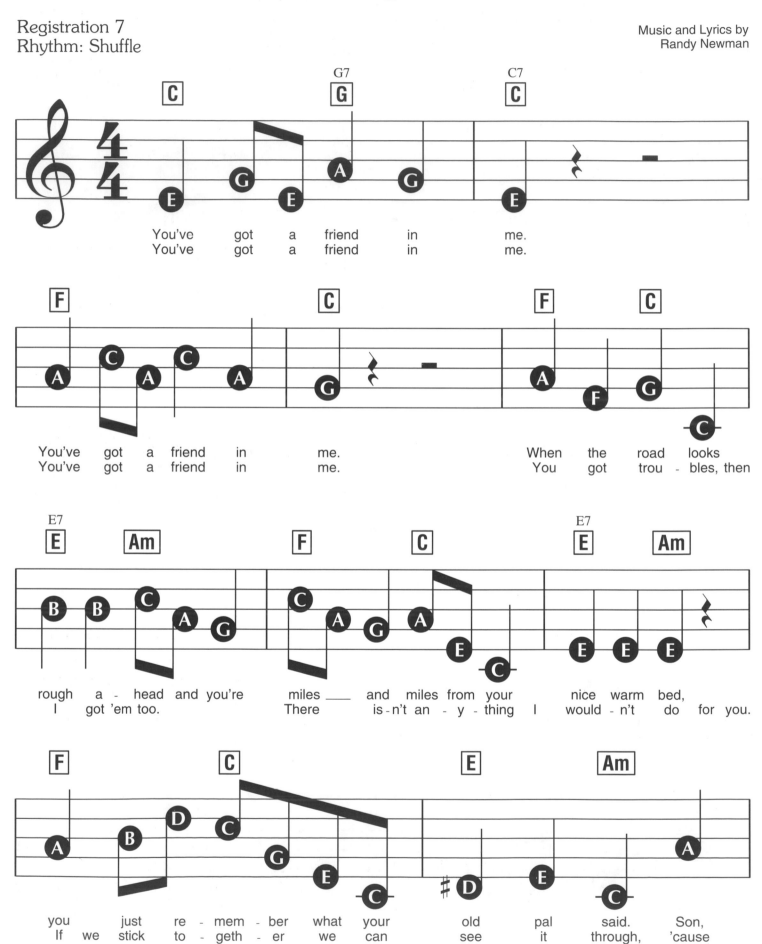

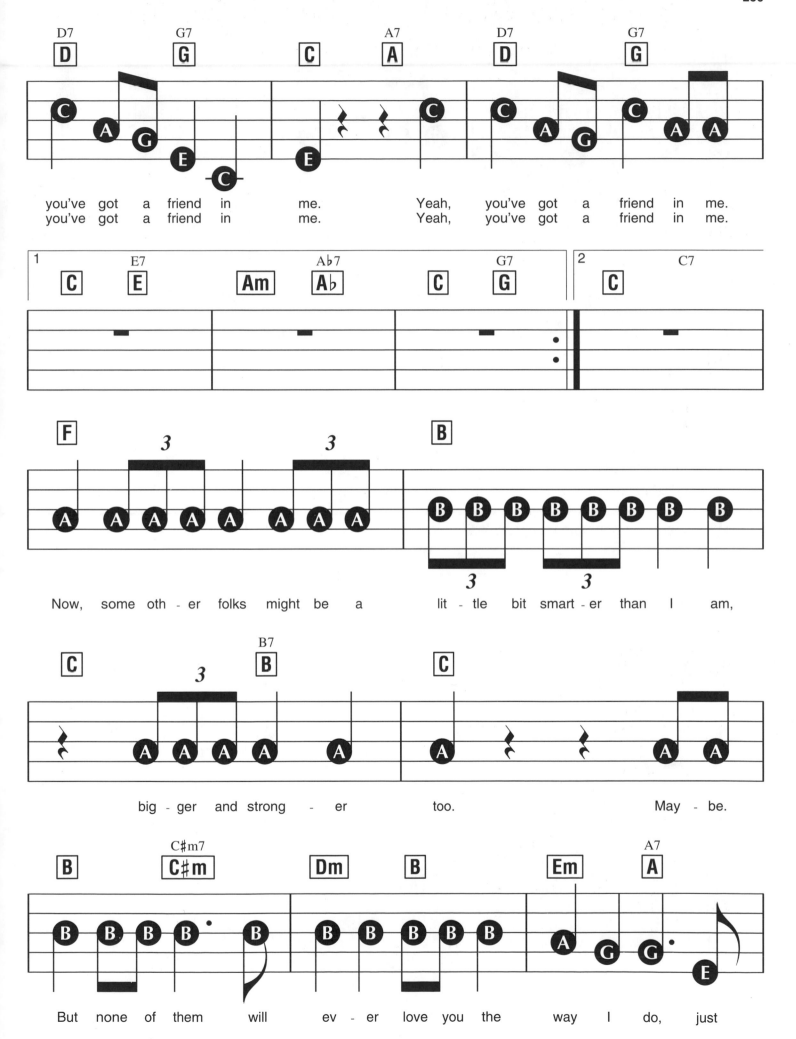

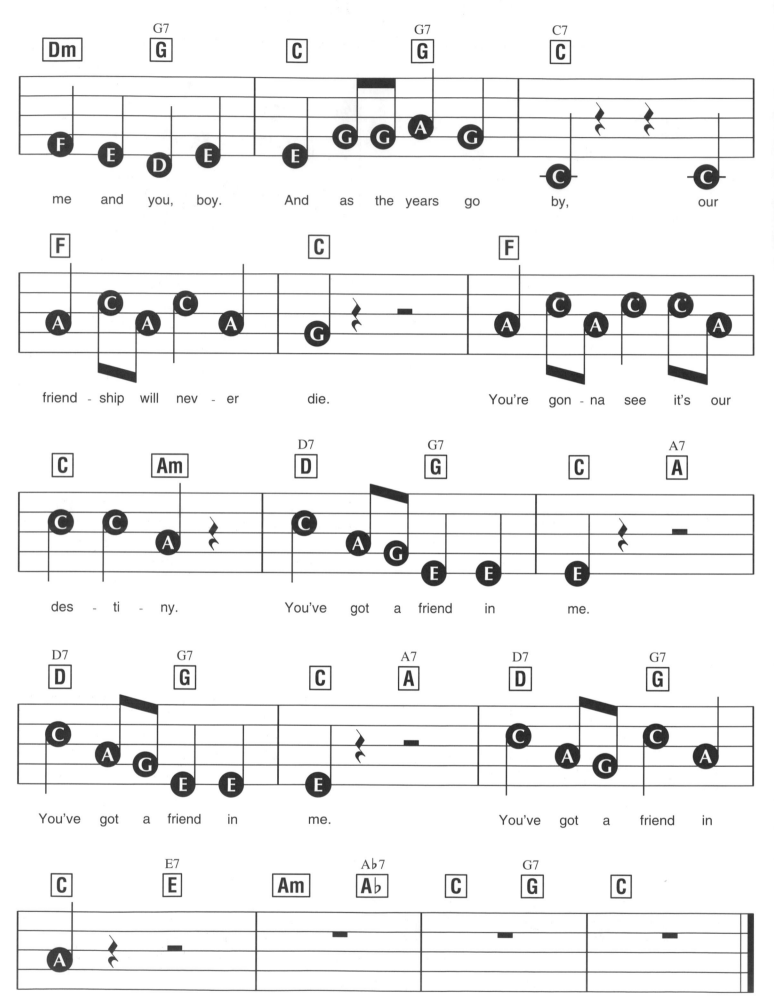

Zero to Hero
from Walt Disney Pictures' HERCULES

Registration 5
Rhythm: Rock

Music by Alan Menken
Lyrics by David Zippel

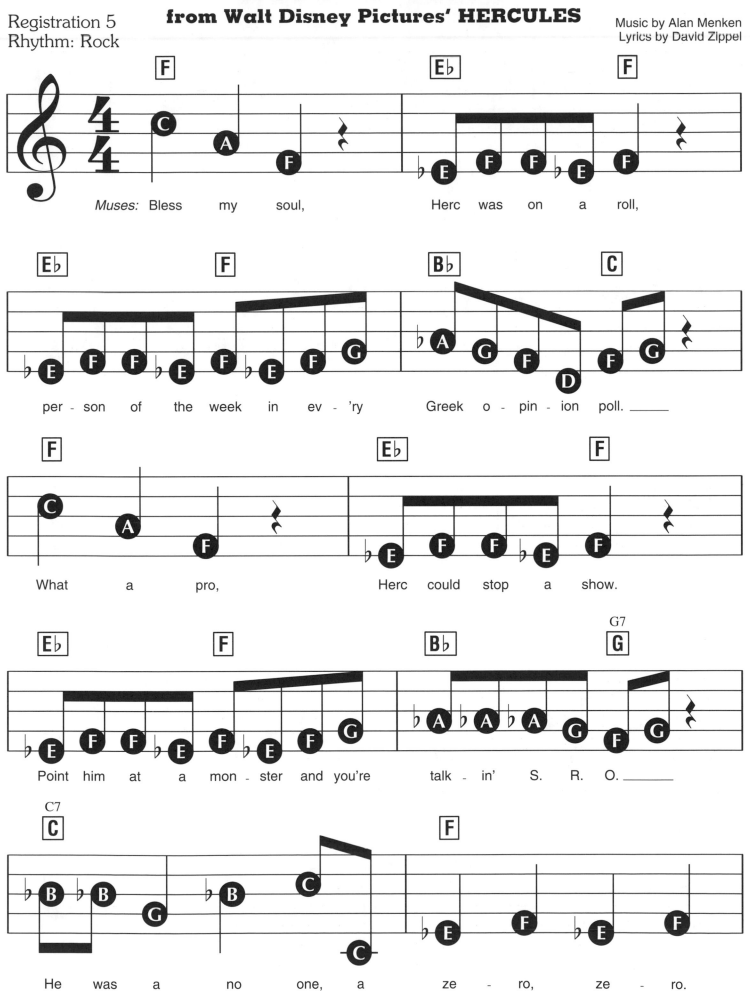

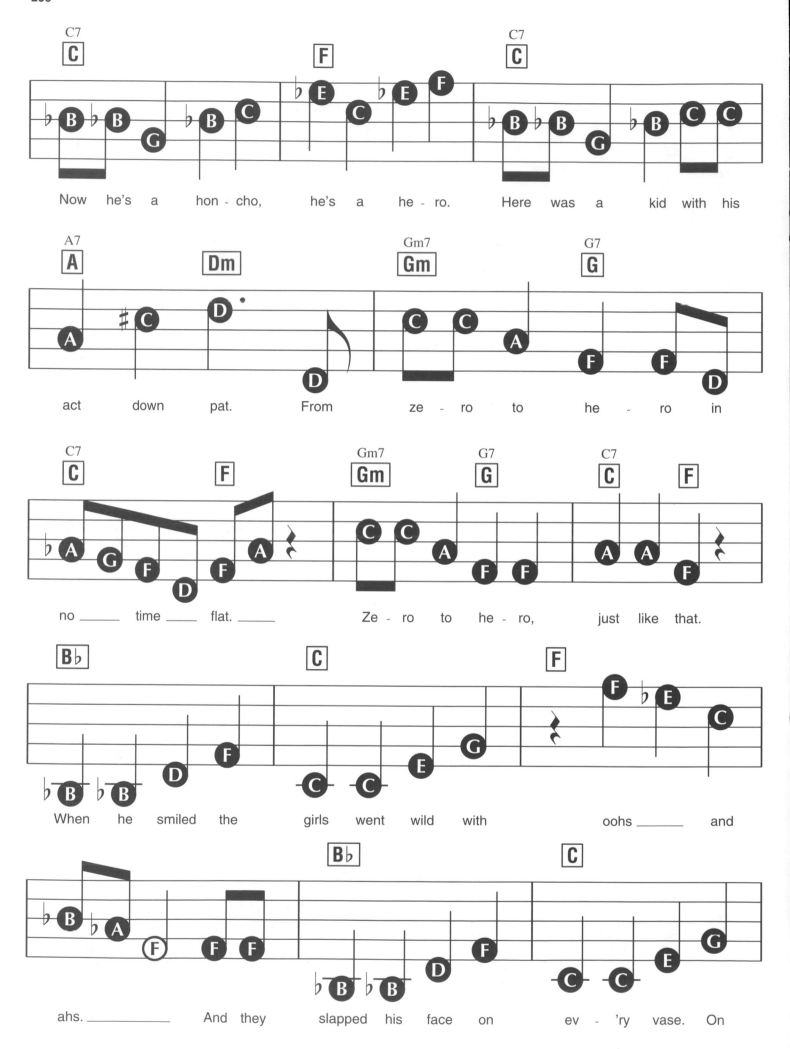

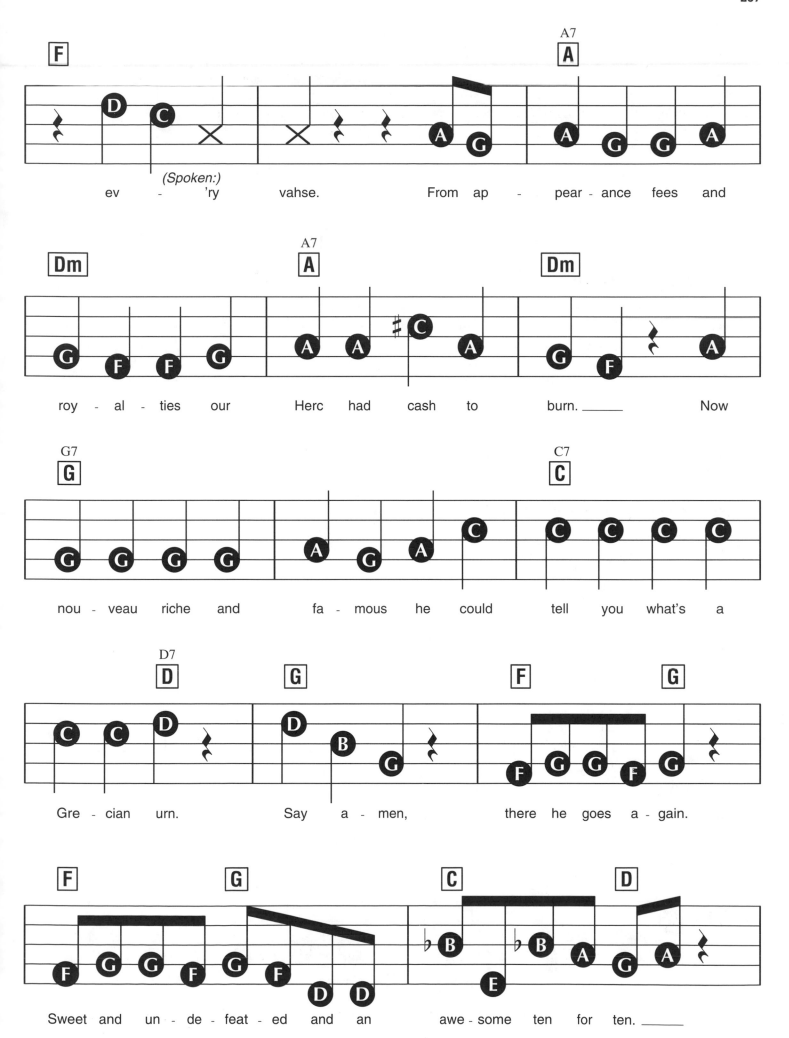

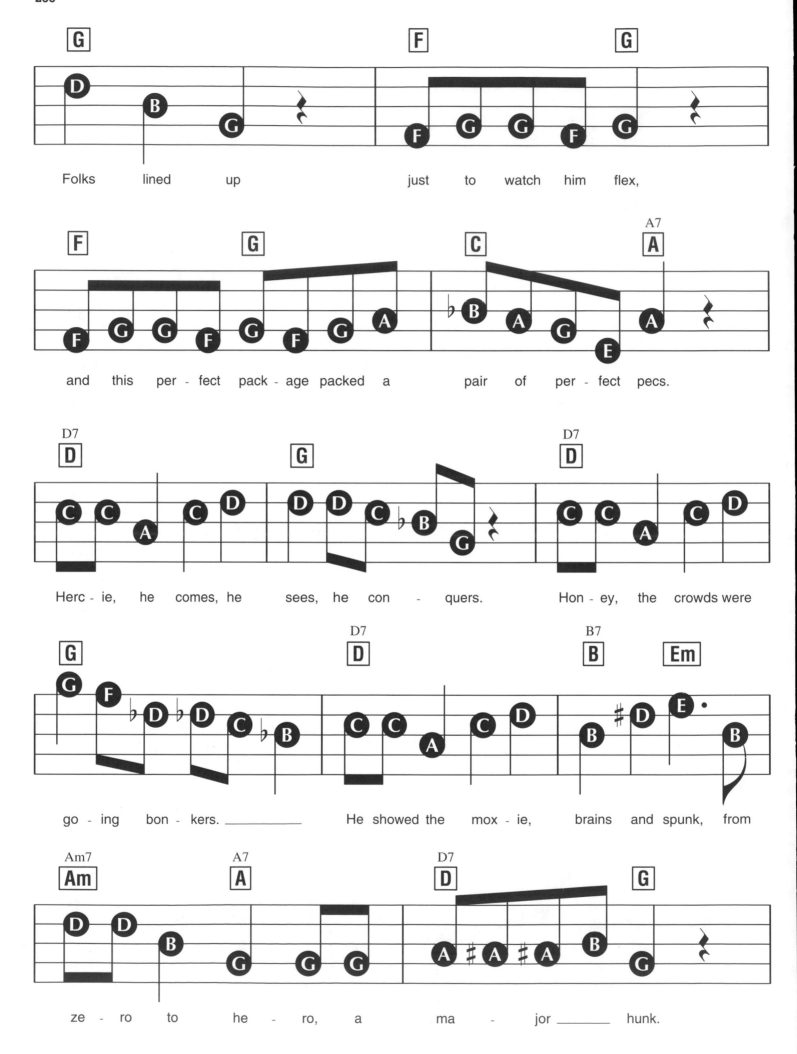

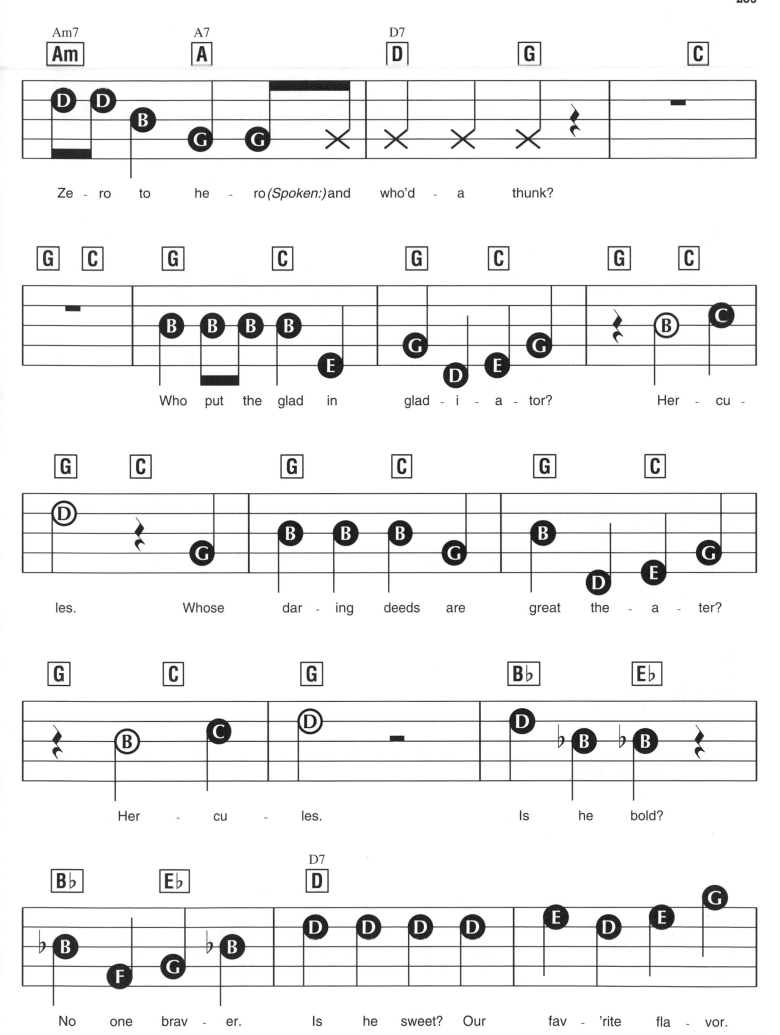

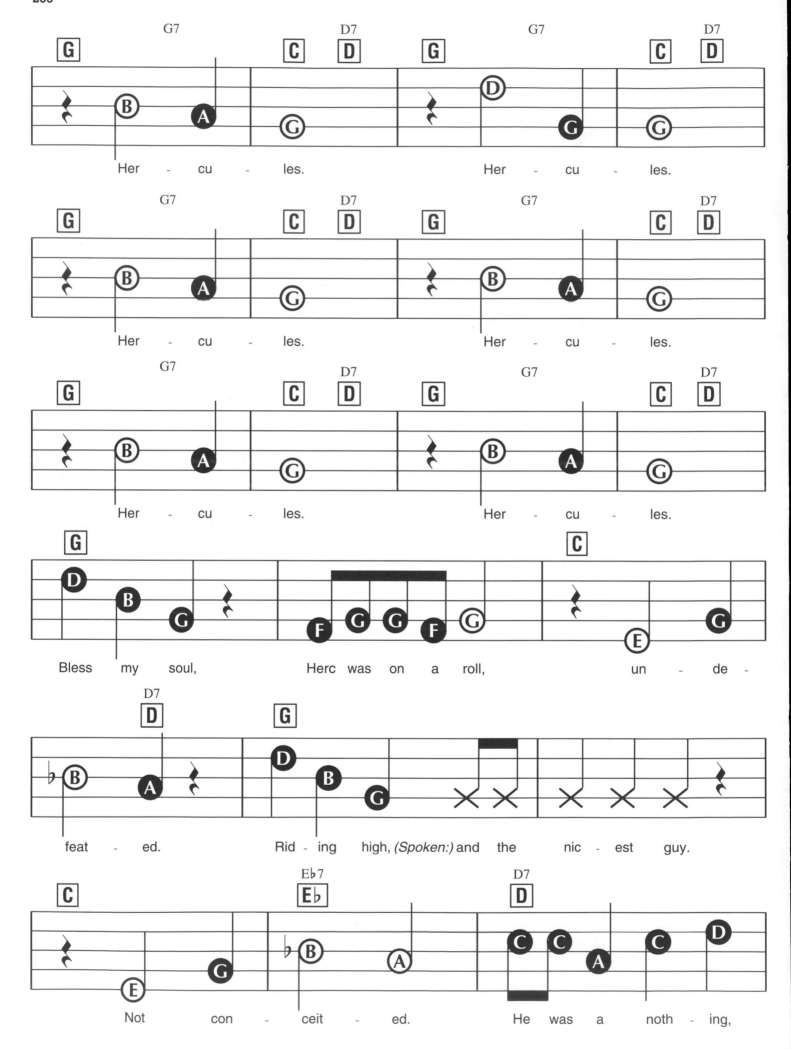

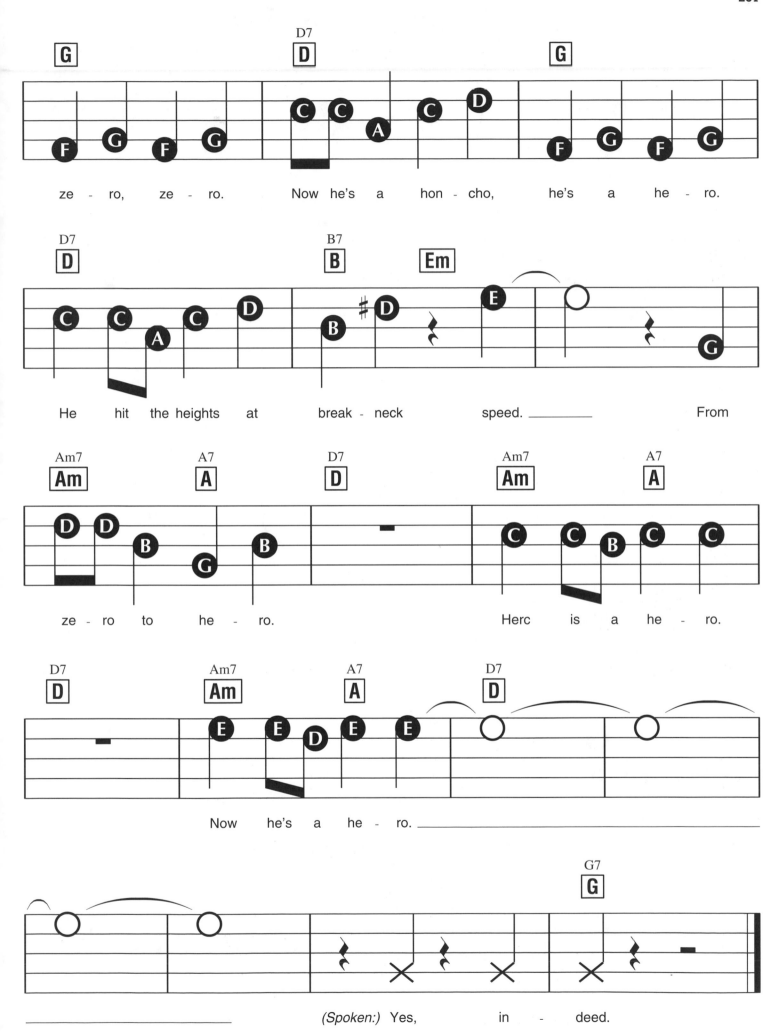

Zip-A-Dee-Doo-Dah
from Walt Disney's SONG OF THE SOUTH

Registration 8
Rhythm: Fox Trot or Swing

Words by Ray Gilbert
Music by Allie Wrubel

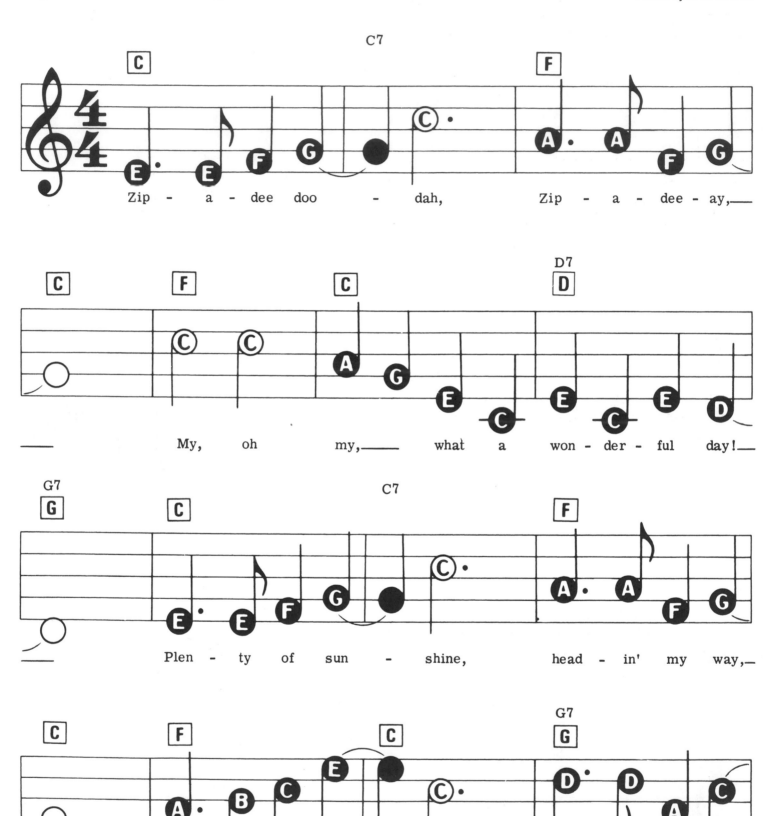

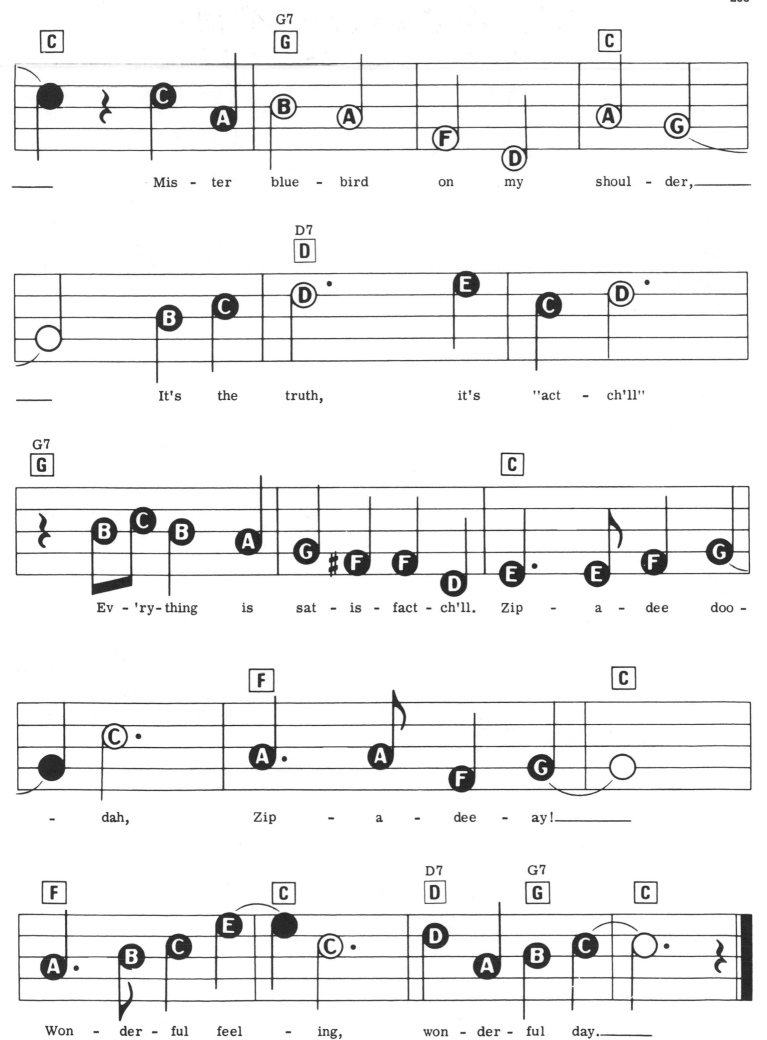

Registration Guide

- Match the Registration number on the song to the corresponding numbered category below. Select and activate an instrumental sound available on your instrument.

- Choose an automatic rhythm appropriate to the mood and style of the song. (Consult your Owner's Guide for proper operation of automatic rhythm features.)

- Adjust the tempo and volume controls to comfortable settings.

Registration

1	Mellow	Flutes, Clarinet, Oboe, Flugel Horn, Trombone, French Horn, Organ Flutes
2	Ensemble	Brass Section, Sax Section, Wind Ensemble, Full Organ, Theater Organ
3	Strings	Violin, Viola, Cello, Fiddle, String Ensemble, Pizzicato, Organ Strings
4	Guitars	Acoustic/Electric Guitars, Banjo, Mandolin, Dulcimer, Ukulele, Hawaiian Guitar
5	Mallets	Vibraphone, Marimba, Xylophone, Steel Drums, Bells, Celesta, Chimes
6	Liturgical	Pipe Organ, Hand Bells, Vocal Ensemble, Choir, Organ Flutes
7	Bright	Saxophones, Trumpet, Mute Trumpet, Synth Leads, Jazz/Gospel Organs
8	Piano	Piano, Electric Piano, Honky Tonk Piano, Harpsichord, Clavi
9	Novelty	Melodic Percussion, Wah Trumpet, Synth, Whistle, Kazoo, Perc. Organ
10	Bellows	Accordion, French Accordion, Mussette, Harmonica, Pump Organ, Bagpipes